# EPIC BIKE
# RIDES
## *of the*
# WORLD

*Explore the planet's most thrilling cycling routes*

Easy   Harder   Epic

# CONTENTS

# INTRODUCTION

Ask a dozen cycling writers for their most memorable bike rides and you get many more than a dozen answers. For some, biking was purely about escapism and involved nothing more complicated than packing some sandwiches and meandering into the distance with the wind at their backs. One or two went a little further and, GPS unit in hand, ventured into the wilds of Patagonia and the Himalaya, powered by nothing more than their legs and a desire to see what was around the next corner.

Those writers with families recommended flat and accessible loops around traffic-free islands or along river paths. A few contributors preferred to case themselves in skin-tight Lycra and seek out heart-pounding ascents, making ardent pilgrimages to the sites of classic races to pay their respects. Mountain-biking writers wrote of thrills and spills on rugged trails on every continent. And more than a few authors agreed that a good ride wasn't complete without a beer or two afterwards with old friends or new.

What was clear, though, is that everybody has their personal interpretation of 'epic'. You can have an epic adventure straight from your front door and be back in time for tea. Or you can follow in the tyre tracks of adventurer Alastair Humphreys and pedal around the world, through 60 countries, for four years.

This book attempts to reflect that diversity and those varying levels of commitment. We can't all take a sabbatical for cycling! We've sought out some of the most entertaining experiences you can have on a bicycle, whether you're a casual rider or a cyclist with a stable of carbon-fibre machines. The settings of these experiences range from some of the world's most remote places – Mongolia, Bhutan and the Outer Hebrides – to its hippest cities and dreamiest islands. Some of these rides take just a couple of

hours, others a day or two, a week, or more than a month. We've usually not tried to specify times the rides might take beyond the distance involved – everybody is different; take as long as required.

Instead, we've given a general indication of whether a ride is easy (in terms of terrain, distance, conditions or climate) or more challenging (bigger hills, longer distances, fewer cake shops). The most important point of these stories is to inspire you to get your bike out (dusting it off and pumping up the tyres first if need be) and explore somewhere new with the wind in your hair.

Cycling is the perfect mode of transport for the travel-lover, allowing us to cover more ground than if we were on foot, but without the barriers that a car imposes. We are immersed in our surroundings, self-powered, independent, and forever pondering the question 'I wonder what's over there?'. The bike rider is free to follow a whim, discover the limits of their endurance, or stop and settle for while. Hopefully, this book will prove that there's no better way of simply experiencing a place, a culture and its people than by bicycle. And as some of these tales tell, arriving on a bicycle opens doors, literally and figuratively.

## HOW TO USE THIS BOOK

The main stories in each regional chapter feature first-hand accounts of fantastic bike rides in that continent. Each includes a toolkit to enable the planning of a trip – when is the best time of year, how to get there, where to stay. But beyond that, these stories should spark other ideas. We've started that process with the 'more like this' section following each story, which offers other ideas along a similar theme, not necessarily on the same continent. Many of these ideas are well established routes or trails. The index collects different types of ride for a variety of interests.

# THE TOUR D'AFRIQUE

*Tour d'Afrique lives up to its name: a ride across the entire continent of Africa. It's tough on the bike and gruelling on the body.*

Through stinging beads of sweat I looked ahead and the road shimmered into the distance – a thin grey line with endless plains of sand on either side. We'd cycled 50 miles (80km) so far and had the same distance to go. The sun was beating down, and the desert wind was relentless. It was like riding into a hairdryer. With added grit. What a crazy place to go cycling.

This was my first day on the Tour d'Afrique, a long-distance race from Cairo to Cape Town, Africa's traditional northern and southern extremities. This annual test of endurance covers around 7500 miles (around 12,000km) divided into eight stages of 14 days, giving four months to ride the continent end-to-end. And while some pedal the whole distance, those with less time can ride just a stage – which is no mean feat in itself. There's also a team relay option, and in 2009 I was part of a Lonely Planet team, with two riders completing each stage then handing on the baton.

The Tour d'Afrique starts at one of Africa's best-known landmarks, the Pyramids of Giza, on the edge of Cairo. After obligatory photos in front of the giant monuments, and one for luck in front of the Sphinx, the peloton heads south to begin its epic journey. Route details change each year, as new roads are built or borders close, or when countries become too volatile to visit, but the Tour d'Afrique follows pretty much the same overall pattern. From the Egyptian capital, riders head to the Red Sea then follow the coast road before tracking inland to reach the Nile Valley and cycle through a landscape of palm trees and crop fields that have barely changed since Pharaonic times.

A ferry ride along Lake Nasser brings the riders to their second country, Sudan, and a demanding few days on sandy roads

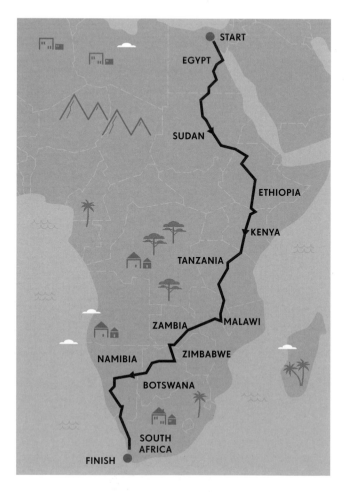

through the Nubian Desert, an eastern extension of the Sahara. In this remote part of Africa, where travel is hard at the best of times, cycling adds an extra level of endurance and excitement.

In Khartoum my own adventure began, as I joined a Lonely Planet teammate on that heat-soaked highway through the endless desert landscape. Distances between towns were long, so we often stopped for a drink and a rest at basic roadhouses, some little more than a lonely shack surrounded by sand. We enjoyed small glasses of sweet black tea, and an unexpected bonus was the availability of glucose biscuits. Together they kept us fuelled for another hour or two of tough cycling.

From Sudan we crossed the border into Ethiopia. Almost immediately, the flat desert changed to a fertile landscape of green rolling hills, and dead-straight roads gave way to frequent bends as we climbed into the Ethiopian Highlands, a range of mountains sometimes dubbed the Roof of Africa.

From the vantage points of the bikes, we were able to see local people working in the fields, kids going to school, everyone just getting on with daily life. We were also joined by a group of Ethiopian cyclists, and a highlight of the trip was riding alongside them as the dramatic scenery rolled past, chatting about life in Ethiopia and the finer points of the local bike-racing scene.

After Ethiopia, the Tour d'Afrique goes to Kenya. The route may be out of the mountains, but the cycling gets even harder with a traverse of the arid Dida Galgalu Desert. When the Lonely Planet team were here in 2009, a freak rainstorm turned dirt roads into mud. One of the riders later reported: 'It was much more than just cycling. It was a matter of survival.'

A day of climbing into the lush foothills of Mt Kenya comes as a welcome relief, enhanced by crossing the Equator, from where

## CAIRO TO CAPE TOWN RECORD BREAKERS

The first Tour d'Afrique in 2003 set a new benchmark in long-distance cycling events, and also set a new world record, with nine riders cycling from Cairo to Cape Town in 120 days. Over the following decade, the record was reduced by several solo riders. In 2015 the record was broken by British cyclist Mark Beaumont, covering around 6718 mile (around 10,812km) in a brisk 41 days, 10 hours and 22 minutes.

*Clockwise from top: Mt Kilimanjaro in Tanzania; carrying cargo by bike; feluccas on the Nile; flowering landscapes. Previous page: a gelada baboon grazing in the Simien mountains of Ethiopia*

it's an easy ride to Nairobi and on to Tanzania through a classic African landscape of savanna grasslands dotted with flat-topped acacia trees. On a bike it's easier to see monkeys, giraffes, zebras and other wild animals that car-drivers might miss, and the vista is further enhanced by the snow-covered peak of Kilimanjaro serving as a backdrop.

The next port of call is Malawi. In this poor country bikes are everywhere, metal beasts of burden carrying vast bundles of firewood, piles of bricks, giant gas canisters, rolls of corrugated iron, even beds. With locals and Tour d'Afrique riders having two wheels in common, it's the perfect opportunity to share a friendly wave or a few words of greeting.

In Zambia, long straight roads cut through a vast empty country to reach yet another classic African landmark, Victoria Falls, where the Zambezi River plummets into a gorge, sending up a cloud of spray that can be seen from far away; a very welcome sight at the end of a hard day's cycling.

Beyond the Zambezi are the relatively developed countries of Botswana and Namibia, but easy conditions are offset by long days in the saddle, including the approx. 129-mile (approx. 208km) 'queen stage' along the Trans Kalahari Hwy. If that doesn't raise a sweat, riders may also encounter elephants on the road – guaranteed to get the heart pumping.

Then comes the last section through South Africa, where once again the bikes bring riders closer to stunning landscapes, with final off-road forays through Namaqualand and the sculptured orange rocks of the Cederberg mountains.

The Tour d'Afrique ends as it began, at a famous landmark: weary but elated cyclists pass the flat-topped summit of Table Mountain to reach Cape Town and the end of a truly epic ride. **DE**

*"On a bike it's easier to see monkeys, giraffes, zebras and other wild animals that car-drivers might miss"*

## TOOLKIT

**Start** // Cairo, Egypt
**End** // Cape Town, South Africa
**Distance** // Approx 7500 miles (approx. 12,000km). The route varies but usually goes via Sudan, Ethiopia, Kenya, Tanzania, Malawi, Zambia, Botswana and Namibia. Riders can opt to do the race (with competitive sections most days) or the 'expedition' (which means just taking part).
**Duration** // Covering the entire distance requires around 120 days, divided into 90 riding days and 30 rest/ sightseeing days.
**When to ride** // The Tour d'Afrique is organised every year, usually mid-January to mid-May, by TDA Global Cycling (www. tdaglobalcycling.com/tour-dafrique).
**More info** // Support trucks carry supplies and camping gear. Some riders may also take advantage of a truck-ride to cut daily cycling distances.

*Opposite: the switchback turns of
the Sani Pass in Lesotho*

# MORE LIKE THIS
## AFRICAN RIDES

### KILIMANJARO CIRCUIT, TANZANIA

If you've got more time to spare after tackling the Tour d'Afrique, a challenging option is the loop around the base of Africa's best-known mountain, Kilimanjaro, a distance of 146 miles (235km). A good start point is Moshi, a popular base for trekkers, and the route goes via Sanyaa Juu and Tarakea. It's well off tourist itineraries, so you'll need a tent. Roads are a mix of terrible dirt and perfect tar, with everything in between, while numerous rivers mean plenty of valleys to cross, so this is not a trip for the faint-hearted.
**Start/End // Moshi**
**Distance // 146 miles (235km)**

### SANI PASS, SOUTH AFRICA TO LESOTHO

The Drakensberg range forms a line of jagged peaks and steep valleys stretching in an arc though the eastern part of South Africa. Sitting at the top of this mountain chain is Lesotho, a separate country, sometimes called the 'Kingdom in the Sky' thanks to its lofty location. Forcing a route up this precipice is the Sani Pass, a tortuous gravel track linking the two countries, and a cycling challenge. You start at the small town of Himeville and follow the road (tar at first, then dirt), gradually climbing to the South African border post. Then it's dirt all the way, a constant grind, with ramps increasingly sheer, and turns increasingly tight, to finally reach the Lesotho border post at the summit. Temperatures can be baking hot, or freezing cold. Either way, thirst can be quenched at the nearby Sani Mountain Lodge, which claims to be the highest pub in Africa.
**Start // Himeville, South Africa**
**End // Lesotho border**
**Distance // 23 miles (37km)**

### MASSAWA TO ASMARA, ERITREA

Of all Africa's countries, Eritrea has the richest cycling heritage, thanks to Italian colonial influence, and today it's the national sport, with a thriving race calendar that includes the Tour of Eritrea. Get a taste of it by tackling the spectacular climb from the port city of Massawa up to Asmara, the capital. Sometimes billed as 'Eritrea's Mortirolo', a nod to the infamously rugged Alpine pass, it's a winding snake of a road with steep gradients and hairpin bends, plus dizzying drops and great views over the sandy plains below. The first 26 miles (42km) is fairly flat (but very hot) then the bulk of the ascent, over 2000m, is in the next 41 miles (66km). Currently, Eritrea's government is cited by human rights organisations as one of the most oppressive in the world, which may deter travellers, but when the tide turns, add the Massawa–Asmara road to your bucket list.
**Start // Massawa**
**End // Asmara**
**Distance // 67 miles (108km)**

# RIDING THE RIF

*Northern Morocco's Rif Mountains aren't on most cyclists' bucket lists. The riding and culture can be taxing, but epic isn't meant to be easy!*

I have a love-hate relationship with hills. I'm big on the cycling challenge, mostly in principle, and I love the reward, especially in practice. As I make long ascents, though, I lose enthusiasm and tend to abandon the two-wheeler's don't-stop dictum. And while I lament the added burden of gear-filled panniers — a necessity for self-supported, multi-day pedals into mountainous places with limited food availability, poor-quality amenities, meagre mechanical backup and unreliable alternative transportation — I depend on it as an excuse when I slow down and, yes, even stop.

This was in my thoughts on my first days of riding in the Rif

Mountains, which parallel the Mediterranean coast of northern Morocco and include several significant climbs. I pondered how the Rif isn't particularly sought out for cycling or, really, any standard form of tourism; but as I was on the first leg of a nine-month, counterclockwise bicycle circumnavigation of the Mediterranean Sea, from Morocco to Gibraltar, geography had dictated my path.

Also top of mind was how the Rif, home to large kif (aka cannabis) plantations, is perhaps best known for its primary export: hashish. Over the decades, this has been both a magnet for and source of friction with tourists. Young backpackers and hippies have long trooped here to avail themselves of the product, even though

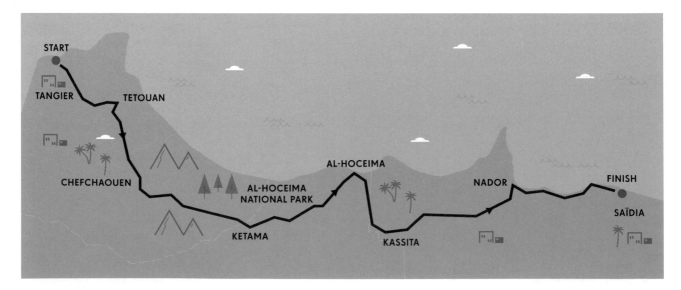

smoking it is illegal. Unfortunately, that means anyone visiting the Rif Mountains today is assumed to be interested in buying hashish. Sellers and touts are constantly pressing their case, sometimes to the point of harassment. Drugs trigger other criminal behavior too, especially smuggling, so police checkpoints are common.

These are important reality checks when pondering a ride in the region. But while it may not seem all that conducive to cycling, the gorgeous mountain scenery, challenging and changeable terrain on fairly good-quality and uncrowded roads, and glimpses of typical Moroccan life away from the touristy commercial hubs make for something genuinely different and extremely appealing. The Rif is worth the journey as long as you're steeled and ready for polite and purposeful self-sufficiency, not to mention some discomfort, as the food and lodging along the way can be basic.

Our path took us east from world-famous Tangier to relaxed, seaside Saïdia on the Algerian border, via Tétouan and blue-painted Chefchaouen, both known for their bustling medinas, and Al-Hoceima and Nador, two coastal communities with fine beaches. These towns all offer solid gastronomic and touristic solace. The many miles between them, however, pass through villages that can lack creature comforts for visitors. The two in which we found ourselves on two different nights were Kassita and Ketama, the latter the notorious kif capital of the region.

Outside the towns, the reliable Rif constants we grew to appreciate were the scenery and the road quality. These were big pluses because the route was rarely flat, even from Nador to Saïdia,

> *"We glided on usually good pavement through valleys of cedar trees, sweated up hillsides and swept thrillingly down"*

when it stayed within view of the sea through hot and arid undulating lands flanked by the Beni-Snassen Mountains. In fact, besides road construction, pass-clinging clouds, lowland midday heat and police checkpoints, the external obstacles were few. We glided on usually good pavement through valleys of cedar trees, sweated along rolling deforested hillsides, slogged up to and then thrillingly down from high elevations, and sliced through coastal headwinds, all while marveling at sweeping vistas and seeking the unseen sources of lamb bleats, cow bells and echoing calls to prayer.

That isn't to say the roads were empty. While motorised traffic wasn't frequent, it was hardly absent. There was also almost always a djellaba-clad man in sight (women were largely absent), even halfway through nine switchbacks, 6 miles (10 km) and 800m of elevation gain to the mountain pass before Kassita. These inexplicable wanderers were present as well on the steep climb between Tétouan and Chefchaouen, the two gruelling ascents between Chefchaouen and Ketama, and the two epic one-day plunging descents to sea level, from Ketama to Al-Hoceima and from Kassita to Nador.

Interestingly, the first words out of these roadside characters'

## MOROCCAN FOOD TIPS

Roadside stalls have slim pickings, but tourism-ready towns promise Morocco's best foods: couscous, tagines, such grilled meats as *méchoui* (lamb), fried sardines, *harira* (soup), salads including *zaalouk*, *shakshouka* and more. Tagines and couscous are often only served at home for special occasions, so accept any invitations. And try street foods, such as *ksra* (anise flatbread), *sfenj* (deep-fried doughnuts) and *kefta* (meat seasoned with ras el-hanout spices).

*Left to right: Chefchaouen; a Berber family; the Straits of Gibraltar; stocking up in the medina of Tetouan. Previous page: the blue town of Chefchaouen*

mouths wasn't 'as-salamu alaykum' (a standard greeting in Arabic) or 'makh dith?' ('how are you?' in northern Berber dialect), it was 'hashish?' Few would accept a single 'no'. One young tout jogged alongside us – up a tough hill – for several miles, determined to make a sale. Another proffered a grapefruit-size ball of congealed hash oil. A Mercedes even followed slowly behind us for a while; it eventually turned back without a word or a wave.

But those quirky moments of awkwardness and suspicion were far less common than the locals' displays of generosity and befuddled curiosity. At roadside stands, where we guzzled cold Orange Crush soda or sipped mint tea, our round-the-Mediterranean project elicited amazed reactions. While we were snacking, another Mercedes discharged some official-looking gents (who we thereafter nicknamed 'the diplomats') who simply wanted to know where we were from and how the biking was.

And at our overnight stops, someone usually took us under his wing and made us feel welcome. This was even the case in Ketama, a place many Moroccans won't go. There, Bayloul Mohamed, a local university student working at our hotel, led us to a tagine meal in an unassuming, unmarked restaurant and taught us all about the region.

Cycling has always transported me – physically, mentally and especially culturally. I hit many highs and lows in the Rif, even without any kif! The challenges were many, but it was a road and an experience that stands out more than most among many epic rides. **EG**

## TOOLKIT

**Start //** Tangier
**End //** Saïdia
**Distance //** approx. 373 miles (600km)
**Getting there //** Tangier-Ibn Battouta Airport, located 7½ miles (12km) southwest of Tangier, is used by Royal Air Maroc, easyJet, Ryanair, Air Nostrum (Iberia Regional) and more.
**Where to stay //** A mix of accommodation is available in larger centres, such as Tangier, Tétouan, Chefchaouen, Al-Hoceima, Nador and Saïdia. For small in-between villages, always research options in advance.
**When to ride //** April to the end of June. September and October are also good, though the kif harvest keeps locals and roads busier than usual.
**What to take //** Everything you need, including tools, spare parts, extra food and drink, and gear for changeable weather.

# MORE LIKE THIS
## SELF-SUPPORTED ADVENTURES

### SOUTHERN NAMIBIA

Namibia has the second lowest population density in the world. Most of its people are in the north, so the south is empty indeed. Not surprisingly, it's dry and unforgiving land. Towns and amenities are few and far between. Roads are mostly loose gravel. But it's also unutterably gorgeous. A seven-day, 621-mile (1000km) unsupported pedal through this astonishing landscape, from Namibia's capital of Windhoek to the South African border, requires planning, packing, perseverance and profound self-reliance. Factoring in the vast distances between towns, roadhouses, campgrounds and great attractions, an ideal itinerary is to head south-west to Sesriem for a visit to Sossusvlei's red dunes and salt pans, then turn south via Helmeringhausen and Seeheim to pause in Hobas and view Fish River Canyon (rivalling the Grand Canyon), and then point south again to Felix Unite, near the Noordoewer international crossing to South Africa.
**Start //** **Windhoek**
**End //** **Felix Unite**
**Distance //** **621 miles (1000km)**

### SOUTHERN SRI LANKA

In stark contrast to Namibia, Sri Lanka (see p152) has high population density, abundant services and variable landscapes that pack significant natural and cultural punch into small distances. The challenges to cyclists are poorly maintained roads, steamy temperatures and the frequent excited calls of 'Where are you going?' (a literal translation of the traditional greeting) from locals. The reward is a cornucopia of pleasures: tea-covered hills, commanding panoramas, and the southern coastal plains and their famous wildlife-filled parks and colourful, religious centres. One five-day, 168-mile (270km) ride commences in hilltop Haputale and enjoys the temperate tea plantations for a day to Ella before hurtling down the escarpment past historic caves, waterfalls and national parks to temple-rich Kataragama. Three days of lowland pedaling pass through Tissamaharama, Embilipitiya and many small villages on the way to the shoreside city of Matara.
**Start //** **Haputale**
**End //** **Matara**
**Distance //** **168 miles (270km)**

### THE LYCIAN COAST OF TURKEY

The coastal road from Antalya to Fethiye parallels the Lycian Way, Turkey's most famous long-distance footpath along ancient Lycia's seafront. Especially memorable for its sheer cliffs and plunging views to the Mediterranean Sea, it winds around the hidden coves and sandy beaches of this so-called Turquoise Coast, but also up and down an uncompromising clutch of hills, including one called Mt Olympos (not the one of Zeus fame). Easily completed in three or four days, the 171 miles (275km) traverse the resort community of Kemer; Kale (Demre), site of the real St Nicholas' restored 6th-century church and the ruins of the Lycian city of Myra; a picture-perfect seaside town called Kaş; and present-day Kınık, site of more Lycian ruins, once the city of Xanthos.
**Start //** **Antalya**
**End //** **Fethiye**
**Distance //** **171 miles (275km)**

*Clockwise from top: on the road in southern Namibia; an ancient Lycian amphitheatre in Turkey; touring tea plantations in Sri Lanka's Southern Highlands*

# CUBA'S SOUTHERN ROLLERCOASTER

*Pounded by surf, overshadowed by mountains and deeply imbued with revolutionary history, this lonely ride along Cuba's Caribbean coast pulsates with natural and historical drama.*

Cuba is full of dichotomies and its roads are no exception. Take Carretera N20 for instance, the 106 miles (170km) of potholed asphalt that runs along the south coast between Santiago de Cuba and the rustic village of Marea del Portillo, a spectacularly battered thoroughfare that could quite conceivably be described as the nation's best and worst highway. Shielded by purple-hued mountains that tumble down to meet the iridescent Caribbean, it scores ten-out-of-ten for craggy magnificence. But, lashed by hurricanes and beset by a severe lack of maintenance, it can be purgatory for aspiring drivers. Not surprisingly, few cars attempt it, leaving the road the

preserve of goats, *vaqueros* (cowboys) and the odd two-wheeled adventurer on a bicycle.

During nearly 20 years of travel in Cuba, I have traversed this epic highway in numerous ways, most notoriously on a protracted hitchhiking trip involving at least a dozen changes of vehicle, from a terminally ill Fiat Uno to a truck where the only other passenger was a dead pig. But my preference, if time and weather allows, is to tackle it on a bicycle. As visceral experiences go, this is Cuba as its most candid. The salty air, hidden coves, and erstwhile revolutionary history conspire to form a proverbial Columbian voyage of discovery that becomes more magical the further you pedal.

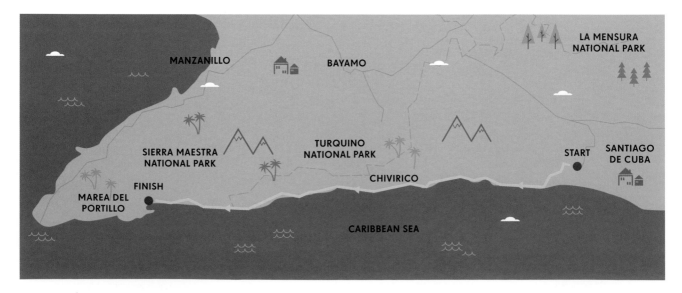

Fidel Castro and his band of bearded guerrillas lived as fugitives in these mountains for over two years in the late 1950s and the sense of eerie isolation prevails. Indeed, so deserted is the road that, in the handful of bucolic hamlets en route, farmers use it to air-dry their coffee beans, kids hijack it for baseball games, and cows parade boldly down the middle of the sun-bleached thoroughfare as if the motor car had never been invented.

Base camp for anyone attempting the ride is Santiago de Cuba, the nation's second largest city and, in many respects, its cultural capital. Heading west from here, the journey is best split into three stages. While route-finding is easy, the ups and downs of the highway as it curls around numerous headlands present a significant physical challenge. Be prepared. Roadside facilities range from scant to non-existent.

The first time I ventured out on a borrowed bike, I carried inadequate provisions and ended up knocking on the doors of isolated rural homesteads to 'beg' for water. Sure, I met some very obliging *campesinos* (country dwellers) offering liquid refreshment (including rum!), but the head-lightening effects of the dehydration probably weren't worth it. To avoid a similar fate, arm yourself with a robust bike and carry plenty of food and water.

The first recently repaired section from Santiago to the small town of Chivirico sees a modest trickle of traffic. Look out for growling *camiones particulares*, the noisy trucks that act as public transport in these parts. Around Chivirico you might spy another unique Cuban-ism, the *amarillos*, government-sponsored transit officials

## *"This remote region has remained utterly unspoiled, a glorious ribbon of driftwood-littered beaches"*

named for their mustard yellow uniforms; their job is to stand by the side of the road and flag down passing vehicles for hitchhikers.

Chivirico also has one of the route's strangest epiphanies, the Brisas Sierra Mar, an unpretentious all-inclusive hotel that springs seemingly out of nowhere 40 miles (65km) west of Santiago. Treat yourself: there is precious little accommodation for the next 62 miles (100km).

West of Chivirico, traffic dwindles to virtually nothing, while the eroded state of the road can make the going ponderous, even for cyclists. Fortunately, the magnificence of the scenery makes slow travel highly desirable.

This remote southeastern region has remained utterly unspoiled, a glorious ribbon of driftwood-littered beaches and crashing surf backed by Cuba's two highest peaks, Turquino (1974m) and Bayamesa (1602m). Such settlements that exist are tiny and etched in revolutionary folklore. El Uvero at the 60 mile (97km) point has a monument guarded by two rows of royal palms commemorating a battle audaciously won by Castro's rebels in 1957. Further west, La Plata, the site of another successful guerrilla attack, maintains a tiny museum. Just off the coast, vestiges of an earlier war lie underwater

## CLIMBING PICO TURQUINO

Cuba's highest mountain, Pico Turquino (1974m), is regularly climbed from Hwy 20, starting from a trailhead at Las Cuevas just west of El Uvero. It's a steep and gruelling 10-hour grunt to the top and back, but no specific mountaineering skills are required. The ascent must be made with a guide, but can be split over two days with a night spent in a basic mountain shelter.

*Left to right: a coast road in the Sierra Maestra; Catedral de Nuestra Señora de la Asunción in Santiago de Cuba; street scene with a 1951 Plymouth in Santiago de Cuba; the Sierra Maestra. Previous page: a rural church in Santiago de Cuba*

in the wreck of Cristóbal Colón, a Spanish destroyer sunk in the 1898 Spanish American war. Today it's a chillingly atmospheric dive site.

By now the steep headlands and tropical temperatures will have turned your legs the consistency of overcooked spaghetti. La Mula, around 6 miles (10km) west of El Uvero, is a rustic *campismo* with basic bungalows where you can recuperate just metres from the ocean.

On day three as the road crosses from Santiago de Cuba province into Granma, I like to pull over at one of the wild, Robinson Crusoe-like beaches and admire the increasingly dry terrain. Dwarf foliage including cacti is common, a result of the rain shadow effect of the Sierra Maestra. Aside from sporadic ramshackle villages, civilisation is confined to occasional *bohios* (thatched huts) dotting the mountain foothills. Sometimes, you'll inexplicably spy a lone sombrero-wearing local pacing alongside the roadside, miles from anywhere, clutching a machete.

The tiny fishing village of Marea del Portillo is equipped with two low-key resorts that guard a glowering dark-sand beach framed by broccoli-green peaks. Don't be deceived by the home-comforts. You've just arrived in one of the most cut-off corners of Cuba. To the north, crenelated mountain ridges shrug off clusters of bruised clouds. To the west sits Desembarco del Granma National Park, famed for its ecologically rich marine terraces. For me, this is paradise personified, a chance to resuscitate my bike-legs, carb-load at the hotel buffet and go off into the wilderness to explore some more. **BS**

## TOOLKIT

**Start //** Santiago de Cuba
**End //** Marea del Portillo
**Distance //** 106 miles (170km) along a rutted but easy-to-follow road.
**Getting there //** The nearest airport is Aeropuerto Antonio Maceo, 4 miles (6km) south of Santiago de Cuba. From here there are daily flights to Havana, and direct flights to Canada.
**Bike hire //** This is rare and unreliable in Cuba. Most serious cyclists bring their own bikes with them.
**Where to stay //** Club Amigo Marea del Portillo (+53 23-59-70-08; www.hotelescubanacan.com); Campismo La Mula (+53 22-32-62-62; www.campismopopular.cu); Brisas Sierra Mar (+53 22-32-91-10; www.hotelescubanacan.com)
**When to ride //** The best time is mid-November to late-March. However, the road is prone to flooding and closures. Check ahead in Santiago.

*Opposite: a Cuban cigar roller in the Valle de Viñales*

# MORE LIKE THIS
## CUBAN RIDES

### LA FAROLA

Hailed as one of the seven modern engineering marvels of Cuba, La Farola (the lighthouse road) links the beach hamlet of Cajobabo on the arid Caribbean coast with the nation's beguiling oldest city, Baracoa. Measuring 34 miles (55km) in length, the road traverses the steep-sided Sierra del Puril, snaking its way precipitously through a landscape of granite cliffs and pine-scented cloud forest before falling, with eerie suddenness, upon the lush tropical paradise of the Atlantic coastline. For cyclists, it offers a classic Tour de France-style challenge with tough climbs, invigorating descents and relatively smooth roads. La Farola starts 124 miles (200km) east of Santiago de Cuba and is thus best incorporated into a wider Cuban cycling excursion. You could also charter a taxi to drop you off at the start point.
**Start // Cajobabo**
**End // Baracoa**
**Distance // 34 miles (55km)**

### GUADALAVACA TO BANES

Talk to savvy repeat visitors in Guadalavaca's popular resort strip and you'll discover that one of the region's most epiphanic activities is to procure a bicycle and pedal it through undulating rural terrain to the fiercely traditional town of Banes 21 miles (33km) to the east. This beautifully bucolic ride transports you from the resort-heavy north coast to a gritty slice of the real Cuba in a matter of hours along a road where you're more likely to encounter a horse and cart than a traffic jam. Some of the resorts lend out bikes but pedalling these basic machines can be hard work; in-the-know visitors often fly in with their own bikes (Holguín's Frank País international airport receives direct flights from the UK, Canada and Italy).
**Start // Guadalavaca**
**End // Banes**
**Distance // 21 miles (33km)**

### VALLE DE VIÑALES

Viñales is a small farming community that does a lucrative side-business in tourism. It sits nestled among craggy *mogotes* (steep, haystack-shaped hills) in Cuba's primary tobacco-growing region. With about as much traffic on its roads as 1940s Britain, the region – which is protected as both a Unesco World Heritage site and National Park – is ideal for cycling. Various loops can be plotted around the valley's multifarious sights, which include caves, tobacco plantations, climbing routes and snippets of rural Cuban life. Riders can hire from the Bike Rental Point in Viñales' main plaza. Or your *casa particular* (private homestay, of which there are dozens in the village) may have bicycles available to rent.
**Getting there // Viñales is easily reached from Havana by bus**
**Distance // Whatever you feel like**

© Mark Read

# TO THE TIP OF PATAGONIA

*Cyclists rub shoulders with gauchos and guanacos in southern Argentina, braving howling wind to reach the tip of the South American continent.*

O ut on the bolt-straight roads of the Argentinian *pampa* (vast plains) my handlebars stay true, but my mind wanders. The open expanse of Southern Patagonia is a pensive place, a vast and empty land that stirs memories and emotion, like a calling to fill its void.

As my legs spin, I hum along to the buzz of knobbly tyres on smooth asphalt. I listen to the snap of my open shirt, which flaps behind me like a cape. I try and clear my head. But like any meditation, I become stuck on certain thoughts, clanking around like coins in a washing machine. Before long, an ostrich-like rhea waddles out of the camouflage of the plains. I smile, my spirits lifted. Then, a guanaco, the camelid native to these parts, breaks rank and jumps daintily over the endless fence line I've been following. It makes a chuckling sound as I pass, as if remarking on the ridiculousness of my toils.

It's a sentiment that seems to be echoed by others. Once, I see the blur of a passenger photographing me from a minivan that hurtles past. What must they be thinking? I guess I must look a little crazy, bearded and unkempt, out here in the emptiness. Later, a couple flag me down to quiz me about my bike. We talk a while by the roadside. I've noticed a distinct soulfulness in Argentinians, perhaps intensified by the thought-stirring sparseness of their land. 'Que lindo este viaje,' the man says, gesturing to his heart, and shaking my hand warmly. 'What a beautiful journey.'

A beautiful journey indeed, and one that captures Patagonia's contemplative character, its windswept isolation and its spectacular vistas. Indeed, the ride down from El Chaltén showcases one its finest moments; the granite silhouette of Monte Fitz Roy is the stuff of picture postcards and mountaineering legends.

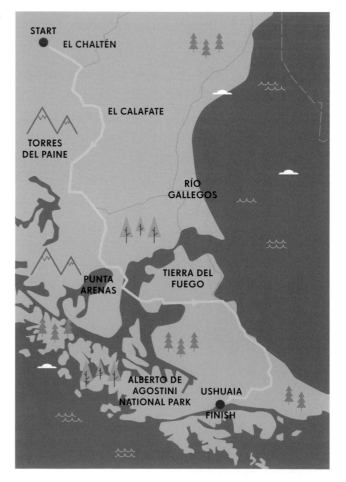

START
EL CHALTÉN

EL CALAFATE

TORRES DEL PAINE

RÍO GALLEGOS

PUNTA ARENAS

TIERRA DEL FUEGO

ALBERTO DE AGOSTINI NATIONAL PARK

USHUAIA
FINISH

Clockwise from top: riding with horses on the Patagonian pampa; portrait of a gaucho; off-road trails run through beech forests. Previous page: heading into the Patagonian hills

I pedal on. As asphalt peters out, I plough my way through deep, corrugated *ripio* (gravel), gliding from one side to the other in search of the truest line. In this light, it's hard to even tell what time of day it is. It could be just before sunset, but in fact it's early afternoon. Scale plays games on the *pampa*, and distance takes on a different quality; perhaps a more mysterious form of measurement is appropriate, like leagues. Only roadside shrines mark the passing of time, and drainage culverts, into which cyclists sometimes burrow to escape the howling winds.

And those winds! They're incessant. Thankfully, my southerly trajectory means they're in my favour much of the time. But when they're not, it's like slamming against a steel wall. A particular tactic is thus required: strategic hops from one wind-free or rain-sheltered enclave to another. Most are abandoned buildings, skeletal husks that resonate former lives. Like hallowed secrets, the exact locations of these sanctuaries are swapped around a carton of wine at a campsite, or scrawled onto a crumpled map out on the road.

Among the most popular is the so-called Pink Hotel on Ruta 40, the legendary road that spans the entire length of this country. An abandoned complex set on a solitary stretch of *pampa*, the Pink Hotel has long shielded a migration of riders from the howling, tent-crushing wind that gathers with gusto each afternoon. On the night I pass through, it's a surprisingly social premises. I'm one of five riders heading south, joined by a French-Canadian couple braving the elements north. We roll out our mats on the hotel's parquet floor and sign the guestbook: the canvas of a graffitied wall, onto which cyclists scrawl their names and a precis of their journeys.

## PENGUIN COLONIES

No visit to Patagonia is complete without an encounter with its most characterful residents. Of the two penguin colonies *en route*, one involves a ferry ride to Isla Magdalena, home to 60,000 pairs of Magellanic penguins. Like drunkards dressed up for a ball, they stagger around in the high winds. The other is at Parque Pingüino Rey in Bahia Inútil, where cyclists can camp near a group of majestic King Penguins that stand up to 1m tall.

*Clockwise from top: King penguins at Parque Pingüino Rey; riding a fully-loaded fat bike; icebergs calving at the Perito Moreno glacier*

Other such places of calm come and go. At a lonely outpost near Tapi Aike, Fabien the police officer ushers me in, as he has done to so many cyclists before me. He feeds me a hearty dinner, and together we watch dubbed movies late into the night. And there's Panadería La Union, about which I hear stories months before I actually arrive. Its location is triple-ringed excitedly on my dog-eared map, and a note scrawled to the side: 'Bakery. Delicious empanadas and cakes. Hosts cyclists for free.'

Breaking the monosyllabic mood of Southern Patagonia, there are also moments of startling eloquence. Sometimes, it's as simple as a lenticular cloud, or a team of muscular horses watching me ride by. At other times, it's raw geology. In El Calafate, I head out to Perito Moreno Glacier. Spanning 2.5 miles (4km) in width, the sight itself is as impressive as the sound it emits: an incessant soundtrack of gurgles and murmurs, of deep, resonant rumbles and thunderous crunches.

I ride on, away from Ruta 40, forging my way closer to the coastline, until finally I cross the Strait of Magellan to Tierra del Fuego, the Chilean and Argentinian archipelago that lies off the southernmost tip of the South American continent. It's named after the myriad of fires once kept by the indigenous Yámana – a hardy folk who walked barefoot through snow. By now, I'm a member of my own impromptu cycling collective, pilgrims drawn from around the globe, pedalling by day and sharing stories by night.

For many, riding to the very tip of the South American continent is the end of long, arduous and undoubtedly beautiful journey; adventures that have unfolded since Colombia, Mexico or even Alaska. And now here we are. Together, we cycle through the gates of Ushuaia. Connected by a rush of similar emotions, we high-five. We hug. We look round in slight disbelief. Yes, we've arrived. Ahead, the road has finally run out. **CG**

*"Together we cycle through the gates of Ushuaia. Connected by a rush of similar emotions, we high-five"*

### TOOLKIT

**Start** // El Chaltén
**End** // Ushuaia
**Distance** // 714.5 miles (1150km)
**Getting there** // Fly or bus into El Calafate, and out of Ushuaia.
**When to ride** // The best time to visit the area is during Patagonian summer – from November to March.
**How to ride** // Head north to south, or face a soul destroying headwind much of the way.
**Where to stay** // Bring a stout tent, and keep your eyes peeled for abandoned houses!
**What to take** // Weather can be notoriously mixed; pack plenty of layers and reliable waterproofs.
**Detours** // Allow time to day hike in Argentina's world class Los Glaciares National Park, explore Torres del Paine in Chile, or connect this route with the 621-mile (1000km) Carretera Austral.

*Opposite: Lake Namtso on the*
*Friendship Hwy, north of Lhasa*

# MORE LIKE THIS
## REMOTE RIDES

### SALAR DE UYUNI, BOLIVIA

Cycling atop the salt crust of Bolivia's Salar de Uyuni – and the more petite but perfectly formed Salar de Coipasa – is an undisputed highlight of many a South America journey. It's a high-altitude ride that takes five or six days, segmented by an opportunity to resupply with water and food at the midway settlement of Llica. As the largest salt flat in the world, cycling here provides an other-worldly experience. There's nothing quite like pitching your tent on a bleached white canvas, seasoning your dinner with the salty ground on which you're sitting, and awakening in the morning to a glow of ethereal, lavender light. This journey can only be undertaken in Bolivia's winter, as during summer the salt lakes are inundated by seasonal rain.
**Start // Uyuni**
**End // Sabaya**
**Distance // 186 miles (300km)**

### CANNING STOCK ROUTE, AUSTRALIA

Riding Western Australia's Canning Stock Route is a monumental challenge. In fact, it's only been successfully completed by a handful of riders. Given the extended sections of soft sand, dunes and corrugation that typify such a vast, remote and unforgiving desert, this is a route that can only be undertaken on a fat bike, sporting a colossal tyre size of at least 4in in width. You'll also need to carry enough food for more than 30 days, and water for four- to five- day stretches at a time. Despite the 51 old wells that punctuate the route, only a handful can be relied upon. But for anyone prepared to tackle this physical and logistical feat, the reward is complete, unmatched desert solitude.
**Start // Hall Creek**
**End // Wiluna**
**Distance // 1243 miles (2000km)**

### FRIENDSHIP HWY, TIBET–NEPAL

Bookended by the cities of Lhasa and Kathmandu, the Friendship Hwy crosses the Tibetan plateaux via a series of high elevation passes, the highest of which reaches 5251m. Given that much of the pedalling takes place at over 4000m – across the Roof of the World, as it's often called – pre-ride acclimatisation is vital, particularly if flying into Lhasa. The journey itself takes 3 weeks, including a detour to Everest Base camp, promising stunning views of the planet's highest peak. Elsewhere, the Himalayan showcase continues, with the likes of Cho Oyu (8241m) and Shishapangma (8042m) prodding into the atmosphere. Leaving the Land of Snows is like entering another world; Nepal's green backdrop provides a sudden and stark change from Tibet's vast and windswept plateau. Given the political sensitivity of the area, independent travel can be limited. Currently, the Friendship Hwy can only be ridden as part of an organised group.
**Start // Lhasa, Tibet**
**End // Kathmandu, Nepal**
**Distance // 594 miles (956km)**

# THE NATCHEZ TRACE PARKWAY

*The Natchez Trace coasts through three Southern states of America, with thousands of years of history beneath your wheels and the sounds of Elvis in your ears.*

A t the northern terminus of the Natchez Trace Parkway, a milepost sticks up like a thumb on the side of the road. For many bikers, the brown sign represents the final lap, an exclamation point punctuating a two-wheeled odyssey that started two states away in Mississippi. For southbound cyclers like me, however, the marker is just the beginning. 'Mile one,' I exclaim ceremoniously, translating the sign's three digits.

Over 10 days, I will pedal 444 miles (714.5km) from Nashville to Natchez, with a small wedge of Alabama in between. During my journey on the National Park Service road, I will roll through thousands of years of history, and not necessarily in order. I will follow in the footsteps of giant sloths and Chickasaw tribes, Kaintucks (Ohio River farmers and boaters) and Elvis, and Civil War soldiers and Oprah.

During hours-long rides, I will share the two-lane paved road with a handful of cars and motorcycles (the maximum speed limit of 50 miles/80km per hour deters rushed drivers), kindred spirits in padded shorts and helmets (peak season is autumn) and countless critters, including armadillos both dead and alive. And in and out of my saddle, I will experience Southern traditions that touch all aspects of life, from grits to music to football.

The New Trace, a straight arrow that dates from 1936 and roughly parallels the original foot trail, is not as arduous as the Old Trace, a meandering dirt path studded with rocks and roots. Nor is it as perilous: the poisonous snakes, tribal attacks and bandits appear only in yellowed accounts.

But the communities are still dispersed like distant beacons. I have to watch the clock and my pace if I want to arrive at my

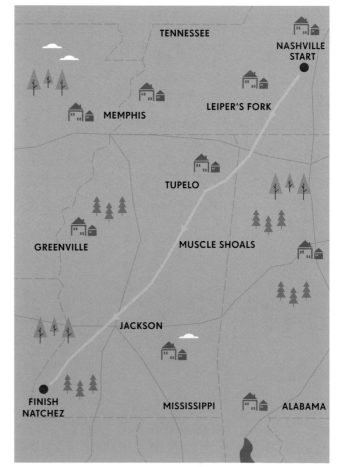

lodging before nightfall – or, in the case of Leiper's Fork, to catch open mic night at Puckett's Grocery & Restaurant.

The 19th-century village, about 15 miles (24km) from the Trace entrance in Tennessee, is a darling among Nashville stars (the Judds, Carrie Underwood) and troubadour musicians seeking an impromptu jam (Aerosmith bandmates). When I enter Puckett's, two young guitarists are electrifying the crowd with a Jimi Hendrix cover. I'm introduced to the unofficial mayor of Leiper's Fork, a towering grey-haired man in a baseball cap named Goose.

'This is one of the prettiest parts of the country, especially on the Trace,' Goose yells into my ear, mentioning the maple and oak trees lining the parkway. He then directs my gaze to the stage, pointing to the keyboardist, who plays with Neil Sedaka, and the guitarist, who tours with Ted Nugent. He widens his sweep to point out Naomi Judd's husband and a CIA agent who I am supposed to forget as soon as I see her.

I don't have much time to ease into the Trace. The longest distance – 72 miles (119km) – falls on the second day. The Tennessee portion is the hilliest, slowing my speed and stretching my energy reserves. Informational placards and historic sites further impede my progress. At the Meriwether Lewis National Monument, I meet a New Orleans-bound skateboarder tending to his injuries after a crash and the Nashville couple who have

*"At FAME Recording Studios, an employee invites me inside Studio A, where Aretha Franklin cut two hits"*

been cheering me on with fist-pumps through their sunroof. We discuss the rumour that the famed explorer died of syphilis. But the National Park refuses to gossip. An interpretive sign by a stone memorial elusively explains that his life 'came tragically and mysteriously to a close.'

In Florence, at Milepost 338, a group of motorcyclists huddle around Tom Hendrix to hear the emotional tale of his great-great-grandmother. As a Yuchi girl, he explains, she was forced to leave her tribal land in Alabama for Indian Territory in present-day Oklahoma. She was restless, however, and reversed course. She spent five years searching for her way back home.

In the 1980s, Tom started to collect millions of pounds of rocks and build the 1½-mile/2.5km-long Te-lah-nay's Wall to honour her life and spirit. The eastern portion runs in a direct line and represents the Trail of Tears; the western section sprawls in many directions, symbolising her meandering return route.

At Muscle Shoals, about 20 miles (32km) off the Trace in

## THE HOME OF ELVIS

The birthplace of Elvis is the B-side of Graceland. In Tupelo you can visit the 15-acre park complex that houses both his humble childhood home and a museum of memorabilia. There's also the legendary Tupelo Hardware Company, which still sells tools and instruments. Inside the store, stand on a black X that marks the spot where the future rock n' roll star picked out his first guitar.

*Left to right: FAME recording studios in Muscle Shoals, Alabama; Elvis's birthplace in Tupelo, Mississippi; riding the Natchez Trace Parkway; hanging out at open mic night at Puckett's Grocery, Leiper's Fork. Previous page: Nashville, capital city of country music*

Alabama, is where some of the biggest names up and down the radio dial have recorded, such as Otis Redding, Etta James, Paul Simon, Bob Dylan, the Rolling Stones and Band of Horses. At Muscle Shoals Sound Studio, a museum guide encourages me to shake a pair of maracas in the booth where Mick Jagger and Keith Richards belted out three songs on 'Sticky Fingers'. A German tourist ducks into a sacred but still-operating space: the bathroom where Richards wrote 'Wild Horses'.

At FAME Recording Studios, an employee invites me inside Studio A, where Aretha Franklin cut two hits and Alicia Keys played the piano for the 2013 documentary film, Muscle Shoals. In Studio B, he tells me that Duane Allman once slept and performed here. For the next 60-odd miles (97km) to Tupelo, I have Southern rock stuck in my head.

For 361 miles (581km), I have biked solo. But one morning, I unexpectedly become a duo. A French-Canadian in striped long underwear sidles up next to me and strikes up a conversation that endures for more than 80 miles (129km). We become a trio when a former turkey farmer from North Carolina joins us.

We count down the final distance together, with the French-Canadian throwing up his arm at significant intervals. At the three-mile (5km) mark, I start to feel a mix of elation and deflation. At the last mile (1.6km) of Natchez, I pedal slower, savouring it as much as I did the first in Nashville. **AS**

## TOOLKIT

**Start** // Nashville, Tennessee
**End** // Natchez, Mississippi
**Distance** // 444 miles (714.5km)
**Getting there** // From Natchez, the airports aren't that close. Alexandria (Louisiana), is 70 miles (113km) away; Baton Rouge (Louisiana) is 90 miles (145km). Catch a Greyhound bus to the start of your ride or hire an airport shuttle. Nearby bike shops can box and ship your wheels.
**Where to stay** // For overnight options, cyclists can pitch a tent at more than a dozen campgrounds, including several bicycle-only sites, or pedal into Collinwood, Tennessee; Florence, Alabama; and Houston and Kosciusko in Mississippi.
**Where to eat** // The Trace does not provide any food concessions beyond the rare vending machine at a rest stop. Pack meals in panniers.
**More info** // www.natcheztracetravel.com

*Opposite: autumn foliage on
the Blue Ridge Parkway,
viewed from Waterrock Knob*

# MORE LIKE THIS
# ALL-AMERICAN RIDES

### RAGBRAI, IOWA

Short for the Register's Annual Great
Bicycle Ride Across Iowa, RAGBRAI
connects the dots of small towns
stretching from the western shores of the
Missouri River to the eastern banks of the
Mississippi River. The ride, held during
the last full week of July, started in 1973
as a six-day excursion, and every year
the organisers plot a new route, shuffling
the eight host communities procured for
overnight stops. Despite the changes,
several constants persist: the course
distance and the direction from west to
east, to avoid strong headwinds and biking
into the sun. The landscape highlights
country life, with red barns, silos, and fields
carpeted in corn, wheat and sunflowers.
And, contrary to pancake jokes, your legs
will learn that Iowa is not flat.
**Start/End // Changes annually, with
the itinerary released in late January
(www.ragbai.com)
Distance // On average 468
miles (753km)
More info // www.ragbrai.com**

### BLUE RIDGE PARKWAY, VIRGINIA
### TO NORTH CAROLINA

The iconic Blue Ridge Parkway rises and
falls like a roller-coaster track running from
Virginia's Shenandoah National Park to
North Carolina's Great Smoky Mountains
National Park. Most bikers budget about
10 days to complete the 469-mile (755km)
route, which crosses four national forests
and features 176 bridges, more than two
dozen tunnels and hundreds of historic
sites. Riders will experience the America
that inspires patriotic songs: uninterrupted
forests, burbling rivers, splashy waterfalls,
vibrant wildflowers or foliage (depending
on the season), and mountains haloed in
clouds. Roadside diversions abound, such
as the Blue Ridge Music Center, Julian
Price Memorial Park and Craggy Gardens.
Time your visit to Waterrock Knob with the
sun's sky spectacle.
**Start // Shenandoah National Park
near Waynesboro, Virginia
End // Great Smoky Mountains
National Park near Cherokee,
North Carolina
Distance // 469 miles (755km)**

### GREAT ALLEGHENY PASSAGE (GAP),
### MARYLAND TO PENNSYLVANIA

The chirps of bike bells have replaced
the toots of train whistles that once
rang through the corridors of the Great
Allegheny Passage (GAP). The 150-mile
(241km) biking and hiking trail (no cars
allowed) sprang from mostly abandoned
railbeds laid between Cumberland,
Maryland. and Pittsburgh, Pennsylvania.
The trail is flat and leisurely, and coasts by
some remarkable landmarks. On the 13-mile
(21km) Frostburg-to-Meyersdale leg, for
example, the wow list includes the Mason–
Dixon Line into Pennsylvania; the 3,300ft-
long Big Savage Tunnel, which was named
after the stranded 18th-century surveyor
who had offered himself up as food to save
his men; the Eastern Continental Divide,
the trail's highest point at 2390ft; and the
curved Keystone Viaduct. Charming towns
such as Confluence, on the Youghiogheny
River, and Ohiopyle, a hyperactive hub of
outdoor activities, entice bikers to hop off
and stay awhile.
**Start // Cumberland, Maryland
End // Pittsburgh, Pennsylvania
Distance // 150 miles (241km)**

# A CIRCUIT OF SAN JUAN ISLAND

*A breezy half-day spin around San Juan Island passes fragrant lavender farms, groves of misty pines, gorgeous coastline, and pods of orcas.*

Nestled between Seattle and the Canadian border in the postcard-perfect Puget Sound, San Juan Island is one of several that comprise the archipelago of San Juan Islands. Each of the islands are filled with stunning sights and quaint diversions that make a lovely escape for casual cyclists. Each island also has a particular appeal for people who love to travel with their bicycle – the laidback cruising on Lopez Island versus the slightly more heart-racing terrain of Orcas Island – but the picturesque San Juan Island is just right, offering maximum views and a taste of adventure that is approachable for a wide range of riders.

I discovered the bicycle-friendly roads that circle San Juan Island offer something new around every bend – rocky outcroppings that plunge into sparkling waves, lofty groves of Douglas fir, migratory birdlife, bucolic farms and miles of coast. But this 35-mile (56km) ride has just as many excuses to get off the bike, including a pair

of picturesque harbour towns, roadside farm stands, and historic sites that speak to the region's colourful past. The biodiversity of such a small island is fascinating – from dense conifer forest and open farmlands to picturesque beaches. Modestly rolling terrain, 247 annual days of sunshine, and breathtaking scenery makes it an ideal destination to ride.

My partner and I began at the island's main port, Friday Harbor, connected by frequent ferry service to Washington. After fuelling up on breakfast at one of the harbourside cafes we were on our way.

Heading south out of town on Argyle Rd, we followed the signs to the American Camp visitor center, one of the two former 19th-century military camps that make up the San Juan Island National Historical Park. A ranger was on hand answering questions about the so-called Pig War, an 1859 boundary skirmish between the British and the US. The conflict owes its colorful name to the incident that sparked it: a dispute between an American farmer and an employee of the Hudson's Bay Company who owned an unruly pig. Fortunately, the pig was the only casualty.

A few more miles south and we reached South Beach, which has incredible views across the Strait of Juan de Fuca to the snow-capped drama of the Olympic Mountain range. We continued south to the Cattle Point Lighthouse along a steep bluff and paused at pull-offs for mesmerising views of Vancouver Island, Olympic National Park and Port Angeles.

Continuing west and north we made our way to Lime Kiln Point

*"Volunteer whale watchers scan the waves for orcas and other species of whales that include gray, humpback and minke"*

State Park – known to the locals as Whale Watch Park – which is one of the island's most popular spots for a picnic. If you're here in the summer, you have a good chance of spotting a pod of orca whales. There are volunteer whale watchers at the most popular overlooks, scanning the waves for orcas and other species of whales that include gray, humpback, and minke. This is a good excuse to park the bike, as the area is great to explore on foot. We wandered around an historic lighthouse, an interpretive centre with hands-on exhibits and displays about the orcas, and an ancient lime kiln. This is where you should top-up your water as well, as the slightly more vigorous riding is about to begin.

Leaving Lime Kiln Point, the road gains a couple of hundred feet of elevation, passing some of the most spectacular coastal sights on the entire ride. Over the hill, we cruised down to San Juan County Park. If you missed the whales at the first stop, try again; the unfortunately named Smallpox Bay is another good spot to look for the pods. This part of the island is home to all kinds of other wildlife as well, including deer and bald eagles. Turning left on West Valley Rd, we rolled past the curious gang at the Krystal

## THE ORCAS OF SAN JUAN ISLANDS

The San Juan Islands host three resident pods of black and white orcas – a population of just over 80 whales, many of whom are known on a first-name basis by the locals. The orcas call these waters home between May to October. If you want to see them up close, consider a kayaking excursion – but your chances are just as good to spot them as they swim near the shore.

*Left to right: the San Juan Islands have three pods of resident orcas; Roche Harbor and Lime Kiln Lighthouse on San Juan Island. Previous page: looking out over the San Juan archipelago with Mt Baker in the distance*

Acres Alpaca Farm – which has a great gift shop of locally made goods – before seeing signs for English Camp. Situated on an open, grassy patch, this is another good place for a rest.

As we continued down the road toward Roche Harbor, we started thinking about lunch. Locals recommended the Westcott Bay Shellfish Company, a small family farm that produces deliciously briny oysters and has no-frills picnic tables where you can enjoy the sun, and shuck your lunch. But we were in the mood for something a bit heartier, so headed into town.

Centred around a tidy port and the stately Hotel de Haro, the marina at Roche Harbor is a charming lunch stop. Lime production was a major industry here during the late 19th century, but these days the small harbor is a magnet for yachting retirees from the Pacific Northwest. Explore the lanes of the historic village before making your way to the San Juan Islands Sculpture Park, a 19-acre park with more than 150 works by local and international artists, including some amazing kinetic sculptures.

Back in the saddle, it was a straight shot back to Friday Harbor – just under 10 flat miles (16km) on Roche Harbor Rd. Halfway back, we passed the lovely Lakedale Resort – a lakeside hotel with some options for glamping – before arriving at the final diversion, San Juan Vineyards. We did a bit of tasting (we earned it!) before bringing a glass out to the patio and taking in the warm evening light. A quick three miles (5km) more brought us back to the start in Friday Harbor, for hot showers and an elegant dinner. **NC**

## TOOLKIT

**Start/End** // Friday Harbor
**Distance** // 35 miles (56km).
**Getting there** // Get to the island via the Washington State Ferry from Anacortes (www.takeaferry.com) or from Seattle's seasonal Victoria Clipper. Seasonal ferries also depart from Bellingham or Port Townsend.
**Bike hire** // There are plenty of bike rental options in Friday Harbor, including high-end road bikes.
**Where to eat/stay** // Friday Harbor is San Juan Island's largest town, and has a host of dining and sleeping options. Romantic B&Bs are scattered all over the island.
**When to ride** // The best time of year for a visit is between late April and early September.
**More info** // For complete information on visiting the island, including cycling resources, see www.visitsanjuans.com.

*Opposite: there are few straight roads
on the Dingle Peninsula, Ireland*

# MORE LIKE THIS
## ISLAND RIDES

### VIEQUES ISLAND, PUERTO RICO

Six miles (9½km) off the southeastern
coast of Puerto Rico, Vieques is a little strip
of paradise – just 21 miles (38km) long
and four miles (6½km) wide. Much of this
enchanted place was owned by the United
States Navy until 2003, when two-thirds
of the island transitioned from a bombing
range to lush nature reserve. Pedal down
its long, dusty roads to find secluded
beaches otherwise inaccessible by car.
Many of the best of these have no names,
but Red Beach is worth seeking out; the
blonde crescent strip of sand lies beyond
the cracked asphalt airstrip of the former
Camp Garcia. Even during the high season
(between late November and May) you'll
have the place mostly to yourself.
**Tour // Black Beard Sports
(www.blackbeardsports.com) has
rentals and leads tours**

### NANTUCKET ISLAND RIDE, USA

Filled with New England ambience, history,
and fresh-air vistas, Nantucket is a relaxing
destination that's perfect to explore by
bike. The island is only 14 miles (22½km)
long and three and a half miles (5½km)
wide, so a dedicated cyclist can spin
around its entirety in one day, but you'll be
better off to take some short rides around
town and to the outlying beaches. Start
with the boutiques and restaurants on
the cobbled streets of historic Nantucket
Harbor before navigating the network
of smooth bike-paths past ocean views,
migratory birds, and windswept beaches.
Refuel on bowls of chowder among the
rows of neat gray-shingled cottages in the
old fishing village of Saiconset.
**Bike hire // The Island Bike Company
(www.islandbike.com) has a range of
bikes, including cruisers and roadies**

### DINGLE PENINSULA, IRELAND

Between the craggy range of mountains
and rocky cliffs that plunge into the Atlantic,
the Dingle Peninsula is a joy for cyclists,
who can ride a demanding day-long loop
that passes historic ruins, roaring coastline,
and amazing beaches. The peninsula
is something of an open-air museum,
dotted with more than 2000 Neolithic-Age
monuments built between 4000BC. and
early Christian times. The village of Dunquin
has many crumbling rock homes that were
abandoned during the famine. You'll also
pass the Gallarus Oratory, one of Ireland's
most well preserved ancient Christian
churches. As you near the end of the loop,
pull off for a quick stop at the 12th-century
Irish Romanesque church with an ancient
cemetery before returning to Dingle Town,
where you'll find plenty of pubs (many of
which are hardware stores by day) to toast
the adventure.
**Start/End // Dingle Town
Distance // 25 miles (40km)**

# FAMILY BIKEPACKING IN ECUADOR

*Picturesque Quilotoa Loop feels suitably off-the-beaten-track, but with a range of comfortable digs along the way, cyclists can recharge before tackling Ecuador's tremendous inclines.*

For those unfamiliar with the topography of South America, let me assure you of this: the Ecuadorian Andes are a deeply crumpled land. A slim band squeezed between the expanse of the Pacific Coast and the vast sprawl of the Amazon, it abounds with microclimates, determined more by geography and altitude than by any season. Within these folds, one steep-sided valley dovetails into the next. Cradled between two volcanic ranges, they form the Avenue of the Volcanoes, as coined by Alexander von Humboldt, the Prussian naturalist who journeyed through the continent in the 19th century.

Big mountains, big views... and, above all, big climbs: adventurous cycling, without doubt. But family friendly? Yes and, somewhat surprisingly, very much so.

We shared our Ecuadorian adventures with three brothers I'd first met while cycling through the country three years prior. Mountain guides by trade, they lived offgrid on an organic family farm outside Quito. In the interim, we'd kept in touch – and we'd all had children. When the chance came to visit Ecuador once again, this time I travelled with my partner and our two-year-old son Sage, so we might experience this beautiful and unfeasibly rugged country together.

In any shape or form, this ride would have been epic enough. Apart from the quiet dirt tracks, small mountain settlements, and fluffy roadside llamas, its backdrop was nothing short of spectacular: high altitude Ecuadorian paramo, the alpine tundra for which the country is known, and the emerald-tinted, 2mile (3.2km) wide Quilotoa crater lake, a definitive highlight along the Avenue of the Volcanoes.

But factor in no less than eight bicycles and five accompanying trailers, charged with a payload of children ranging in age from

six months to three years, and such a journey takes on an even more memorable character. Despite the afternoon downpours and the occasional synchronised meltdowns, our pint-sized expedition proved to be an incredible life experience for everyone.

Together, we blazed a trail of family mayhem through the countryside. We rubbed shoulders with poncho-clad horse riders, picnicked amongst fields of quinoa, visited an indigenous market, and lingered in village playgrounds.

We kept distances short, and tried to harmonise riding times with napping schedules. When our three toddlers needed a break,

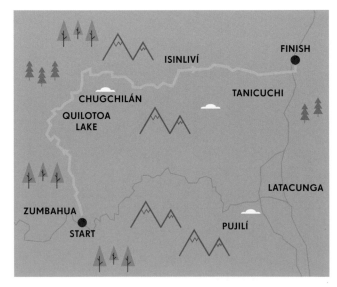

*Clockwise from left: keep spirits and sugar levels up with regular stops at street markets; healthy meals; towing the full team; feeding time; a laden fat bike with trailer. Previous page: pedalling into the wilds of Ecuador*

"Reaching the summit was rewarded with a feast of local produce, cheese and ripe avocados that had filled our panniers"

we stopped and played football, helped them climb trees, or just explored the land. And what a land it was. A fertile patchwork of vertiginous fields clung to steep-sided slopes, surrounded by both soaring peaks and crumbling canyon cliffs. Pigs scuffled around by the road, men sauntered by with machetes on their hips, and women crammed their colourful shawls with fresh corn, their felt hats peeking out through the foliage.

The route itself looped south-east through Ecuador's Central Sierras. After stopping to applaud the natural watery wonder of Quilotoa, and scout briefly along the knife edge of its crater, it took us through the small settlement of Chugchilán, where we detoured into the dewy delights of the Illiniza Cloud Forest. There, fingers of mist curled through the trees, enveloping the land, filling every nook and cranny with silence. When the sun occasionally permeated through, it was subtle and shadowless, painting the mountains in gigantic, camouflaged swatches.

Up and down we rode, rarely a flat moment for respite. Climbs had our derailleurs clattering frantically through the gears, spinning our legs in the lowest cadences we could find, the ballast of our toddler cargo weighing us down. In immediate riposte, descents demanded we pull on brake levers like reins on a horse, lest our trailers shunt us forwards. Added to this, the terrain was often bumpy, sometimes even cobbled. Yet when I looked back to check on Sage, more often than not he was sound asleep, oblivious to our efforts.

Travelling over the winter holidays, we celebrated Christmas in Isinliví, a picturesque settlement perched in one of the region's verdant valleys. As we came to appreciate, South Americans know how to party, whatever time of the year. The main square awash with revellers, countryside cowboys and a roving brass band that relentlessly circled its stony streets. To Sage's delight, it even boasted an antiquated funfair, featuring a merry-go-round that spun with dizzying speed.

Isinliví was also our last staging post before we tackled the longest climb of the trip, a Herculean undertaking that involved 1000m in altitude gain, on an unpaved road at that. Inevitably, this final undertaking had us all off the bikes and pushing, our Lilliputian team of toddlers enthusiastically lending a helping hand too. When the summit finally came, it was rewarded with a feast of local produce, cheese and deliciously ripe avocados that had filled our panniers. Then, with a last gaze out towards the highland paramo, we dived into the whirligig descent that lay ahead, the flags of our trailers snapping in the wind.

Despite the diminutive daily distances, I won't lay claim that family bikepacking is easy; without doubt, it poses its own set of mental and logistical challenges, quite apart from any physical toils. But I couldn't more highly recommend trying one out, wherever it may be in the world, for however many days you may have. Gather the troops and brew up a plan. Choose a route that everyone will enjoy. Take the time to luxuriate in being off the bike as much as you are on it. I can guarantee that such undiluted family time will warm the heart and feed the soul. For everyone involved. **CG**

## MARKETS

Ecuador's markets are not to be missed: vibrant colours, towering displays of food and a real sense of community. Fresh fruit juices and delicious snacks abound – grilled plantain is safe to eat, and a sure-fire toddler favourite. Usurping the main square each Saturday, there's Zumbahua's market – at the beginning of the Quilotoa Loop. Or, as a separate trip, don't miss Otavalo, the best place to stock up on beautifully knitted jumpers and ponchos for children.

*Clockwise from left: cosy cargo; public transport; climbing gravel roads, one step at a time*

## TOOLKIT

**Start //** Zumbahua
**End //** Lasso, on the Pan-American Hwy.
**Distance //** 68 miles (110km)
**Getting there //** Both Zumbahua and Lasso can be easily accessed by bus from Quito.
**Where to stay //** Hostal Llullu Llama in Isinliví. For eco-minded luxury, the Black Sheep Inn, near Chugchilán.
**What to take //** Pack light and make use of traveller-friendly accommodation en route.
**Climate //** Put aside several days in Quito to acclimatise before heading into Ecuador's high country.
**Hot tip //** Ecuador's inclines can be long and unreasonably steep (but ultimately rewarding!). Trucks regularly ply Ecuador's mountain roads. For a few dollars, flag down a driver, and enjoy a lift to the top of the next mountain pass.

*Opposite: riding through
downtown Salida, Colorado*

# MORE LIKE THIS
# FAMILY BIKEPACKING RIDES

### SALIDA, COLORADO, USA

The Great Divide Mountain Bike Route
(GDMBR) is famed for its Herculean race,
in which self-supported riders tear across
the Rockies. But broken up in bite-size
portions, it also has all the ingredients for
a series of wonderful family bikepacking
adventures. Indeed, it doesn't get much
better than the high grasslands and
aspen groves above Salida, Colorado,
especially during the technicoloured
splendour of autumn. There, a dirt road
loop can be formed using Aspen Ridge
and the backbone of the GDMBR. Salida's
polished, historic redbrick downtown –
distantly echoing an insalubrious past as
a Wild West railroad settlement – also
features a park in which to picnic, a
playground, a climbing wall and a river to
soak in. Kid trailers are almost as common
as the dual suspension mountain bikes that
roam the streets.
**Start/End // Salida, Colorado**
**Distance // 52 miles (84km)**
**More info // www.bikepacking.com/
routes/family-bikepacking-salida**

### WHITE RIM, UTAH, USA

Even within the vast expanse of the
American South West, Utah holds its own
particular appeal. There's an inordinate
number of national parks and natural
wonders vying for attention: a medley
of canyons, cliffs, buttes, arches and
tabletops, hewn over millennia from its
quintessential red rock. The White Rim Trail,
in the south-eastern portion of the state, is
a rare bicycle touring gem, simply because
it's difficult to imagine how a ride could be
more perfectly formed. Located in the heart
of Utah's Canyonlands National Park –
eroded into shape by the mighty Colorado
and Green Rivers, this 97-mile (156km)
loop boasts a succession of one superlative
panorama after the next. Combine this with
a wellpacked dirt road, sublime camping
potential and complete, utter desert
silence, and it's everything you seek in a
weekendsized adventure.
**Start/End // near Moab, Utah**
**Distance // 97 miles (156 km)**
**More info // www.nps.gov/cany/
planyourvisit/whiterimroad.htm**

### CONGUILLÍO NATIONAL PARK, CHILE

The Conguillío National Park lies at the
northern tip of the Chilean Lake District,
and envelopes the 3125m Llaima Volcano.
It's a lunar landscape where islands of
fertile earth lie stranded between lava
flows frozen in time – or at least until
the next eruption. Quiet mountain roads
make for great, if challenging, family
bikepacking, combining an exploration of
the park with a ride to Lonquimay, through
the neighbouring Reserva China Muerta.
Dotted through the area, standing nobly
in tranquil groves, are the enchanting
*Araucaria araucana* or 'Monkey Puzzle'
trees, so named as it was thought that
climbing them would flummox even a
monkey. These bizarre, bandy, Seussian-
like creations reach up to 40 m high, their
tentaclelike branches surely protecting
them from any primate intrusion while also
fascinating children.
**Start // Melipueco**
**End // Lonquimay**
**Distance // 50 miles (80km)**

# COLORADO
# BEER BIKE TOUR

*Year-round sunshine, world-class cycling, and hundreds of breweries – quench
your thirst after a long day on the bike with some of America's best craft beer.*

get off the bike, legs full of lead and heart thundering, face tingling from the wind and mouth full of cotton. If this was a typical ride, I'd grab my water bottle and find the nearest cheeseburger. But taking in the scenic regions of Colorado's north by bike is anything but typical. On this ride, I'll savor the marriage of the region's two perfectly complementary pastimes at every stop: mind-blowing cycling and mouthwatering beer. A blissful 20-mile (32km) descent from the mountains and an icy pint of citrusy, grassy, dry-hopped double IPA? This is my kind of recovery regimen.

Colorado has long been a hotspot for road cycling and mountain biking, and boasts more microbreweries per capita than anywhere else in the US. For a beer-loving cyclist, it's a no-brainer.

I start in the state's capital, Denver, which has transformed from a frontier cow town into an urban capital of the American west. The city itself might be destination enough for casual cyclists – an excellent bike network includes long, leisurely routes

along the Platte River Parkway, the Cherry Creek Bike Path, and trails to neighbouring suburbs. You can even use the excellent B Cycle program, which has bikes stationed throughout the city. But one look at the peaks of the '14ers' (local speak for a 14,000ft mountain [4267m]) looming on the horizon, and I knew that a serious two-wheel adventure was ahead.

Denver is the perfect embarkation point for my beer-themed trip. I was a month early for the endless tasting at September's Great American Beer Festival – but consoled myself with a fun, boozy overview of the city's breweries from the Denver Microbrew Tour. A few of my favourites include the Great Divide Brewing Company, where the spectrum of seasonal beers are all beautifully balanced (be careful, many of them are over 7%), an outpost of the excellent Breckenridge Brewery, and the weekly rotation of taps at the Denver Beer Co.

Fully hydrated and rested up, I hit the road. My next major stop would be Fort Collins, a college town that perfectly merges Colorado's beer and bike cultures. Although a serious cyclist could do the trip in a long day, I took the 100-mile (161km) route into two days with an overnight in Greeley. With the pancake-flat roads and a tailwind, I blasted out of Greeley for a cruise through the unending green expanse of the Pawnee National Grassland, a magical sea of swaying hip-high grasses that were once prime buffalo hunting land. There's something hypnotic about the rhythmic sway of the prairie.

*"Riding west brought me to Fort Collins, the essence of the trip, its bike-packed streets dotted with great breweries"*

Navigating a few extra miles brought me to the Pawnee Buttes, two 300ft formations that leap dramatically out of the flatlands. Aside from free-roaming cattle, these back roads are mostly free from traffic, and toward the end of the day I caught the flash of a white-tailed antelope bounding through the fields.

Riding west brought me to Fort Collins, which straddles Colorado's topographical divide, at the point where the Rockies begin their rise. This town is the essence of the trip: the bicycle-packed streets of Fort Collins are dotted with great breweries. And the city is mad about cycling: the Fort Collins Bike Library offers free bikes to anyone who passes through.

This first stop in Fort Collins is the New Belgium Brewery. This employee-owned operation has brought its passion for bicycles, beer and sustainability to an international audience in recent years. The guides give me a playful walk through the facility that ends in a carnival-like tasting room before I head back to town for a stop at the Odell Brewing Company, a remarkable small brewery with the best IPA of the trip. If the sun was up, I would have hit the beer garden at Equinox Brewing, but the jagged horizon suggests

## THE COLORADO TRAIL

With some 535 miles (861km) of twisting singletrack, jaw-dropping views, and rollercoaster elevation, the Colorado Trail is one of the world's great long-distance mountain bike journeys. Riding the entire trail – from Denver to Durango – takes about 20 days, and requires re-supply in mountain towns along the way. For the more casual rider, there are numerous day-rides that will give you a taste of this epic adventure. For complete information: www.coloradotrail.org.

*Left to right: autumn colours at Boulder Creek; not a town for indecisive drinkers; Colorado is singletrack heaven for mountain bikers. Previous page: Denver at dawn*

that a good night's rest is in order.

Anyone could close this loop by riding straight south on the relatively flat roads that skirt the edge of the Rockies. I've got a pint of stout or two to work off, so I'm up for the challenge of climbing Rist Canyon to Stove Prairie Rd. This route (loved by locals and a recent stage for the USA Pro Challenge) is tough, but the scenery is incredible. Ahead, mountains roll into view in shades of purple and blue. Behind, plains reach out in a checkerboard of green. All day, I'm surrounded by pines, massive boulders and rushing creeks. Heading south on Stove Prairie Rd, I lose all that elevation through the sweeping curves that lead to Loveland. Of course, there are plenty of places to fuel up in this small town as well, starting with the family-owned Loveland Aleworks, where the creative selection of taps is frequently rotating. This stop includes a pucker-inducing explosion of summer flavour with the Strawberry Sour.

The next day, I take the 35 miles (56km) between Loveland and Boulder in a few hours, allowing plenty of time for exploring the Boulder Creek Bike Path to end the penultimate day. Snuggled up against the Flatirons, this bohemian college town is in love with the outdoors. After chatting with the local characters on the Pearl St promenade, I grab a beer at Avery Brewing, and take a self-guided tour from the catwalk. The evening ends with some noodling guitar warriors at the Draft House, which brings in local bands every weekend. Another half-day in the saddle brought me back to Denver for a well-earned rest for my legs and my liver. **NC**

## TOOLKIT

**Start/End** // Denver
**Distance** // about 350 miles (563km) in five or six days.
**Getting there** // Denver International Airport is an easy connection to many cities in the US and has several daily routes to Europe, Japan, Canada and Latin America.
**Bike hire** // A number of Denver shops will rent bicycles suitable for multi-day trips, including The Bicycle Doctor (www.bicycledr.com), and Bicycle Village (www.bicyclevillage. com). The big REI (www.rei.com) in Denver also rents bikes and camping equipment, and can arrange bike shipping.
**Where to drink** // The Beer Drinker's Guide to Colorado has reviews and maps to Colorado breweries. Denver Microbrew Tour offers a great brewery overview.
**More info** // See www.bikedenver.org and www.denvergov. org, which has downloadable bike maps.

*Opposite: showing you the way
to the next whisky stop in Kentucky*

# MORE LIKE THIS
## REFRESHED RIDES

### CALISTOGA WINE TOUR, USA

A weekend amble through California's wine country is an extremely popular way to get a taste of the region north of San Francisco. Although Napa's roads can get clogged with tourists, a good alternative is to ride the relatively quieter roads surrounding Calistoga. Pedal north out of town on Hwy 29 and take Old Toll Rd up a side valley. A steep, shaded climb will pass a couple of family wineries before rejoining Hwy 29 and reaching the summit at the Robert Louis Stevenson State Park – an excellent place to rest, picnic, and take in the views. Coast downhill to Middletown and east through the lovely valley that's home to the Guenoc and Langtry Vineyards. Then climb Butts Canyon and descend into the flowering meadows of Pope Valley. From here, connect to the celebrated (car-free) Silverado Trail, through the adorable downtown of St Helena, and head back to the start.
**Start/End // Calistoga**
**Distance // 62 miles (100km)**

### VALLEY BEER TOUR, USA

The region of Western Massachusetts and southern Vermont gets called the Napa Valley of Beer for good reason – the clutch of creative craft breweries and excellent brew pubs makes it a beer-lover's dream. Start this trip in Springfield, a half-day train ride from New York City. Here, you can enjoy old world beer-making traditions at The Student Prince, one of the best German restaurants in Western Mass. After a stein and a schnitzel, make your way along back roads to North Hampton, a college town with a number of great brew pubs, including the 40 taps of local and far-flung beers at Dirty Truth and the rowdy outdoor beer garden at the Northampton Brewery. This ride ends just across the Vermont state line at the The Whetstone Station Restaurant and Brewery, where riders can enjoy a view of the Connecticut River and refined small plates.
**Start // Springfield, Massachusetts**
**End // Whetstone Station Restaurant & Brewery, Vermont**
**Distance // 66 miles (106km)**

### KENTUCKY BOURBON TOUR, USA

A ride filled with rich history, heady spirits, and Southern American charm, this trip takes in six of the best distilleries along the scenic, rolling rural roads of Central Kentucky. The terrain is moderately challenging (particularly with a couple of samples under your belt), so this is recommended for more experienced cyclists. Start in Lexington at the Jim Beam distillery, where you can get a detailed map of the region and turn-by-turn instructions. Along the route, you'll sample America's oldest spirit at the Heaven Hill Distillery, Maker's Mark, Four Roses, Wild Turkey, and Woodford Reserve. In addition to the delicious bourbons, you'll find rolling hills of bluegrass and picture-perfect horse farms.
**Start/End // Lexington**
**Distance // 30 miles (48km)**
**More info // www.kybourbontrail.com**

# NORTH AMERICA'S PACIFIC COAST

*With the shimmering Pacific horizon to your right and an endless ribbon of blacktop ahead, this ride traces the dramatic western edge of North America.*

For cyclists who live to ride, this is a once-in-a-lifetime trip, the kind of experience that's a culmination of years of daydreaming and months of planning. I'd wanted to ride an extended stretch of the Pacific Coast Hwy for years, but the challenge is no joke: the jagged western edge of the continent has plenty of long, tough climbs and lonely stretches of blacktop that demand tenacity and self-sufficiency. But the rewards make it one of my favourite rides. Sunsets enflame the horizon, dizzying cliffs drop into the crashing surf, and redwood giants tower above. Over the years, I've ridden plenty of beautiful miles on Hwy 1, but none more exciting than the stretch between Seattle and San Francisco – an epic 980 miles (1577km) with incredible sights, great camping and plenty of diversions.

Scores of cyclists make the southbound trip on the Pacific Coast Hwy every year – mostly in the summer. I took the trip solo, but the camaraderie of the riders who gather around nightly fires at the hiker-biker campsites balanced a month of solitary days in the saddle. I met John and Margaret, a pair of sweetly sardonic teachers sporting classic '80s touring rigs, gadget-obsessed twin sisters from Victoria BC on their way to Los Angeles, and a handful of grizzled vagabonds attempting solo trips to Mexico and beyond. And everyone had a story – about troubleshooting a mechanical nightmare in the rain, or a truck-driving redneck with an axe to grind, or climbs that seemed never-ending.

Although I was determined to camp – there are established campgrounds every 50 to 60 miles (80 to 96km) along the route with sites designated for cyclists – there are also plenty of opportunities for so-called 'credit-card' touring, for riders who travel light and prefer a soft bed.

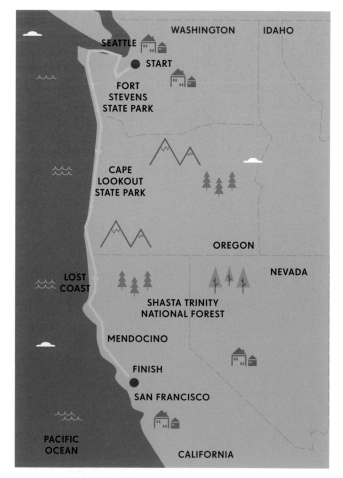

The complete trip between Seattle and San Francisco can be done in 15 days (for a powerhouse cyclist with very little gear), but I took twice as long with a fully-loaded touring bike. Although I met plenty of riders ticking away miles on a tight schedule, I knew quickly that this wasn't my style. The flexibility of my itinerary enabled some of the trip's rewarding memories: pints of world-class beer at the Six Rivers Brewery, naps under swaying redwood trees, and clifftop whale-watching. In other words, little pieces of heaven.

Before leaving Seattle, I spent an extra day or two fuelling up on the city's excellent food scene. Exploring the narrow alleys and bustling stalls of Pike Place Market, I got some fancy campfire supplies for the days ahead, and dug into the city's best: steaming bowls of ramen and fresh-that-day crab.

I began my detours as soon as the trip began, tacking on several days to ride around the Olympic Peninsula. With misty rides on near-empty roads, the trip began with a surreal tranquility. It didn't take long to get what I came for: brackish ocean breeze and mind-blowing vistas, as I cruised along spine-tingling cliffs, shovelling down snacks at quirky little roadside bodegas.

It took a long three days to get around the whole thing, but it was worth every minute: views of the Strait of Juan de Fuca, quiet farms, remote beaches and ancient forests. The camping was a superlative highlight.

More of the best Pacific Coast lies in the coastal campgrounds of Oregon, which make up the bulk of the trip. I loved Fort Stevens State Park, a 4200-acre park that has incredible biodiversity – everything from gusty dunes to freshwater wetlands – and a number of historic military sites from the WWII fortification of the coast. Many of the coastal Oregon parks further south made me consider lingering a bit longer than planned, like Cape Lookout State Park, where the beachside hiker-biker sites are blissfully

## CONTINUING ON...

Although the ride from Seattle to San Francisco is a favourite section of the Pacific Coast because of the quality of the scenery, the relatively quiet roads and the superlative options for camping, a cyclist with enough time and energy can keep pedalling for weeks along the Pacific. The stretch from San Francisco to Los Angeles is also a scenic stunner, though narrow shoulders and heavier traffic make it more of a challenge.

*Clockwise from top: fog rolls in off the Pacific along the North California coast; the Avenue of the Giants; campfires at dusk on Cannon Beach, Oregon; Pike Place Market, Seattle. Previous page: Cape Sebastian State Park in Oregon*

remote from the RV sites.

Although the camping in Oregon is the best on the trip, I discovered the most jaw-dropping vistas south of the California border. The ride here is a constant parade of awe-inspiring natural beauty, particularly when you get to the smoothly paved Avenue of the Giants, a byway surrounded on all sides by towering old-growth redwood trees. (If you're into mid-century kitsch, there are even several that you can ride through, near Leggett.)

Riding along the edge of the so-called Lost Coast, I paused for a breather and saw the white flumes of whales, in their migration to Mexico. As I pedalled further south, I slowed for the seaside holiday towns lining the coast of Northern California. In one of them, historic Mendocino, there's a tidy grid of cute shops and four-star restaurants next to gorgeous headlands. I also paused for fresh seafood in Point Arena – which has an amazing bakery and an historic theatre.

By the time San Francisco got near, I was in great shape for the most challenging section of the ride, Sonoma County. Thankfully, this also has the best views, with rock formations in the waters that rival the dramatic power of the famed Big Sur coastline south of San Francisco. Here, Hwy 1 offers paved rollers along the cliffs – three days in the rhythm of 20 minutes of lung-burning climbing followed by 5 minutes of glorious descending.

Reaching the coastal farms that supply San Francisco's famed foodie culture, I knew the end was near, and stopped into Point Reyes Station for fresh oysters and locally made triple cream cheese at the Cowgirl Creamery. By the time I crossed the Golden Gate – 28 days and 980 miles (1577km) after my departure – this epic trip proved that the most magical part about going somewhere was the process of getting there. **NC**

*"The ride is a constant parade of awe-inspiring natural beauty, particularly when you get to the Avenue of the Giants"*

### TOOLKIT

**Start** // Seattle
**End** // San Francisco
**Distance** // 980 miles (1577km)
**Duration** // Just over two weeks, though it's much more enjoyable with three weeks or more.
**Getting there** // If you fly in and out of Seattle, you can return with your bike via Amtrak at a modest additional fee, or ship your bike for a flat fee through REI (www.rei.com).
**Where to stay** // Hiker-biker campsites at the Oregon State Park System are only US$5 and they never turn away cyclists – even if the park is sold out.
**What to read** // *Bicycling the Pacific Coast* by Vicky Spring & Tom Kirkendall
**When to ride** // You can do this trip any time of year, but summer and autumn are best.

*Opposite: riding the Côtes-d'Armor
in Brittany, France*

# MORE LIKE THIS
## WATERSIDE RIDES

### CRATER LAKE RIM RIDE, USA

Riders in the Pacific Northwest get a certain far-off look in their eye when they talk about the otherworldly ride along the edge of Crater Lake, one of the most rewarding day-long rides in the Western United States. The gorgeous, deep blue waters of this volcanic lake in southern Oregon have a visual power that leaves a big impression – it reflects the surrounding peaks and sky like a mirror, inspiring panoramas that will take any cyclist's breath away. (Or maybe that's the 3000ft of elevation change at high altitude.) A strong cyclist could do the 35-mile (56km) loop around the lake in three or four hours. But, regardless of your skills, the spectacular road is almost never flat – you'll be climbing or descending most of the day.
**Start/End // Crater Lake Visitor Center**
**Distance // 35 miles (56km)**

### GERMANY'S BALTIC COAST

With the sea as your constant companion, a multi-day tour of Germany's Baltic Coast offers gorgeous beaches, rugged cliffs, regional seafood and the bustle of historic coastal villages. Begin this summer tour of the coast in Flensburg and head east, towards Fehmarn Island, an excellent place to observe migratory birds. Along the way, you'll see many of the seaside resorts lining the Bay of Lübeck that have been resplendently restored. A stop several days later in Lübeck will allow you to refuel with the city's famed marzipan treats before you pedal on to the quaint Unesco-listed towns of Wismar and Stralsund – two Hanseatic League trading centres of the 14th and 15th centuries. The second island on this trip, Rugia, presents more excellent cycling, with dramatic cliffs, white beaches, and the wild beauty of Jasmund National Park.
**Start // Flensburg**
**End // Jasmund National Park, Sassnitz,**
**Distance // 279.5 miles (450km)**

### THE FRENCH ATLANTIC

A trip along France's longest cycling trail, appropriately named La Vélodyssée, can be enjoyed as a day-long cruise or a multi-day epic; the full trail is about 745½ miles (1200km) stretching from Brittany in the north to the Spanish border. With the Atlantic in view for most of the ride, this journey is best be done at an easy pace that allows you to savour the region's pleasures – including cute seaside B&Bs, historic sea ports, and beautiful beaches. Although each of the route's 14 sections has distinctive charms, seafood lovers should make it a point to include the path from La Barre-de-Monts to Les Sables-d'Olonne, which will allow you to tuck into fresh oysters. The section between Arcachon and Léon is also stunning, as the path passes deep forests and inland lakes.
**Start // Brittany**
**End // Bayonne**
**Distance // 745½ miles (1200km)**

# MOUNTAIN BIKING IN MOAB

*Few places get mountain bikers as excited as Utah's Moab – a desert dreamscape of slickrock and singletrack revered for its riding culture and infamous 24-hour race.*

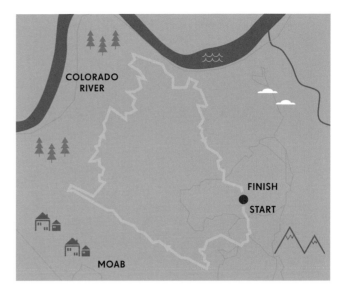

When my riding partner dismounts and picks up his bike, I figure there's no shame in doing the same. I had a feeling that any attempt to ride this particular section of trail would end with me biting some dust, sprawled on my back with all the grace of an upended blister beetle – again – but I might have given it a stab.

That's if I weren't exploring Behind the Rocks with Mountain Bike Hall of Fame grandee John Stamstad, and if he considers something to be unrideable, then the argument is effectively over. Stamstad is the emperor of endurance cycling – a reputation he earned, in part, right here – on the route of the legendary 24 Hours of Moab cycle race that annually ran through the Utah desertscape from 1994 to 2012.

Having effectively invented solo 24-hour mountain-bike racing and pioneered the pursuit of Great Divide racing across America, Stamstad once set a world record by cycling a mountain bike across off-road terrain for 354.5 miles (570km) in 24 hours.

Suffice to say, when he gets off his bike, it's for good reason. This spot is named Nose Dive, and bits of broken bicycles lie scattered in the dust all around – the bleached bones of the foolish few who have attempted to ride the dive. 'I used to be able to pick a line through here,' Stamstad laments. 'But the jeeps have destroyed it now. You can't ride out of it anymore, so there's no point killing yourself on the descent.'

Stamstad never actually won the 24 Hours of Moab – not least because the last time he did it, he insisted on riding a single-speed bike (and still came second) – but he's done so many laps of the legendary circuit that he could ride it with his eyes shut (and very possibly has). The race route is a shortened version of the Behind the Rocks Lunatic Loop, a 28-mile (45km) trail that is probably Moab's least popular. A 'sandy sufferfest' is how the guy in Poison Spider Bicycles described it when he heard where we were heading.

But I'm desperate to experience the epic course, and now the event is in hiatus, this is the only way. My legs are eternally grateful that we only have to ride the route once, and the rest of me soon discovers that July is not a month when even Stamstad would want to be riding multiple loops for 24 hours on the trot. We're out early in the morning – long before the day comes to the boil, when temperatures in the rare shade simmer at around 100°F (38°C) – but perspiration quickly drenches my face and fills my eyes.

Stamstad shows me around every nook and cranny of the course, recounting tales from the trails as we roll. At one point I go sailing over the bars during a technical descent, and he thoughtfully attempts to spare my blushes by describing how he once passed the erstwhile race leader at this very place, as the guy lay on the ground with concussion. I'm obviously travelling somewhat slower, and it's only my pride that gets concussed.

I get back into the saddle and we continue, rounding a stunning golden edifice of almost Uluru proportions, which my companion grinningly informs me is known as Prostitute's Butte, because of how it looks from the air. The trail then runs across a seductive section of Moab's iconic slickrock – smooth Navajo sandstone that appears sketchy, but actually grants knobbly tyres an uncanny amount of traction, allowing riders to roll over the most unlikely gradients while remaining rubber side down.

The 15-mile (24km) race circuit finishes shortly afterwards and we seek shelter from the inferno of the midday sun. At a diner in town, the menu includes an 'All-day Mountain Bikers' Breakfast', which delivers a carb-laden load that would keep most riders fuelled for the duration of a 24-hour race.

Once the worst of the heat has passed, we explore the more popular routes that slither across the slickrock and skim the rim of the canyon, making Moab a hallowed haunt for mountain bikers, irrespective of the race. Incredibly, these classic tracks were laid down during the Jurassic period, and no human intervention has been required to make or maintain them as perfect MTB trails.

That said, the mega-popular, world-renowned 10-mile (16km) Slickrock Trail itself follows a series of white dots painted onto the rocks, which do jolt you out of the amber-tinted ambience of the natural surrounds somewhat, so Stamstad takes me on the wilder Amasa Back Trailhead route instead.

This adventure, another 10-miler, sees us ascend over 1000ft, climbing across sandstone all the way to a magical mesa top, with an astonishing vista across the Colorado River and Kane Creek. Beyond the rust-coloured desert, the La Sal Mountains on the horizon still have a dusting of snow, which seems almost impossible from the furnace of the canyon.

Numerous drop-offs, technical climbs and steep descents keep us on our game throughout this return route, and rolling around close to the canyon rim – which plunges away with hair-raising severity – demands serious concentration, but it's not just the elevation that gives me goosebumps here.

Riding back to the trailhead, as thunder rumbles in the distance and forked-tongued lightning licks the distant range, it feels like I've ascended some sort of higher plane of mountain biking. And then I'm bounced out of my whimsical reverie by a red rock that has waited 200 million years just to throw me over the bars of my bike and bring me back to earth. **PK**

## 24-HOUR RACING

Another Mountain Bike Hall of Famer, Laird Knight, created 24-hour MTB racing – where riders attempt as many loops of a technical off-road course in 24 hours as possible – as a team pursuit. In 1996 Stamstad entered a 24-hour race in Canaan as a team, but all four names on the sheet were a variation of his own. He did the event solo, beat most of the field and invented a new form of endurance racing.

*Left: navigating the sandstone Amasa Back trail. Previous page: looking out over the mesas around Moab*

## TOOLKIT

**Start/End** // Behind the Rocks/24-Hours of Moab route: US-191, just beyond Kane Springs Picnic Area; Amasa Back Trailhead: Amasa Back car park; Slickrock Trail: Sand Flats Road.
**Distance** // Behind the Rocks: 15 miles (24km); Amasa Back Trailhead: 10 miles (16km); Slickrock Trail: 10 miles (16km).
**What to ride** // A dual-suspension mountain bike.
**Tour** // Ride independently, or consult the experts at Poison Spider Bicycles (www.poisonspiderbicycles.com) for guidance, or to arrange a spot on the Porcupine Shuttle, which leaves daily, taking bikers to do the epic 32-mile (51km) 'Whole Enchilada'.
**When to ride** // Spring and autumn deliver ideal conditions.
**More info** // www.utahmountainbiking.com

*Opposite: Finale is the base for an*
*Italian 24hr mountain bike race*

# MORE LIKE THIS
# 24HR MOUNTAIN BIKE RACES

### THE 24H OF FINALE LIGURE, ITALY

Moab may have been the spiritual home of 24-hour MTB racing up until 2012, but the format conceived by Laird Knight and taken to the extreme by John Stamstad has spawned many classic events all over the world. One of continental Europe's biggest all-day bike bashes is the 24-hour of Finale Ligure in Northern Italy. Since its launch in 1999, this iconic race has seen teams and soloists compete on separate singletrack circuits, both with stunning sea views over the Mediterranean. Around the race, the Mountain Bike Festival of Finale takes place, with various bike-related activities, plus entertainment, food and drink.
**Start/End // Camping Terre Rosse**
**Distance // It's a 4-mile(6.7km) circuit for solo riders, and a 6-mile (9.75km) circuit for team riders.**
**More info // www.24hfinale.com**

### THE STRATHPUFFER 24, SCOTLAND

Just in case the concept of doing a 24-hour mountain-bike race around a technical course doesn't sound tricky enough, this event in the Scottish Highlands takes place in the icy grip of midwinter, when the trail is cloaked in inky darkness for roughly 17 out of those 24 hours. Tough teams of two, four and 10 take part in the race, with some superhard soloists also braving the chilly challenge. Tracks in the Torrachilty Forest are often under a layer of snow, which covers rock gardens, tree roots and other assorted obstacles. The event is held in mid January and begins with a Le Mans-style run to the bike.
**Start/End // Torrachilty Forest, which is 3 miles (5km) from Strathpeffer**
**Distance // 7-mile (11km) circuit**
**More info // www.strathpuffer.co.uk**

### TRANS BAVIAANS, SOUTH AFRICA

Billed as the toughest single-stage mountain bike race in the world, the Trans Baviaans is a 24-hour MTB challenge of a completely different ilk. Instead of sending riders around loops while the hour hand travels around the clock face, this super-demanding race takes place across an unmarked linear course through the heart of the beautiful Baviaanskloof Wilderness Area. The route is punctuated by checkpoints that teams must visit, and the 143-mile (230km) distance from Willowmore to Jeffrey's Bay needs to be completed within 24 hours. It's only open to teams, and demands sharp navigation skills as well as high levels of endurance.
**Start // Willowmore**
**End // Jeffrey's Bay**
**Distance // 143 miles (230km)**
**More info // www.transbaviaans.co.za**

# RIDE THE
# WHITEHORSE TRAILS

*Just under the curve of the Arctic Circle, in Canada's ultra-remote Yukon Territory,
Whitehorse offers magical mountain-bike trails beneath the midnight sun.*

Studying a guide to Whitehorse's mountain-bike tracks is a like eyeballing a plate of spaghetti dished up by an excessively flamboyant and generous chef. Some 435 miles (700km) of rideable trails have been mapped within the city limits of the Yukon Territory's capital – 186 miles (300km) clicks of sensational singletrack, and 248.5 miles (400km) of delicious doubletrack and dirt roads.

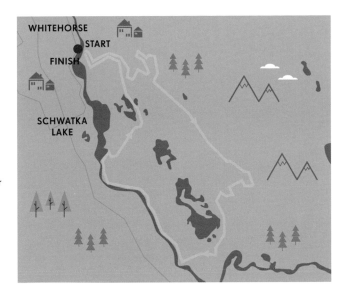

I can't think of another metropolis in the world that offers an off-road feast comparable to the bikers' banquet served up here. But this tasty tangle of tracks also makes it difficult to decide where to start. Or finish. Or go in the middle. You could potentially pedal for days – weeks even – and not cycle over the same bit of dirt within this mind-blowing maze of interconnecting spruce-fringed paths.

It's possible to splice several trails together into one epic continuous ride, instead of doing little circuits, but it definitely helps if you know the lay of the land – or roll with someone who does. Which is why I'm grateful to be following the flowing lines

being etched in the earth in front of me by local guru, Sylvain Turcotte, owner of Whitehorse MTB base Boréale Explorers, and a pro trail hound.

We're riding around a super scenic combination route on the outskirts of Whitehorse, on the Grey Mountain side of the mighty Yukon River – an emerald waterway that elbows right through this enigmatic territory, before crossing the border into Alaska.

You can reach the trailheads directly from the CBD, with the wilderness beginning as soon as you leave the city streets, pass through Rotary Peace Park, cross the bridge and set off up Grey Mountain Rd. Our route – one of myriad options – begins with a gentle ascent to the Upper Riverdale Trail, which quickly delivers a cracking vista back across Whitehorse city and the great green Yukon.

Crossing Grey Mountain Rd, we follow the Yellow Brick Rd, a trail that leads (via several short connecting tracks) not to a wizard, but to the next best thing: the brilliant blue Boogaloo Trail system, which is every bit the 'buffed out, fast-flowing and glorious piece of singletrack' that David, another local guide, had promised it would be.

Although this isn't like Vancouver's notoriously gnarly North Shore scene, the trails do boast plenty of technical features. There are chicken runs alongside some of the scarier obstacles, in case you veer onto a track that's beyond your skill level, but routes are clearly signed and graded according to International Mountain Bike Association (IMBA) standards: green circle routes are easy, blue square trails more challenging, black diamond tracks demand

*"The Southern Tutchone – First Nation people of the Whitehorse region – used the banks of the Yukon as a trading route"*

technical skill (or blind bravery) and double black diamond runs are only for highly experienced and/or pain-impervious riders.

Other clues to how tricky a trail might be can be found in the extra colourful vernacular employed in the name – SFD (Straight Fucking Down) being a prime example of a track that delivers exactly what it swears it will.

Leaving Boogaloo behind we venture further up the flanks of Grey Mountain and tie together a bunch of blue and black tracks – including Payback, SFD, Girlfriend and Juicy – for a long, flowing (and occasionally eye-wateringly rapid) descent around Chadburn Lake to the start of the iconic Yukon River Trail.

This open and undulating trail traces the east bank of the Yukon River for 4 miles (6.6km), rolling spectacularly along the steep ridge and occasionally ducking and diving into the forest. The loose-dirt path isn't overly technical, but it is narrow and demands full focus, because one lapse of concentration or ill-timed gaze at the lovely views might result in a high-speed tumble all the way into the freezing embrace of the river.

This path is steeped in history. For centuries before the arrival of Europeans, the Southern Tutchone – First Nation people of the Whitehorse region – used the banks of the Yukon as a hunting and

trading route. And in the late 1890s, prospectors (including the author Jack London) with heads and hearts running hot with gold fever, rushed this way, in a desperate scramble to reach Dawson City and the Klondike to stake their claim. What they would have given for a sturdy dual-suspension steed I can only imagine.

The route rages on, clinging to cliffs and sidestepping bluffs, right through the historic ruins of an old boom town, Canyon City, an important stop-off during the 1898 Klondike Gold Rush – stampeders would stop here before nervously negotiating potentially lethal rapids just downstream.

It's not a bad spot for riders to calm their own nerves before pedalling the precipitous Rim Trail, which tiptoes along the edge of Miles Canyon and ultimately leads down to the shores of Schwatka Lake, where glacial waters await those brave enough to make the plunge.

And then there's a decision to be made. Head back to Whitehorse or explore more trails around the Hidden Lakes? The day is getting old, but that scarcely matters. It's midsummer, a time when the Yukon lives up to its nickname as the land of the midnight sun.

Whitehorse occupies a position on the globe so far north that the sun barely sets for several weeks around the summer solstice, and the sky never gets properly dark. There's even a 24-hour mountain-bike race here where using lights is against the rules. As Robert W Service, the bard of the Yukon, once observed: 'There are strange things done in the midnight sun'.

We ride on towards the Hidden Lakes. To pass up the opportunity of finding more cycling gold in these hills really would be strange. **PK**

## CARCROSS

Canada's newest mountain-bike mecca is in Carcross, home to the Tagish First Nation. Around Montana Mountain, a trail network of 46.5 miles (75km) – including 22 miles (35km) of singletrack – has been developed from old mining paths in a groundbreaking project involving local indigenous youth groups and cyclists. 'Mountain Hero', the star route, is an IMBA epic-rated trail featuring 12.5 miles (20km) of climbing and a 5-mile (8km) descent to Nares Lake.

*Left to right: taking a break by the lake near Carcross, Yukon; shredding forest singletrack in Whitehorse, Yukon (and overleaf). Previous page: cornering in Carcross, south of Whitehorse*

## TOOLKIT

**Start / End** // Whitehorse
**Distance** // 31 miles (50km)
**Tour** // You can ride independently (free) or with a local operator such as Boréale Explorers (www.be-yukon.com), which provides good-quality bikes, expert guidance and yurt-based accommodation in the midst of the trails.
**What to take** // A decent dual-suspension mountain bike, along with a helmet, some armour and all the usual spares and tools. Carry bear spray (seriously) and insect repellent.
**When to ride** // Unless you have a fat bike (a mountain bike with supersized tyres) tracks are only rideable May to October. Check out June's 24 Hours of Light MTB festival.
**More info** // See www.yukonbiking.ca. Printed waterproof maps can be purchased in Whitehorse's two local bike shops, Cadence Cycle and Icycle Sport.

*Opposite: Riding high over
Rotorua, New Zealand*

# MORE LIKE THIS
## MOUNTAIN BIKE TOWNS

### FORT WILLIAM, SCOTLAND

At the epicentre of Lochaber, the self-proclaimed Outdoor Capital of the UK, Fort William is a mountain bikers' trail town that hosts a highly popular stage of the annual Mountain Biking World Cup, but also offers pedalling punters a broad range of cross-country riding tracks. The Nevis Range has everything from gentle green-graded forest trails through to black-diamond rocky runs, and there are more at Lochaber MTB centre. Test yourself on the Witch's World Champs, a red route entirely comprised of singletrack with over 270m of climbing, which was designed for the 2007 World Championships in Leanachan Forest, and also explore Laggan Wolftrax in nearby Strathmashie Forest.
**Start/End // The Witch's Car Park**
**Distance // 5 miles (8.5km)**
**More info // www.ridefortwilliam.co.uk**

### WHAKAREWAREWA TRAIL, ROTORUA, NEW ZEALAND

The Whakarewarewa trail network on the southern outskirts of Rotorua on New Zealand's North Island offers 81 miles (130km) of super sweet singletrack, with trails for all abilities snaking through a fantastic forest of Californian redwoods and New Zealand natives, including a killer loop formed by linking Tokorangi, Katore, Gunna Gotta, Paddy's Run, Tickler, Be Rude Not 2, Pig and Exit tracks. This trail town extraordinaire has hosted every international MTB event going, from the UCI Mountain Bike & Trials Championships (held on Mt Ngongotaha in 2006) to the Crankworx Mountain Bike Festival and the opening round of the Enduro World Series (both in 2015). Since 2013 it has staged the annual 10-day Rotorua Bike Festival each February.
**Start/End // Nursery Rd (or Long Mile Rd car park)**
**Distance // 9 miles (15km)**
**More info // www.riderotorua.com or www.skyline.co.nz**

### ALICE SPRINGS, AUSTRALIA

There are world-class mountain-biking parks scattered all across Australia, but arguably the best 'trail town' in the big burnt country is found slap bang in the Red Centre – in a town called Alice. From the middle of rusty, dusty downtown Alice Springs, you can ride straight into the magical MacDonnell Ranges, where hundreds of kilometres of truly terrific singletrack threads through the ochre peaks, around the red bluffs and out into the desert. The terrain screams iconic Australian outback, and this is fast becoming the Southern Hemisphere's answer to Moab. From the trail centre recently opened at Telegraph Station, you can explore an excellent figure-of-8 route by combining Apwelantye, Arrwe and Ilentye trails. The centre rents bikes and provides guidance, proper signage appears at trailheads and junctions, and professional trail builders are still adding to the network of tracks already established by highly active local riders.
**Start/End // Telegraph Station trailhead**
**Distance // 14 miles (23km)**
**More info // www.outbackcycling.com/ alice-springs/mountain-biking; www. centralaustralianroughriders.asn.au**

# THE MINUTEMAN BIKEWAY

*Play Paul Revere on a ride from Boston's northern outskirts to Lexington – scene of the first battle of America's Revolutionary War – along the Minuteman Bikeway.*

I t's not every day you come face to face with a national hero. But in suburban Massachusetts I eyeballed two of them, just a hop and a skip apart. Or, more accurately a push and a pedal – because cycling's the way to do it.

There's a clue to the heritage of my route in the name. The Minuteman Bikeway snakes 11 miles (18km) between the outskirts of Boston and a disused railroad depot at Bedford, tracing – roughly speaking – the route taken by Paul Revere on his famous night ride of 18 April 1775. But though patriotically named for the best-trained colonial militia – ready at a moment's notice to take arms against oppressive British redcoats – this isn't a Disney-fied tourist route, but a popular commuter cycle path. It's also the perfect way to access some of the most important historic sites in the area during a Boston city break, so I hired a bike and grabbed a map for the relaxing half-day ride.

Having braved the city's morning rush-hour, at Boston Common I joined the blissfully traffic-free cycle path west along the Charles River, the shouts of coxes berating college rowing crews drifting across the water. Through Harvard Sq and on to Belmont I zigzagged through quiet back roads and among the beautifully restored wetlands of the Alewife Brook Reservation to northern Cambridge.

A granite column marking the bikeway's terminus is etched with alewifes, reflecting this spot's traditional name. I felt a pang of disappointment: I'd pictured an exuberant tavern-keeper's partner, sloshing foaming flagons. But no: an alewife – pronounced more like 'all-wuff' – is a tiny fish found in the nearby Mystic River. No matter. The road to independence beckoned.

In fact, the bikeway's genesis was revolutionary in more ways than one. This tarmac ribbon replaced the former Boston–

Lexington railroad; after it was mothballed in the late 1970s, local activists battled to transform the route into today's cycle trail, opened in 1992. The Minuteman project was at the vanguard of the Rails-to-Trails Conservancy, a movement formally created in 1986 that backs communities across the US working to convert disused lines.

As I trundled past the monolithic milepost I thought of Revere and his nocturnal mission to warn Lexington and Concord's rebel militia of the arrival of the British. And almost immediately a reminder of another, less well-known episode of that crucial night appeared at Spy Pond. In the 19th century, before modern

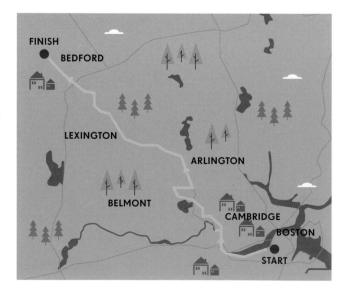

Scenes from the American
Revolutionary War: Captain William
Smith's home on Battle Rd between
Lexington and Concord; a reenactment
with Redcoats in Lexington; the statue
of Paul Revere in Lexington

refrigeration, ice was harvested commercially here, and today it's a popular ice-skating venue. But on 19 April 1775 it was just a country lake, where Mother Batherwick was out gathering dandelions – or so a signboard here proclaims – when she spotted British soldiers retreating from Lexington. Far from fleeing, the bumptious old woman took them prisoner – quite how, the board doesn't say. But among the clapboard houses and swaying trees shedding their autumn foliage, it added fascinating detail to my burgeoning picture of that momentous day.

Just a couple more minutes' pedalling brought me to Arlington and the steely – or, rather, bronze-y – gaze of Hero Number One: Uncle Sam. Yes, the Uncle Sam, or so his hometown claims: Samuel Wilson, a merchant born here in Arlington, won renown supplying the US army during another war against the British in 1812. His statue doesn't look much like the goateed fellow on the recruitment posters – but then it's debatable whether he truly was the inspiration for the national figurehead.

I doffed my bike helmet respectfully, just in case, and scooted onwards, past the brown timber walls of the Old Schwamb Mill – the country's oldest continuously operating mill site, where wood has been shaped since around 1650 – and on to Arlington's Great Meadows, roughly halfway along the trail. Pausing in the shade of a tree bedecked with flaming fall hues, I listened to a cricket chirping its final song of summer. Boston – and thoughts of war – seemed a long way distant.

The bikeways skirts around the centre of Lexington, and I decided to save that treat for later, pushing on for another half hour to Bedford. At the official end of the Minuteman sits gleaming railcar No 6211, a restored 1950s relic of the Boston and Maine Railroad and a reminder of the web of railway lines that once radiated out from Boston. Today most are silent – except, on some at least, for the whirr of pedals and bike chains.

Content to have completed the trail, I returned to Lexington to delve a little more into the events of 1775. For a spot with such a momentous historic legacy, Lexington is a pleasantly understated town. I scooted past vintage houses studding its wide streets, spotting the Buckman Tavern, mustering point of the militia on that fateful April morning, and the 1698 Hancock-Clarke Parsonage, where Revere warned Samuel Adams of the approaching British regulars.

At Battle Green, site of the fateful skirmish, I stood in the shadow of Hero Number Two: Captain John Parker, tall on his rocky plinth, clasping his rifle ready to defend his hometown. It was Parker who led the local militia in their stand, losing his cousin and seven other rebels to redcoat arms in the first battle of the American Revolutionary War.

There's something apt about arriving at Lexington, like Revere, on a saddle rather than in a car or bus seat. It might not be the most dramatic ride, nor the most challenging, but the Minuteman provides a journey into the past – an exhilarating way to explore the history of Massachusetts' insurrectionary forebears. **PB**

## WHERE DID WAR REALLY START?

Ralph Waldo Emerson claimed the shot signalling the start of America's Revolutionary War was fired at the North Bridge in Concord. Residents of Lexington, six miles (9.5km) east, counter it was earlier, on their Battle Green, when militia briefly fought British regulars. Consider both sides: cycle to Concord along the unsealed Battle Road Trail from Lexington (or the Reformatory Branch Trail from Bedford), or catch the Liberty Ride trolleybus.

*Previous page: Harvard University in Cambridge, Massachusetts*

## TOOLKIT

**Start** // Alewife Station, North Cambridge, Massachusetts
**End** // Bedford Depot Park/South St, Massachusetts
Distance // 10.5 miles (17km)
**Getting there** // Alewife 'T' Station is on the red subway line. www.mbta.com
**Bike hire** // Urban Adventours (www.urbanadventours.com) hires hybrid bikes from US$40 for 24 hours. Lexington's Ride Studio Cafe (www.ridestudiocafe.com) provides bikes, parts, advice and great coffee.
**Where to stay** // The Inn at Hastings Park (www. innathastingspark.com) is a boutique hotel with terrific food close to Lexington's Battle Green.
**When to ride** // The trail is open year round; it's snow-ploughed in winters.
**More information** // www.minutemanbikeway.org.

*Opposite: Dolomites scenery in the Val di Funes in Bolzano province*

# MORE LIKE THIS
## RAIL TRAILS

### CICLABILE DELLE DOLOMITI, ITALY

Scenery doesn't get much more spectacular than the limestone ranges of the Dolomites in northeast Italy. This largely traffic-free bike path, formerly known as the 'Long Way of the Dolomites', follows a railway line through the provinces of Belluno and Bolzano that was built during WW1 and many of the original stations, tunnels and bridges remain. The bike path also runs beside the Boite River and through such pretty alpine towns as Vodo, Venas and Valle at the foot of the peaks of Pelmo and Antelao. Trains to Venice and Padua depart from the finish town of Calalzo di Cadore.

**Start // Dobbiaco**
**End // Calalzo di Cadore**
**Distance // 37 miles (60km)**

### ROUTE OF THE HIAWATHA, USA

Mind the bears! In winter this 15 mile (24km) rail trail closes because hibernating bears hole up in the tunnels. With 10 long tunnels, including the 1.6 mile (2.5km) Taft Tunnel, this family-friendly rail trail through the Bitterroot Mountains between Idaho and Montana is the perfect habitat for the cantankerous mammals. The Route of the Hiawatha is one of America's most scenic and historic rail trails, and features not only tunnels, but seven trestle bridges along its downhill route from the East Portal trailhead. Pair this excursion with the 73-mile (117km) rail trail the Coeur d'Alenes, which follows the route of the Union Pacific railroad across northern Idaho from Mullan, a mining town on the mountainous Montana border to Plummer near the Washington border.

**Start // Shuttles operate from the Lookout Pass Ski Area**
**End // The Coeur d'Alenes concludes at Plummer**
**Distance // 88 miles (142km)**
**More info // www.ridethehiawatha.com; www.friendsofcdatrails.org**

### RATTLER & RIESLING TRAIL, AUSTRALIA

The Clare Valley in South Australia is the backdrop for these rail trails and its Riesling wines – arguably the best in the world – your reward at the end of a day in the saddle. The Rattler Rail Trail (named after the trains that plied the Spalding line that it follows) connects Riverton and Auburn, where it meets the Riesling Trail. Once you've made it to Auburn (and neither of these trails are in the slightest bit challenging), the quaffing can begin. Clare Valley is home to around 30 cellar doors, with crisp, acidic Riesling the speciality but the local cool-climate Shiraz is also very good. Some of the wineries are on the route of the rail trail but many are only a short detour down shady roads. The Riesling Trail starts in Auburn and continues to the town of Clare.

**Start/End // Riverton and Clare, via Auburn**
**Distance // The Rattler is 12 miles (19km), the Riesling Trail is 22 miles (35km)**

# BUENOS AIRES' BIKE PATHS

*The chaos, colour and character of the Argentinian capital's barrios is best viewed from two wheels, as you ride through its past to its present.*

From Jorge Luis Borges' short stories of knife fighters and tango dancers who owned the street corners of the old city, to the elegant tree-lined avenues that hark back to the city's golden age, street life is central to the Buenos Aires' lore and legend.

It's no different today – sidewalk cafes where the city's handsome citizens while away hours, vendors selling everything from feather dusters to hammocks, and the city's famous dog walkers wrangling hounds of every shapes and size: it all happens on the street. You don't even need to go inside a museum to see some of the city's best art – a thriving street art scene means you can enjoy contemporary masterpieces without ever dismounting your bike.

I'd lived in Buenos Aires before the bike paths were laid, and was used to traveling by taxi, bus or on foot. But when I returned on a recent visit I was delighted to find a new way to enjoy the city, cycling swiftly and safely through the cobbled streets of Palermo, sneezing at the plane trees that drop their fine fluff during the springtime, and admiring the purple blooms of jacaranda along Avenida del Libertador.

My favourite ride takes you from La Boca to Parque de la Memoria, an easy 5½ miles (9km) if you go direct, but you'll want to meander through the city's cycleway network, taking in the sights and sounds of several *barrios* (neighbourhoods), each one very distinct.

La Boca is the logical place to start, because while it may not be the spot where the city was first founded by the Spanish (that honour belongs to Parque Lezama, which you'll ride past soon enough), it represents Argentina's birthplace as a polyglot,

immigrant nation. It's here that the hundreds and thousands of migrants poured off their ships and into the boarding houses and poor neighbourhoods of the city's south. 'The history of Buenos Aires is written in its telephone directory,' penned English writer Bruce Chatwin, and more than half those names are Italian, mixed up with German, Welsh, Irish, French and Spanish.

The backbone of your ride is El Bajo – the wide multi-laned thoroughfares of Paseo Colón and Avenidas Libertador and Figueroa Alcorta. The *porteños* (locals or people of the port) refer to it as El Bajo (meaning 'low') because it's the low-lying land sloping down towards what was once the banks of the wide brown waters of the Río de la Plata. The city has turned its back on the river, blocking the view with high-rises, and you'll not catch a glimpse of the water at this end of town unless you choose a detour through the swanky remodeled docklands of Puerto Madero or take a ride through the leafy Parque Ecológico.

From La Boca, the next neighbourhood heading northwards is San Telmo. Once the home of the well-heeled, a yellow-fever epidemic saw them abandon their now-crumbling mansions for the northern end of town. On Sundays, San Telmo's Calle Defensa is taken over by street stalls selling handicrafts and bohemian fashion. There's usually a grungy young tango band or two, while

> *"A thriving street art scene means you can enjoy contemporary masterpieces without dismounting your bike"*

Plaza Dorrego hosts an afternoon open air *milonga* (tango party). For a bit of literary history, take a ride up Calle México to the old Biblioteca Nacional, the National Library where Borges was director for years, and wrote many of his most celebrated stories.

Just a little further along Defensa, and you'll hit the Casa Rosada, or Pink House – Argentina's seat of government. Famous as the place from which Eva Perón made her stirring, strident speeches, it looks over Plaza de Mayo, the political heart of the country, which is usually filled with protestors of various stripes. Up Avenida de Mayo you can get a feel for the city's more opulent past, with the ornate facades of once-elegant buildings now dark with soot.

Back on the Bajo, you'll head further north to Recoleta, and then on to Palermo. It's worth ducking up into the heart of each barrio and along its smaller streets. You'll find plenty of bars and restaurants with outdoor tables where you can eat while keeping

## SHOPPING IN THE MARKETS

You can even shop on two wheels in Buenos Aires, especially if you hit the city's famous markets. There's San Telmo on Sundays and Plaza Francia, Recoleta from Friday to Sunday. But the loveliest is the Mercado de las Pulgas – the Flea Market – on Avenida Dorrego and Avenida Álvarez Thomas, where you'll find everything from priceless antiques to kitsch urban trash. It's open from Tuesday to Sunday.

*Left to right: street scene from San Telmo; Plaza de la Republica; tango in la Boca; refreshments in San Telmo. Previous page: an avenue of jacaranda trees in Buenos Aires*

an eye on your bike – a good idea in this city.

The end of your ride takes you along the beautiful Avenida del Libertador, through the Palermo Woods with their artificial lakes and beautiful rose garden. The place to rest after cycling this wonderful city is at one of its newest parks, Parque de la Memoria. Here you'll finally come face to face with the river; its dulce de leche waters lap against this quiet green space, dotted with sculptures. A wall bears the names of the thousands of Argentines who disappeared during its Dirty War, when the military government attempted to cleanse society of any political dissidents by murdering them or driving them into exile. It's a solemn but beautiful spot, and its sadness doesn't inhibit the young lovers who go there to smooch between classes at the nearby university. Irrepressible Argentines.

Any time of day is a good time to cycle, as this is a city that truly never sleeps. On a recent evening ride, I stopped for a refreshment on Libertador to find an elderly woman and her pooch rendezvousing with her middle-aged daughters and their own canine companions for coffee and cake. It was midnight, and we shared a joke as joggers padded past and the cars racing by helped light the summer evening. Portenos love their city, and know how to enjoy its beauty and its chaos. **SG**

## TOOLKIT

**Start** // La Boca
**End** // Parque de la Memoria
**Distance** // 5½ miles (9km), but detours recommended
**Getting there** // International travellers arrive at Ministro Pistarini Airport at Ezeiza. Flights from nearby countries land at Palermo's convenient Jorge Newbery Airport.
**Bike hire** // Some hotels have free bikes for guests: try Casasur Bellini in Palermo. Biking Buenos Aires (www.bikingbuenosaires.com) rents bikes by the hour and day.
**Bike share** // See www.turismo.buenosaires.gob.ar/en/article/cycling-ba for a downloadable map.
**Tours** // Biking Buenos Aires (www.bikingbuenosaires.com) has a good selection, including one dedicated to street art.
**When to ride** // Spring, from mid-October to December.
**Bike purchases/repairs** // Try Canaglia Bicicletas.

*Opposite: ride the bridges and*
*canal paths of Amsterdam*

# MORE LIKE THIS
## CITY RIDES

### BARCELONA, SPAIN

By fringing its medieval streets with
a modern maze of bike lanes (107
miles/172km of them), Barcelona has
evolved into a cycling city in the last
decade. Its 'Bicing' scheme is aimed at
inhabitants, but bike-hire facilities and
cycle-tour experiences are ubiquitous. Take
a spin to Montjuïc Castle, a 17th-century
hilltop fortress and former prison with
spectacular city and sea views, or do an
urban loop from Plaça Catalunya, through
the Barri Gòtic, past Santa Maria del Mar
to Ciutadella Park. Ride up passeigs de
Lluís Companys and de Sant Joan, under
the Arc de Triomf and swing a right to
the Sagrada Família at Gran Via,
before returning via La Casa Batlló
and La Rambla.
**Start/End // Plaça Catalunya**
**Distance // 5 miles (9km)**

### MONTREAL, CANADA

With its savagely hilly topographical profile
and harsh seasonal weather conditions,
Montreal has been described as an unlikely
cycling city, yet that's exactly what it has
become, with well over 373 miles (600km) of
bike trails slithering around town – almost
155 miles (250km) of them entirely separate
to road traffic – and more than 5000 public-
use bikes available for hire. Each summer,
some 30,000 people rock up in Jeanne-
Mance Park to take part in the annual
Tour de l'Île de Montréal, a road riding
challenge that has several distance options
(the 15-mile/25km or 31-mile/50km classic,
and the 40-mile/65km or 62-mile/100km
Découverte). The routes – which roll around
the Island of Montreal and span the mighty
St Lawrence River across Jacques Cartier
and Champlain bridges, over Île Sainte
Hélène and through Parc Jean-Drapeau,
to explore Longueuil and Parc Michel-
Chartrand before returning to the start
– can be ridden at any time, but roads are
closed to motorised traffic during the event.
**Start // Parc Ave**
**End // Jeanne-Mance Park**
**Distance // Ranges from 15 miles to**
**62 miles (25km–100km)**

### AMSTERDAM, THE NETHERLANDS

Bikes form part of the fabric of Amsterdam,
possibly the planet's most cycle-friendly
city. Each day, 400,000 riders trundle
along 249 miles (400km) of dedicated
cycle paths, which wend around every
corner and canal in this 17th-century city.
Unsurprisingly, the city and its surrounds
are as flat as a Dutch pancake, so cycling
is easy. Bikes in the Dam are typically
low-slung cruising machines, ridden with a
jaunty upright gait. Pedal around the city
centre, taking in the main sights, or loop
out along the banks of the River Amstel to
Ouderkerk aan de Amstel, before riding to
Abcoude and the fortress town of Weesp,
via the Bullewijk, Waver, Winkel and Gein
rivers. Then trace the River Vecht to Castle
Muiderslot, passing through Diemerpark,
back to the centre.
**Start/End // Amsterdam**
**Centraal train station**
**Distance // 28 miles (46km)**

# THE COVERED BRIDGES OF VERMONT

*Drink in the flaming fall foliage – and gallons of gloopy maple syrup –*
*on a cycling circuit between a handful of the US Northeast's most winsome towns.*

The flaming fall foliage in Vermont is a knock-out. Quite literally – it left me sparked out, flat on my back and gasping for breath.

Cycling along the leafy back lanes of Addison County, I was savouring the gentle burn in my calves on the short ascents, then the whispered kiss of the September breeze on my face as I freewheeled down. Alternately puffing and purring, I was happily drinking in the ubiquitous woodscapes of crimson and incandescent amber when suddenly it seemed I'd been drinking a little too deeply. Concentration broken by the vistas while pelting joyfully downhill, I turned a corner to be faced with an unexpected T-junction. On jammed the brakes. The bike stopped dead. I didn't – and flew over the handlebars, with just time to think: so this is what they mean by fall in New England...

Fortunately, both the bike and I survived pretty much unscathed – only my reverie had been punctured. Dusting off my bike, I vowed to focus more on the road and less on the scenery.

That's easier said than done in these parts. Riding through central Vermont in autumn is like cycling through a succession of mesmerising screensavers. Forested hillsides glow with traffic-light hues, red and amber and vibrant green. Red Dutch-gabled barns rise from cornfields, wooden covered bridges span serene waterways and pumpkins are piled at roadsides. It's idealised New England turned up to 11 – and biking heaven.

That comical tumble came just a couple of hours into a 100-mile (161km) triangular ride between three of the most charming burgs in the Champlain Valley, midway from Massachusetts to Montreal. This broad, undulating dale, bounded by the Green Mountains to the east and New York State's Adirondacks to the west, is

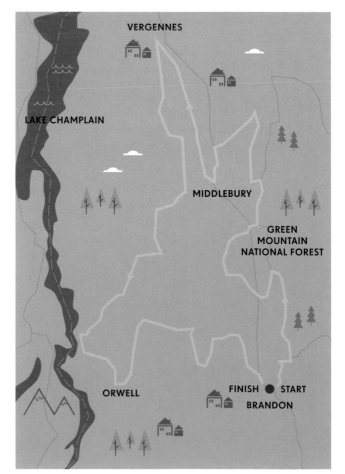

becoming renowned for inn-to-inn cycling tours, as is Vermont in general – with good reason.

For starters, it's predominantly rural – only Wyoming has a smaller population than Vermont, and the state's tallest building is only 11 storeys – and most of its roads are wide, quiet and eminently bike-friendly. The food's terrific, all artisan this and that, craft beers and, well, oceans of maple syrup. And it's breathtakingly beautiful.

My three-day jaunt began in Brandon, an artsy little settlement of clapboard houses where wicker chairs rock on shady verandahs. I'd timed my trip well. A handful of chilly nights had kickstarted the leaf-peeping season, so when I saddled up on a crisp September morning, the hilltops were already smouldering with fall colours.

I tootled languidly along Park St and out past traditional farmsteads, glancing at the map to confirm my deliberately tortuous path. The plan was to pedal about four hours each day, covering 30 or 40 miles (48 to 64km) – but the blue line marking my route staggered across the page like a drunken spider, partly to avoid busy roads, partly to take in the most scenic patches.

A speedy pace was impossible anyway, because photo calls came thick and fast. I'd no sooner pack away the camera after one viewpoint than another materialised. First came the Falls of Lana, cascading 20m or so down the forested hillside. Then I skirted Lake

*"I made a circuitous loop north, waylaid by whimsical road names demanding to be checked out"*

Dunmore, wooden jetties jutting into placid waters. I might manage half a mile (800m), then be waylaid for ten minutes snapping grazing cows, hayfields and grain silos, or a barn-cum-antiques-store from which spilled toy cars, rusty signs, vintage hoes and whirligigs.

It was mid-afternoon when I meandered into that night's halt, Middlebury. The archetypal Vermont college town (Robert Frost lectured here), it's blessed with white-spired churches, galleries, cafes and views over the burbling Otter River. I strolled along its brick-built main street and explored the Henry Sheldon Museum – 'Bringing Vermont History to Life since 1882' – and Vermont Folklife Center, showcasing local arts and crafts.

Next morning I fuelled up at the farmers market, its stalls laden with breads, cheeses, goat's milk soap, and mountains of pumpkins the glowing ochre of late afternoon sun. Not to mention maple syrup. Bottles and jugs and flasks and flagons of maple syrup.

Loaded with portable calories, I pedalled back into the countryside en route to Shoreham, ten miles (16km) or so from

## FROM SAP TO SYRUP

Vermont produces more maple syrup than any other US state. Native American peoples taught settlers how to tap maple trunks in late winter (late February/early March) to collect the sap that oozes out as it rises in the morning and falls at night. To make syrup, they'd throw hot rocks into hollowed-out logs filled with sap; today, wood-fired evaporators are used. Forty gallons of sap produce just one gallon of syrup.

*Left to right: quiet roads and colourful leaves in Vermont; Middlebury College; maple syrup; Halloween scene. Previous page: Lake Champlain*

Middlebury. But why go direct when you can enjoy the even-more-scenic route? Instead of heading directly west, I made a circuitous loop north via Vergennes, waylaid periodically by whimsical road names demanding to be checked out: Lemon Fair Rd, Bittersweet Falls Rd, Snake Mountain Rd. The latter traced a ridge providing panoramic views across the broad sweep of the Champlain Valley, Middlebury's college and steeples rising from a sea of autumn colours to my left.

Bolstered by a breakfast mountain of blueberry pancakes in Shoreham, on my final morning I pedalled through a murky pea-souper and whizzed past the turn-off for Larrabee Pt, where a ferry crosses Lake Champlain to New York State and historic Fort Ticonderoga, then halted to investigate a roadside army of painted wooden creatures. In the adjacent barn I found the gallery of sculptor Norton Latourelle, who has carved a Noah's ark of dogs, birds and rabbits – plus a curious long-necked beast labelled 'Champ'.

'He was first seen long before your Loch Ness Monster,' Norton grinned. 'The early French explorer Samuel de Champlain described him as a "20-ft serpent, thick as a barrel and with the head of a horse".'

A tall tale, to be sure. But a search for a mysterious water creature might provide just the excuse to return and pedal some more of Vermont's snaking, sensational byways. **PB**

## TOOLKIT

**Start/End //** Brandon, Vermont
**Distance //** about 99 miles (160km) Brandon–Middlebury–(Vergennes)–Shoreham–Brandon
**Getting there //** Rutland Airport is 22 miles (35km) south of Brandon. Cape Air (www.capeair.com) flies from Boston Logan.
**Tour //** Inn to Inn (www.inntoinn.com) offers a four-night package, including half-board accommodation, maps, route notes, bike hire and baggage transfers.
**Bike hire //** Green Mountain Bikes (www.greenmountainbikes.com) rents bikes from U$30 per day; bikes can be delivered to inns.
**When to ride //** April to October. Foliage season is mid-September to mid-October, when rates rise and accommodation gets booked out.

*Opposite: Tofukuji temple
in autumn hues*

# MORE LIKE THIS
# FALLING LEAVES RIDES

### SONOMA COUNTY, USA

Sonoma County is where California's
velo and vino cultures collide in a happy
claret splatter every autumn. For a classic
Wine Country ride, leave the hub-town
of Healdsburg, ride along Westside and
turn right onto West Dry Creek Rd, an
undulating 9-mile (14km) avenue that's one
of California's most popular cycling roads.
At Yoakim Bridge Rd, cross the valley to Dry
Creek Rd, hang a left and climb Canyon
Rd before enjoying the descent into
Alexander Valley. Turn right, roll through
Geyserville, cross Russian River and take
Hwy 128, Red Winery and Pine Flat roads
back towards Healdsburg, via Jimtown,
with valley-hugging vineyards to the right
and hills ablaze with autumnal colours on
your left.
**Start/End // Healdsburg**
**Distance // 32 miles (51km)**

### KYOTO, JAPAN

Less commercialised than spring's pink-
and-white eruption of cherry blossoms,
the kaleidoscopic quality of Kyoto's *koyo*
(leaves) in autumn is equally sensational,
especially when seen from the saddle. From
mid-September, a crimson tide – the 'koyo
front' – surges south across Japan from
Hokkaido. A great place to see the fiery
foliage at its reddest intensity is Tōfukuji
Temple, which can be explored during an
easy cycling loop from Kyoto station. Allow
two hours (with stops) for this route, which
wends west from the spaceship-like station
along shared bike-pedestrian paths, then
heads south along Higashinotoin-dori,
before going west again to Toji Temple.
From this impressive pagoda-topped World
Heritage site, built in 796, pedal east,
across the Kamo River, to explore the great
Zen Tōfukuji temple. The amazing maple
trees are best enjoyed from Tsutenkyo
Bridge. From here, head north until you
reach Meiji-jingū shrine, then go east and
trace the river back to the centre.
**Start/End // Kyoto City Hall**
**Distance // 7 miles (11km)**
**More info // www.cyclekyoto.com**

### TRANSYLVANIA, ROMANIA

Beyond the clichés of vampire counts
and creepy castles, Romania offers
intrepid travellers multiple mind-bending
experiences, one of the best being
an autumn-time cycling tour through
Transylvania's colour-infused Carpathian
Mountains. This quiet corner of Europe
boasts wonderful wildlife (including bears,
lynx and wolves) and stunning landscapes
punctuated by peaks and Saxon-era
villages. In the heady embrace of the
Făgăraş Mountains, try a two-wheeled
traverse of the Transfăgărăşan, a spin-out
trip along a forest-flanked road, which flows
around hairpin turns on its spectacular
route from Bascov (near Piteşti) to Bâlea
Lake. The Tour of Romania and the Sibiu
Cycling Tour both pass this way, and horror
fans can visit the village of Arefu and see
Poenari Citadel, a 13th-century castle and
one-time residence of Vlad the Impaler,
inspiration for Bram Stoker's Dracula.
**Start // Bascov (near Piteşti)**
**End // Bâlea Lake**
**Distance // 73 miles (117km)**

# VANCOUVER AND WHISTLER

*Short, slippery and very steep: take on the world's most adrenaline-charged mountain bike trails in the forests southwest of Canada's British Columbia.*

'Stay low, and keep your arms bent,' my tutor, Kevan, instructs me, as I edge towards a 2ft step-down. I hesitate, then, as my mountain-bike tyre rolls over the slippery root and into air, he tells me to extend my arms, pushing the bike down into the drop. 'You have to absorb the terrain,' he tells me. There's no respite: the trail keeps snaking downward, around trees, over huge roots and rocks, at a relentlessly steep gradient. 'Fear,' Kevan says, 'is a lack of confidence in your ability.' Thanks, Kevan. And this is one of the easiest trails at Whistler Bike Park in British Columbia.

Fear is one reason I've come here: I want to acclimatise to the level of mountain bike riding in this southwest corner of Canada in the relatively controlled surroundings of Whistler Bike Park, 70 miles (113km) north of Vancouver. Every summer the ski resort's lifts and gondolas are taken over by mountain bikers in body armour and full-face helmets, bearing burly full-suspension mountain bikes. Despite the protective kit, the injury rates among the summer mountain bikers are 10 times those of winter's skiers and boarders.

Whistler was a bike park pioneer, and ski resorts across the world – from Canada to New Zealand and Europe – now resound to the thrum of knobbly tyres on downhill trails. Most offer specialist bikes and kit for hire, and also tuition or skills classes, so they're good places to build your off-road repertoire, namely jumps, drops and near-vertical slopes.

Later in my day with Kevan, I pedal along wide logs, 4ft or 5ft off the ground. The next step is to ride 'skinnies', planks just 4in or 5in across. There's little that is technically difficult about this, provided you have a sense of balance and can pedal in a straight line. They're more a psychological leap than a physical one. Richie

Schley, a veteran Canadian pro mountain biker agrees: 'It's a mind game,' he explains to me. 'None of us just got on a bike and did crazy stuff immediately. Put some logs on the ground and practise jumps. Learn the basics. Take baby steps.'

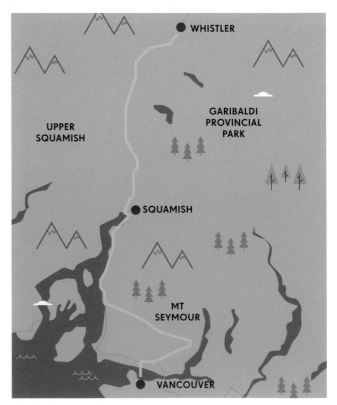

Ready or not, my time's up. I head back down the Sea to Sky Hwy to Vancouver for my rendezvous with epic mountain biking, Vancouver-style.

'Follow me,' says my new guide, Johnny Smoke. We pedal past a chain-link fence to the top of a trail called CBC. It's named after the Canadian Broadcasting Corporation's TV mast at the top of Mt Seymour.

On first inspection, the North Shore of Vancouver is an affluent suburb on the north side of the Lions Gate Bridge, backed by three densely forested, 4000ft mountains: Cypress, Grouse (also known as Mt Fromme) and Seymour. But to mountain bikers, the North Shore is a legendary destination, one that begat a new style of mountain biking: freeriding – big air, big stunts, big risks.

In the late 1980s, before full-suspension mountain bikes, local cyclists started riding down these mountains. In these steep, coastal forests of lofty hemlocks and cypresses they built their way over and around natural obstacles. Bogs were bridged, massive tree stumps breached by log ladders. Trail builders, most famously 'Dangerous' Dan Cowan and Todd 'Digger' Fiander, constructed ever more outrageous stunts. Video producers came to film local bikers riding higher and narrower ladders and plummeting off ever-larger drops. The trails' names gave some clue of what to expect: Flying Circus was a terrifying network of five-inch wide ladders suspended 5m up in the trees.

Today there are about 125 mapped trails on the North Shore. Most tend not to be longer than half a mile (1km). But they are steep and contorted. It's dark inside the old-growth forests and the Jurassic-sized roots and rocks are slippery; one misjudgement and you will slam into a clavicle-cracking tree.

## THE TEST OF METAL

Between Vancouver and Whistler lies the logging town of Squamish, home to a cross-country mountain bike race called the Test of Metal. The event celebrated its 21st year in 2016, making it Canada's most successful bike race. The challenge? It's 42 miles (67km) long, but more than half of the route is technically demanding singletrack. It takes the winners around 2.5hrs to complete and the average human being up to 6 hours.

*Clockwise from top: what goes down must go up – taking the road to the top of the North Shore mountains; and coming down; woodwork at Whistler. Previous page: riding Whistler's ridge*

These trails are the reason that the baseline standard of riding among North Shore locals is more than a step above the rest of the world and why this corner of Canada has produced so many of the world's most skilful (or at least fearless) mountain bikers. Thanks to that group of pioneering riders, a quarter of a century ago, the next generation, and the one after that, grew up with an expanded sense of what was possible (or sensible). Skills – and a devil-may-care attitude – were passed down the line.

Come 5pm, and convoys of pick-ups and cars bearing mountain bikes often worth more than the vehicles, converge on the logging roads heading up Mt Seymour and Mt Fromme. Bikes are checked, armour strapped on and then, after a hard day at the office, it's play time for Vancouver's lawyers, dentists, shop workers and plumbers. Young or old, male or female, the North Shore doesn't discriminate.

Neither does the CBC trail, where Johnny Smoke has brought me. It's a 0.8 mile (1.25km) double-black diamond entree that links to a couple of classic North Shore trails, Pingu and Pangor. I begin gingerly. Most of the features are ground level, thankfully, and a lot of work has been done on the surface in recent years, so steep chutes are paved with stones. It twists and turns through a primeval Pacific rainforest. Every synapse in my brain is firing; the North Shore demands total concentration as we segue from trail to trail.

Then, with my arms aching from braking, I burst, wide-eyed, out of the forest and onto a suburban street. It will take a few more runs before I can follow Richie Schley's best advice for riding the Shore: 'Never hesitate.' **RB**

## TOOLKIT

**Start** // Whistler's longest cross-country trail is Comfortably Numb, which starts from the Wedgemount parking lot.

**End** // Whistler Village

**Distance** // 12 miles (19km)

**Getting there** // Vancouver's international airport receives flights from all over the world.

**Where to stay** // There are bike-friendly B&Bs on the North Shore. At Whistler, accommodation options include within the resort's hotels and lodges, and private house rentals. It's also possible to rent an RV in Vancouver and book a place at a campground (or during the summer, overnight for free in Parking Lots 4 and 5).

**Terrain** // Trails are graded like ski runs, from green (easy) to black and double black diamonds (hard). An intermediate trail here is more challenging than a hard (black) trail elsewhere.

**More info** // North Shore Mountain Bike Association (www. nsmba.ca); Whistler Bike Park (www.whistlerblackcomb. com); Test of Metal (www.testofmetal.com)

*Opposite: miles of smiles at Mt Buller
mountain bike park in Australia*

# MORE LIKE THIS
## MOUNTAIN BIKE PARKS

### MAMMOTH BIKE PARK, CALIFORNIA

There's an ever-growing number of bike parks knocking on Whistler's door. In the Sierra Nevada, just beyond Yosemite National Park if you're coming from San Francisco, Mammoth Mountain has 80 miles (129km) of purpose-built singletrack, accessed by the resort's gondola. Trails range from long cross-country routes to steep and rough downhill tracks with berms and North Shore-style wooden features. The Pioneer Practice Loop around the Adventure Center is an easy trail for beginners and young riders, with instructions for each new feature. A huge range of intermediate terrain then opens up. The most advanced tracks have been used for National Championships. Just remember that you are at an altitude of 9000ft (giving 3000ft of vertical descent) and take it easy the first few days!
**Start/End // Adventure Center, Main Lodge (where the gondola departs)**
**Distance // Longest trails are Off the Top, Beach Cruiser, and Downtown at 13.3 miles (21km); shortest trail is Richter at 0.3 mile (0.5km).**

### SAMOËNS, FRANCE

The French Alps have the highest concentration of bike trails accessed by ski lifts, with the supersized Portes du Soleil valley networking 13 resorts that all open for summer bikers; Les Gets and Morzine are among the most popular choices for foreign visitors. But if you want to get away from the crowds you don't have to go far (though bike parks in Austria and Italy are also tempting), only to the neighbouring Vallée du Haut Giffre. More than 30 trails await, ranging from easy green routes around the mountain villages, intermediate blues through alpine pastures to steeper red and black-graded freeride tracks with jumps and berms. The trails tend to be more natural in style than those of the Portes du Soleil bike parks, crossing streams, and descending through forests. In 2015, Samoëns hosted a stage of the Enduro World Series.
**Start // Tête de Saix (for many downhill trails), easier blue and red trails start lower down**
**End // Samoëns**
**Distance // The longest trail is 8 miles (13km), the shortest 0.6 miles (1km).**

### MT BULLER, AUSTRALIA

Bouncing wallabies, the scent of eucalyptus, and raucous birds: you know when you're mountain biking in Australia. Arguably the country's best bike park, though still dwarfed by resorts in the northern hemisphere, Mt Buller in central Victoria has enough purpose-built trails for a long weekend of dusty action. Four downhill tracks run from the resort hub, the longest at around 1.5 miles (2.5km). There's a wider range of cross-country trails including the 25 mile (40 km) Australian Alpine Epic Trail that swoops across the Victorian High Country and requires more endurance than technical skill, with 2187m of descent (and 1245m of climbing). Stonefly, at 6 miles (9.5km), requires a bit more technical skill. Interestingly, the nearby town of Warburton is beginning to develop its own mountain bike trails, in a rainforest landscape of giant trees that has more in common with the Canadian North Shore.
**Start/End // Mt Buller Village**
**Distance // 25 miles (40km) for the intermediate-graded Australian Alpine Epic**

# MANHATTAN CIRCUMNAVIGATION

*An epic ride of America's most famed city that leaves behind the crowds to reveal waterside glimpses of hidden New York.*

The bicycle renaissance is thriving in New York, which is a surprisingly rewarding cycling city. Locals reading that sentence may be tempted – in a very New York kind of way – to roll their eyes and mutter something about the rest of the world being behind the times. New York is very bike friendly, from Central Park's wide-open boulevards, which are closed to cars for much of daylight hours, to an ever-increasing network of bike lanes criss-crossing iconic landmarks, and exhilarating bridge crossings. Visitors to the city only take partial advantage of this. Few make their way any further than the far end of the Brooklyn Bridge, which is a shame. There is more fun to be had on two wheels by going further.

The jewel in the crown of New York cycling is the Manhattan Waterfront Greenway. This path snakes its way around almost the entirety of Manhattan Island, rolling for 31 glorious miles (50km). Looking at this ribbon of green on the map, I reasoned that this would be a suitable way to venture beyond the known city into places that tourists don't stray. To do so, I needed to take to two wheels. I wanted to roll through unknown neighbourhoods, and explore the extremities of Manhattan. The interior, I figured, couldn't be comprehensively mapped without becoming a resident, but the perimeter could be fairly efficiently circumnavigated. So I joined those hiring a bike, but set out with what I felt were grander ambitions.

As with any circular ride, there's no 'right' way to go, but the prevailing view seems to be to head up the west side to the far north of the island, then back down the east side and complete the loop via the southern tip of the city.

My bike hire location was near Union Sq, meaning I crossed Chelsea and the Meatpacking District as the morning rush petered

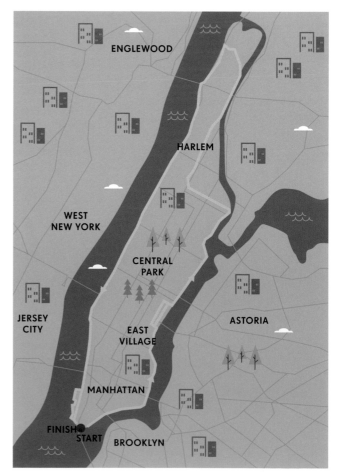

out, and I hit the Hudson bike path just south of the High Line. It was at this point that my perception of the city changed. Endless blocks of busy streets, stuffed with pedestrians and cars and honking taxis that made up the New York of my imagination was replaced by the broad Hudson River. A human scale emerged. It was more than a little strange to suddenly be away from the noise of the city, and instead be able to hear the grind of my wheels on the tarmac path, and the gentle yet firm calls to attention from runners overtaking pedestrians. These warnings became more shrill and direct as we approached the cruise terminal and scores of bemused new arrivals found they were blocking the recreational route of speeding locals. Here was an instant reminder that I was still where I thought I was, in boisterous New York.

The Hudson Greenway, as this section is known, stretched on, and I found as I rode it that my sense of the topography of the city was shifting. Landmarks of northward progression – in particular Central Park – rolled past without notice. From the water I could tell I was leaving Midtown by the visible drop in the height of buildings I was riding parallel to. Fellow travellers on the route were thinning out too. Few tourists head out to lap the island, and on weekdays there aren't many commuters outside of peak times. I even experienced feelings of solitude while moving around the world's most famous city.

Fort Washington Park, marked by the Washington Bridge and the Little Red Lighthouse, felt like a signpost that I was leaving known areas behind and heading into unknown Manhattan. The far north of the island is stranger, and more remote from the familiar parts of

## BRIDGE RIDES

The bridges connecting Manhattan with the outer boroughs and New York are iconic landmarks on a circuit of the island. If you only ride one, the iconic wooden boardwalk on Brooklyn Bridge is it, but most can be cycled. The newest is also the oldest – the High Bridge connecting Harlem with the Bronx dates from 1848, when it was built as an aqueduct. Today it carries pedestrians and cyclists high above the Harlem River.

*Clockwise from top: street scene in NYC; One World Trade Center; restore burned calories with a pastrami on rye sandwich. Previous page: crossing iconic Brooklyn Bridge*

Brooklyn and Queens.

Fort Tryon Park is home to one of the city's most marvellous oddities: The Cloisters. This annex of the Metropolitan Museum of Art proved an ideal stop on my way, as much for the remarkable merging of five medieval abbeys into one whole, as for the works of art inside. Beyond here, shortly before Manhattan stops, cyclists dip inland through Inwood Hill, emerging on the east side of Manhattan for the first time on a path running along the Harlem Greenway. This was originally a horse-racing strip for weekending Manhattanites from which cyclists, ironically, were banned. Today a bike path follows it south until another detour takes you on a signed path through Harlem. This showed another side of the city. It was school graduation day and a happy, carefree atmosphere prevailed on the streets. Like so often on a bike, I pedalled through as an unnoticed observer.

Beyond a small diversion around the United Nations complex between 54th and 37th Streets the Greenway then trundles happily down to Battery Park. South of the Williamsburg Bridge I started to pick up more cyclists, and couldn't resist a few additional miles across the Manhattan Bridge, racing subway trains crossing the water, and returning via the busy but exhilarating Brooklyn Bridge bike and pedestrian path.

Once I'd cleared the crowds at Battery Park it was a short pull back up the Hudson to complete the loop. Bike safely returned, I had one final problem: New York is too exciting a city to relax and put your feet up. I briefly puzzled as to how to fill the rest of the day. The answer came in the form of the Staten Island Ferry, leading to another of the city's boroughs. Which looked like a good place for a bike ride itself, another day. **TH**

*"I found as I rode the Hudson Greenway that my sense of the topography of the city was shifting"*

### TOOLKIT

**Start/End** // The beauty of Manhattan Waterfront Greenway is you can start the loop wherever you want.
**Distance** // 31 miles (50km)
**When to ride** // Spring and autumn are best to avoid the city's frigid winters and sticky summers, but if paths are clear and you've got suitable clothing it could be done anytime.
**Bike hire** // For quality hybrid- and road-bike rentals try Danny's Cycles (www.dannyscycles.com; hybrid $10 per hour, road bike $15 per hour), with six locations around New York.
**More info** // The New York City Bike Map (www.nyc.gov/html/dot/html/bicyclists/bikemaps.shtml) has details on cycle routes across Manhattan and beyond. A print copy is most useful and can be picked up in bike shops and tourist offices.

*Opposite: don't miss watching a keirin race in a Tokyo veldrome*

# MORE LIKE THIS
## CITY RIDES

### TOKYO

Japan's magnificent sprawl may seem, on first glance, to be the antithesis of a cycling destination. With a little help it can be an equally surprising place to ride. Tokyo Great Cycling Tours' six-hour Edo-Tokyo Culture Ride visits Ryōgoku sumo stadium, Ueno Park and concludes at the Imperial Palace. Book in advance. Another side of Japan's cycling culture can be found at one of 47 velodromes around the country that are used for highly popular Keirin races. Keirin cycling is one of the few sporting events in Japan on which gambling is permitted, and entry to race meets is cheap. In Tokyo, visit the Keiokaku and Tachikawa velodromes for race meets.
**Tour // Tokyo Great Cycling Tours (www.tokyocycling.jp) offer a variety of guided rides that are part cycling trip, part exploration of Tokyo's well-known/ less-heralded sights**

### MEXICO CITY

Mega-cities don't seem to offer much promise for anyone considering cycling. They have vast populations, strained transport networks and a sense of controlled chaos. Mexico City, however, is emerging as an exception to the rule at the same time as its reputation as a city destination is growing. Here is a capital with millennia of history, reflected in dozens of museums and galleries, and the varied food and nightlife scene you'd expect when 21.2 million people come together. The major thoroughfares remain hard going, due to traffic and tarmac conditions, but, as with elsewhere in the world, bike tours exploring the city are popular with visitors and cover far more ground than you might on foot. With wheels you can explore some of the designated bike paths that criss-cross the city, including one that runs from Bosque de Chapultepec to the Centro Historico.
**Bike hire // Rent bikes for free for up to three hours at locations in the centre, including from a booth by the Catedral Metropolitana. Ecobici (www.ecobici. df.gob.mx) is a commuter bike service that gives 45 minutes of free riding**
**When to ride // Sunday mornings, when several downtown streets are closed to traffic, opening up a 16-mile (26km) unbroken, car-free route**

### BROOKLYN-QUEENS GREENWAY

The 40-mile Brooklyn-Queens Greenway offers another grand day out, running from Little Bay Park in Queens to Coney Island, linking such attractions as New York Aquarium, Brooklyn Museum and Brooklyn Botanic Garden. By tackling the route over a day or two you can further discover the outer boroughs and also explore the many parks and dedicated bike routes that demonstrate the continued growth of cycling in New York. Best time to try it? Avoid the sticky heat of midsummer in New York and the snow of deep winter.
**Start // Little Bay Park, Queens**
**End // Coney Island**
**Distance // 40 miles (64km)**

# MAI CHAU CYCLE RIDE

*Pedal through gorgeous rice terraces and
timeless village life to see an enthralling slice of Vietnam
in the classically Asian style – by bike.*

I n a narrow lane outside of Mai Chau, I stop my bike to let traffic pass. A water buffalo lumbers towards me, taking up the entire space of the lane. Its calf wanders docilely behind, trailed by a wizened old farmer. In these rural passages, this is as close to a truck, sidecar and driver as I will see.

I'm cycling through the valleys that run like a delta from the town of Mai Chau in northern Vietnam. Pyramids and domes of limestone rise out of the valleys, creating an inland version of Halong Bay. Everything between the mountains, however, is almost ruler flat, with rice terraces underscoring the heavily forested peaks in an archetypal Asian rural scene. It's a landscape so beautiful and yet so kind on my legs, a cyclist might have created it.

For two days I'll pedal through these valleys without any real destination – A to B is not the goal here; I'm riding simply to immerse myself in the place and its rural life. Roads lead to lanes, which lead to unmarked trails along the levees of the rice terraces. Nowhere here is out of bounds to a bike.

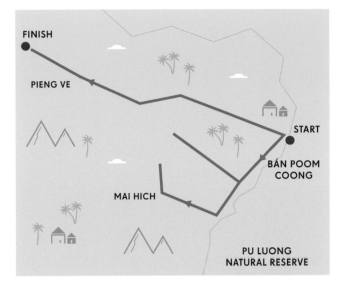

I'm here in rice-harvest season, a time when the valleys, each layered with rice terraces, become a living landscape. At dawn, clouds of smoke already rise from the fields as workers burn the residue from the harvest. Rice harvesters splash through the sodden fields, scythes in hand, trousers rolled to their thighs.

Each morning I set out riding early, into the relative cool of the humid days. Atop each bank between the rice terraces are timeworn footpaths that now double as singletrack for my mountain bike. Overnight rain has made the paths slick and slow, but I'm in no hurry. Cows wander the tracks, chickens dash across them, and a man herds a flock of ducks towards home. The rice fields are dotted with buffaloes and rice harvesters bowed to their work – an archipelago of conical hats in a sea of yellow rice. Faces turn as we pass. Smiles are exchanged, sometimes a titter of laughter as my back wheel slips through the mud.

For a few hours this day, I curl through the fields on my bike. Lines of villages sit crouched at the foot of the mountains like avalanche debris. The roadsides, like aisles in a greengrocer, have corn, taro, banana, cassava and papaya plants alongside, filling every patch of ground not already flooded with rice.

The pedalling is easy – flat, almost traffic-free – and the joy is in the freedom to simply disappear inside the scene and the landscape, which is so clearly delineated into nature and agriculture – the mountains so dense with forest, the valley floors so bare of anything but crops and the occasional clusters of

*"Children pedal alongside me, urging me on for a good-natured sprint: their bikes have one gear, mine has 27"*

bamboo rising like giant florets of broccoli.

Mai Chau may be a popular traveller destination, but its tourist patina fades the further I pedal. Lanes lead into villages occupied by families of minority White Thai people, their homes crouched on stilts. Workers push bicycles overburdened with rice stalks, ever-smiling even though I feel weary just watching them.

Briefly in these flattest of valleys, I do the unthinkable, following a road that climbs onto the slopes at the valley's edge, hoping for a view back over the fields. The road steepens and my legs feel as though they're leaving the valley, but in most other regards the valley comes with me. Villages creep up the slopes, and rice fields are benched into the hills, surrounded now by forest.

Children flood through the gates of a school, their day of study done. Kids crowd the road, and I begin a game with them, growling in jest as I pass. Children scatter like birds, screaming and laughing, then they crowd around again, their eyes and smiles keen for more. When I finally ride on, children pedal alongside me, urging me on for a good-natured sprint race. Their bikes have one gear, mine has 27. They quickly fall behind.

## THE RICHES OF RICE

As you pedal through so much rice terracing in the valleys around Mai Chau, it won't surprise to learn that Vietnam is the world's fifth-largest rice-producing nation, growing around 30 million tonnes of milled rice a year, putting it behind only China, India, Indonesia and Bangladesh for output. More than 80% of the country's arable land is given over to rice.

*Left to right: aerial view of Mai Chau; streetside scene near Mai Chau; fill up on fresh fruit; vive Vietnam. Previous page: sundown over the rice paddies of Mai Chau*

Further up the hill, I turn back and tuck in behind a motorcycle as it descends towards the valley. Wicker panniers hang from its sides, with large pigs squeezed tightly inside them. I tail the motorcycle all the way to the valley, the pigs watching me from inside their mobile cells.

The next morning the valley echoes with rooster calls long before dawn, making an early start no difficulty. I pedal out from my homestay as dawn mist lingers in the valleys, wrapping itself like a scarf around the mountains.

This day I will range further out from Mai Chau, still pedalling through the web of valleys, but immersing myself ever deeper into the rural landscape. Concrete lanes and dirt footpaths wind aimlessly through the rice fields, taking me to anonymous places I'd never find travelling on anything but a bike.

The mountains close in, narrowing the valleys, and I roll quietly through village after village, each one teeming with life – dogs, puppies, roosters, ducks and children swirling like electrons. More quietly, an old woman sits beside a path, chewing betel nut as her buffaloes graze around her. She seems oblivious to my bike, even as I pass.

In many ways this day is a large-format version of my previous one – its few hours stretched into a full day – but I feel as though I could ride like this forever, watching the perpetual cycle of the seasons, the rice, the villages and the people from my very own cycle. **AB**

## TOOLKIT

**Start/End //** Mai Chau
**Distance //** Flexible. From 3 miles (5km) to 31 miles (50km), there are no set routes.
**Getting there //** Mai Chau is a three- to four-hour drive west from Hanoi.
**Bike Hire //** Ask at homestays in and around Mai Chau.
**Tours //** Mai Chau Lodge (www.maichaulodge.com; VND168,000-294,000 per two-hour ride) and Mai Chau Ecolodge (www.maichau.ecolodge.asia; $US8-14 per half-day ride) offer bike tours for guests.
**Where to stay //** Homestays in the White Thai village of Pom Coong make an excellent alternative to nearby Mai Chau.
**Where to drink //** The stylish rooftop bar attached to the Mai Chau Sunset Hotel (www.maichausunset.com) provides a perfect end to a cycling day.
**When to ride //** September and October are arguably the finest months for cycling here, with the rice harvest under way.

*Opposite: cycle to timeless Zhaoxing village in Guìzhou, China*

# MORE LIKE THIS
## SOUTH EAST ASIA RIDES

### CENTRAL VIETNAM

To get a more detailed picture of Vietnam from a bike saddle, the country's wishbone-thin central strip is your best bet. Begin in the former royal capital of Hue and pedal south. Between here and the beach resort of Nha Trang, the coast is backed by the lush highlands, making it easy to switch landscapes and the intensity of the challenge. Stick to the coast for the gorgeous French colonial town of Hoi An, where you can ferry across the river to quiet coastal riding in Son my (My Lai), the sombre site of a Vietnam War atrocity. Turn up into the highlands past here and the hills step up beside you in rice terraces before you enter coffee country across the top of the highlands. Stop in at the hill station of Dalat before enjoying a rollicking descent towards Nha Trang and beach and island bliss to end the journey.
**Start // Hue**
**End // Nha Trang**
**Distance // 435 miles (700km)**

### MEKONG DELTA, VIETNAM

Imagine a place where hills don't exist, and rice terraces roll out endlessly to the horizon. This cycling fantasy is the Mekong Delta region of southern Vietnam. To ride here is to potentially cycle over more water than land, as Southeast Asia's longest river washes out towards the ocean in braids beneath your wheels. Around half of the country's rice comes from this water world: you'll pedal past rice field after rice field, and over a multitude of bridges that might offer views over floating markets – scenes that are about as classically Vietnam as it gets. Many cyclists combine their delta with their deities, pedalling on across Cambodia to the ruins of Angkor Wat. This is a popular itinerary for cycling tour operators, with shuttle services taking out the worst of the highway stretches.
**Start/End // Ho Chi Minh City**
**Distance: 186 miles (300km)**

### GUÌZHOU, CHINA

If the fields of Mai Chau have only whetted your appetite for rice terraces, a cycle journey through the little-visited Chinese province of Guìzhou might beckon. Around the towns of Yongle and Leishan, the hillsides are hooped with terraces. Roads curl through them, passing waterlogged fields where planters or harvesters will be just as intrigued by you as you are by them. Cresting hills to find yourself looking down onto a village such as Zhaoxing, with its drum towers, canals and wind and rain bridges, is like stumbling into a Xanadu. Tourist infrastructure in the Guìzhou countryside is minimal, to say the least, so it's worth considering a tour.
**Start // Guiyang**
**End // Yangshuo**
**Tours // SpiceRoads (www.spiceroads.com) or Red Spokes (www.redspokes.co.uk)**

# BIKEPACKING
# IN MONGOLIA

*Criss-crossed by myriad faint tracks, Mongolia offers almost endless scope for
backcountry touring. And there's no better place to camp after a long day's ride.*

Consider first that just 10% of Mongolia's roads are paved. Next, the country is among the least densely populated in the world. Factor in that land is collectively owned, and as a result, prime camping real-estate abounds. Lastly, savour the knowledge that motorised traffic is incredibly scarce. On an overcrowded planet, Mongolia is a breath of fresh air, and nothing short of a cyclist's paradise.

While much of the country is rife with two-wheeled potential, our journey focused on Central Mongolia's Khangai Mountains, a region of rolling steppe, pine forests, meadows and clear brooks. Dirt roads unravelled in every direction, with barely a fence line to be seen; sometimes they were a dozen tyre-tracks wide, as if such space made aimless driving irresistible. We roamed wherever the whim took us, and camped whenever we ran out of steam. When the tracks themselves ran out, we tacked across the steppe like ships out at sea.

More often than not, we were within eyesight of Mongolia's distinctive *gers* (tents). Synonymous with its steppe, these portable

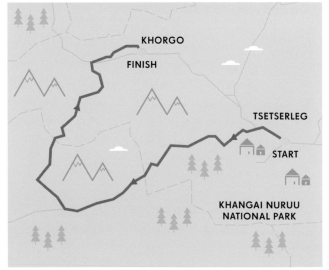

KHORGO

FINISH

TSETSERLEG

START

KHANGAI NURUU
NATIONAL PARK

*Clockwise from left: Mongolian meat pies known as khuushuur; the family yurt; on the (very) open road; temples and traditional costume. Previous page: water crossings are common*

enclaves are relocated throughout the year to wherever the best pastures lie. Perfectly proportioned and beautifully painted within, each off-grid home included a standard inventory of Mongolian accessories: a flock of sheep, a herd of yak, a team of horses, a motorbike, a solar panel, a satellite dish... and some laundry hanging out to dry.

Inevitably families waved us down, force feeding us the nation's favourite tipple, a pungent brew made from fermented horse milk called *airag*. Out on the open expanse of the grasslands, we'd exchange words with shepherds in a medley of Mongolian, English and charades, or simply pass round shots of potent, homemade vodka, grimacing knowingly at each other.

To a soundtrack of thundering hooves, men tore across the steppe, and children trotted alongside us, riding their small and muscular horses as naturally as they drew breath. By the tender age of two, most have learnt to ride. Just a few years later, many have graduated to the role of jockeys, competing in the epic, 15.5-mile (25km) races that form a highlight of Nadaam, the country's annual sporting championships.

Once, the kids we'd watched so gracefully round up sheep on horseback galloped over to our tents, challenging us to a game of football. It was a hard fought battle, of which Genghis Khan would have been proud. With typical Mongolian decorum, it culminated with cups of fresh milk and a platter of dried cheese, before warm farewells – and Facebook profiles – were exchanged by all.

Like their prized horses, our bikes proved ideal for the variety of terrain that we faced, and the many river crossings we

> ## "To a soundtrack of thundering hooves, men tore across the steppe, and children trotted alongside us"

encountered. Some we rode through, water cresting over bottom brackets and hubs. Others were thigh deep, requiring bags to be shed and bikes shouldered. Not that they were cause for complaint. Such impromptu challenges were either the perfect excuse for lingering lunch spots while we discussed the best route across, or they made for welcome river baths, bodies and clothes parched dry after just a few moments back in the saddle.

Onwards we pedalled, over the Khangai's high passes, each marked by distinctive *ovoos* (traditional cairns, usually piles of rocks and/or wood). These sacred monuments stood tall and stark against the horizon: collections of tree trunks stacked up like kindling, they embodied the country's spiritual duality; animal bones and skulls were clues to its Shamanistic traditions, while Buddhist prayer flags echoed those found on the Tibetan plateau. Mongolians walk around these structures three times in a clockwise direction, adding a stone to the pile, or perhaps milk and vodka, in reverence to the Sky God Tengri. Certainly, there was no shortage of big skies here.

Eventually, our ride took us in a broad loop around Terkhiin Tsagaan Nuur, the White Lake, to our destination of Tariat, a ramshackle metropolis by local standards. In typical cyclists' fashion, we celebrated our arrival with a hearty plate of Mongolian

fare: *buuz* – a round of fresh dumplings, packed with an equal ratio of mutton and gristle. In the countryside, the best that restaurants might rustle up were subtle variations on a theme, like noodle soups with very similar flavours or, for more variety, *khuushuur*: fried pockets of meat and (yes, again) fat. As for any hints of greenery, the odd sliver of diced carrot appeared more for colour than for aspirations towards a balanced diet. Sadly, I have to concede that outside of capital Ulaanbaatar, Mongolian cuisine left something to be desired.

A capital which, incidentally, reflects the country's present day cultural and socio-economic melange; the dichotomy of its glassy high-rises bankrolled by multinational mining, its brutalist architecture dating back to years as a Soviet satellite state, and its collection of ancient, gold-gilded temples that wouldn't be out of place in Tibet. Of the latter, my favourite was the Choijin Lama Temple, once home to the state oracle, whose prophetic predictions helped the government navigate state affairs. Now encircled by office towers, it stands like a bastion to the old world, crammed with a bewitching collection of such religious relics as the mummified body of a seated monk, and a trumpet made from a human thigh bone encased in silver.

But it was the simple act of experiencing the vastness of Mongolia's steppe that resonated most for me. There are few places in the world so richly endowed with its sense of immeasurable space. It was on the steppe that my spirit soared towards Tingri, as we pedalled our bicycles ever onwards along Mongolia's beguiling ribbons of dirt. **CG**

## NADAAM FESTIVAL

Legend has it that the Nadaam festival (celebrated each July) was conceived by Genghis Khan to ensure his population remained ready to do battle at a moment's notice. As such, Nadaams revolve around horse riding, archery and Mongolian wrestling. A highlight of any visit, some festivals are large and extravagant affairs, while others pop up on the steppe for a matter of hours, only to disappear in a cloud of jeep dust and galloping horses.

*Left to right: bareback horse-riding; uncrowded camping; fat bike riding*

## TOOLKIT

**Start** // Tsetserleg
**End** // Tariat
**Distance** // 298 miles (480km)
**Get there** // Tsetserleg is an 8hr bus ride from Ulaanbaatar. Tariat has daily bus connections back to Tsetserleg.
**Bike hire** // Mountain bikes and gear are available from the Fairfield Guesthouse (www.fairfield.mn) in Tsetserleg.
**When to ride** // Summer offers warm temperatures and long days, tempered by regular afternoon storms. From September onwards, it's colder but clearer, with fewer flies and mosquitoes.
**What to take** // Roads are unmarked and signposts are rare, so get comfortable with using a GPS.
**More riding** // To extend the route by 3 to 4 days, continue onwards to Mörön, gateway to beautiful Lake Khövsgöl, on the border with Russian Siberia.

*Opposite: magical Thingvellir National Park in Iceland, on its Ring Rd*

# MORE LIKE THIS
# BIKEPACKING RIDES

### COAST TO COAST, SCOTLAND

Although there are several iterations of the Scottish Coast to Coast route, the most comprehensive begins in Aberdeen on the east coast, and culminates in the Ardnamurchan Peninsula, the most westernmost point in the UK. The route is a backcountry mountain biker's heaven, with trails ranging from loch side singletrack to sinewy, technical, rocky chutes, tempered by roughly hewn 4WD tracks, and gentle forest fire roads in between. Notably, the ride passes through the Cairngorms National Park, which boasts some of the finest and most scenic natural mountain biking in the UK. Allow at least a week for the ride, whether you're bikepacking it independently, or joining a guided tour.
**Start //** Aberdeen
**End //** Ardnamurchan Peninsula
**Distance //** 217.5 miles (350km)

### CARRETERA AUSTRAL, CHILE

The Carretera Austral is another Patagonian epic, and a rite of passage for Chilean and foreign cyclists alike. The road's construction was implemented during Pinochet's regime, with the aim of connecting the most remote communities in Chile's waterlogged southern territory: work began in 1976, with the last segment finally completed in 2000. Set to a backdrop of dense forest, vast fjords and glacier-gouged mountains, riding the Carretera is a cinematic experience, blighted only by the fast tourist traffic that ply the roads over Christmas; the southern part of the route is more wild. Given its location in the southern hemisphere, the Carreterra Austral is best ridden from November through to March, though rain is always a possibility. Given that road conditions are predominantly gravel, most cyclists allow three to four weeks to complete the ride, generally pushing onto El Chaltén, across the border in Argentina, to finish their tour.
**Start //** Puerto Montt
**End //** Villa O'Higgins
**Distance //** 770.5 miles (1240km)

### RING RD, ICELAND

There's a reason why Iceland features on the to-do list of so many cycle tourers. Glaciers, geysers, lava fields, volcanoes, lunar landscapes and thunderous waterfalls are just a few of its geological delights, and reason enough for its nickname: the Island of Fire and Ice. The paved Rte 1 – otherwise known as the Ring Rd – is a popular undertaking, though head inland, following its network of highland dirt roads, to where the most remote and challenging terrain is to be found. A strong armory of waterproof clothing is de rigueur for cycling in Iceland, as inclement weather is rarely far away. Be sure to bring a sturdy tent too, as incoming fronts roll in from the Atlantic, bringing stout winds in their wake. Touring is best undertaken in the European summer, when the days are endlessly long, and the temperatures milder.
**Start/End //** Reykjavík
**Distance //** 828 miles (1332km)

# CYCLING THE SETO INLAND SEA

*Explore southern Japan's secret stash of great road riding in Shimanami, where roads lead up hills, over bridges and end with a soak in an onsen.*

**W**hen I think about Japan, words like 'polite', 'clean', 'punctual', 'neon', 'awesome toilets', 'sumo' and possibly 'keirin' come to mind. I've always known there's a deep-seated cycling culture there somewhere, but 'cycling' isn't a word that's immediately apparent. But after a week of riding around the Seto Inland Sea and Hiroshima in the southwest of Japan, those perceptions changed.

My usual 'Saturday morning riding mates', Danny and Paul, negotiated leave passes and booked plane tickets. Our first destination was the town of Onomichi at the start of the Shimanami Kaido cycleway, which traverses a group of connected islands via roads and staggering bridges. We took the high-speed Shinkansen train down to Onomichi from Tokyo and were greeted by Aki, who would be our Japanese guide for the week. After checking into the Onomichi U2 Cycle Hotel, in a beautifully renovated 70-year-old shipyard warehouse, and unpacking our bikes, a light ride in the sunshine seemed like the perfect thing to loosen up the legs and get into the spirit of our road-trip.

Ten minutes later my heartrate was at 180bpm and Aki had Danny, Paul and me strung out like we were coming into the bell lap of a criterium. Aki was on a timeline and needed to get us to a spectacular climb we wanted to visit and back before sundown. This apparently meant that we needed to average 45km/hr. From then on, Aki earned the nickname 'Akimov' (after legendary hardman, Russian pro cyclist Viatcheslav Ekimov).

We followed the Shimanami cycleway around Japan's Seto Inland Sea, exploring a rustic side of the country as we rode over spectacular suspension bridges that would be icons of most cities. Here, these feats of engineering are commonplace. In fact, the

cycleway boasts the world's longest series of suspension bridges as well as the longest suspension bridge in the world (by length).

From Onomichi, we hopped from island to island, all of which seemed to be places where much of the old Japan survives. Tourists don't visit these areas, but the bike often brings us to places we'd otherwise never have a reason to go.

The Shimanami cycleway is impressively set up for cyclists: the entire route was marked by a blue line painted on the road wherever it wasn't obvious. At each bridge was a toll where you toss a ticket into a basket. As we made our way along the cycleway, we started to feel like we wanted to discover something different. Big bridges and bike paths were good, but we wanted to get off the beaten path and explore. Lucky for us, Akimov knew exactly where to take us.

Instead of going the more travelled path to Imabari we headed west towards Kure and ventured to roads, villages and mountains that not many other cycling tourists would have seen. Akimov drove the pace through towns that were hundreds of years old, pathways that traversed the edges of mountains, and coastline roads that hugged the inland sea. Terraced land plunging into the sea, tiny trolleys on a single metal track were used to collect the harvest, and small villages nestled into the base of the hills. It was one of the most memorable days on a bike in my life.

It was beginning to get dark and we finished the ride just short of Hiroshima where we were aiming. We got transport to our hotel and called it a day. Courier services are extremely well set up and affordable in Japan, and shipping your luggage to your hotel on the other side is a good option.

## PEACE PARK MEMORIAL MUSEUM

Hiroshima is a city best known for being hit by an atomic bomb on 6 August 1945. Its Peace Park Memorial Museum is a building dedicated to both documenting that moment in history and striving for world peace. The museum can be a confronting display of what humankind can 'achieve' but the event is well documented and preserved as a lesson to ensure that it will never happen again.

*Clockwise from top: taking a detour to a ski station; riding past a local shrine; an orange daifuku. Previous page: many bridges to cross in Shimanami*

Our next day's ride, to Nukui Dam, was Akimov's stomping ground and he knew the roads well. Just like the previous day, we encountered a wide range of terrain in a relatively small area. Aki's local knowledge paid off when he took us to the top of a climb that seemed to be slightly off the route we had set. The road ended and Aki hopped off his bike and began walking up a steep grassy hill. We looked at each other and shook our heads. We protested but Aki wouldn't have a word of it and just kept walking.

We had no option but to follow and when we reached the top we understood why Aki was so insistent. The views were magnificent but it was still no place for carbon road bikes. Aki kept walking down the other side towards what looked like some singletrack below. We still wondered what we were doing but when we got to where Aki was taking us, to our amazement, it was paved singletrack. I'd never seen anything like it. We were in the middle of nowhere, and the next thing we knew we were riding singletrack that mountain bikers could only pray for, but on our road bikes. On bitumen. Only in Japan... We would never question Aki's judgement again.

I've always known that there's no better way to experience a country than by bike and our trip to Japan highlighted this once again. The bike took us to parts of Japan we'd never otherwise consider going and made us friends along the way. Now when I think of how to describe Japan, 'cyclist's playground' is on the list. **WW**

## TOOLKIT

**Start** // Onomichi
**End** // Nukui Dam
**Distance** // 75 miles (120km)
**More info** // Fly to Tokyo and take the high-speed train south to Onomichi.
**When to ride** // The Shimanami Cycling Festival takes place in October. Spring and autumn are ideal times to cycle.
**Getting around** // A Japan Rail Pass (www.japan-rail-pass. com) offers unlimited travel in a week around much of the country, but doesn't include express trains. The passes are only for tourists and can't be bought in Japan, so you need to purchase before arriving.
**What to take** // You need cash to pay for most small purchases, such as food, train passes and entertainment. Be aware that most ATMs don't use the Cirrus or Plus networks.

*Opposite: descending Mt Etna's*
*volcanic slopes on a mountain bike*

# MORE LIKE THIS
# VOLCANIC ISLANDS

### CANARY ISLANDS, SPAIN

Japan is not the only volcanic destination of interest to cyclists. Iceland and New Zealand appeal, of course, but for road racers, Tenerife in the Canary Islands, between Africa and Europe, is the top destination for winter training. The reason is Mt Teide, the volcano at its dark heart. This is where champions such as Chris Froome grind out hard miles over the winter months, climbing and descending the summit, which is the highest point in Spain. The pros sleep at altitude at the Parador Hotel near the top, but there are plenty of accommodation options elsewhere on the island. Cheap and frequent flights and bike rental shops make Tenerife appealing to the serious amateur looking to gain a bit of fitness over the winter. See also Mallorca.
**Start // Santa Cruz de Tenerife**
**End // Mt Teide summit**
**Distance // 31 miles (50km)**

### SICILY, ITALY

Where Tenerife will suit serious training cyclists, Sicily has much more to offer touring cyclists, including the UNESCO World Heritage sites of Syracuse (founded by the Ancient Greeks) and the beautiful baroque towns of the Val di Noto, plus distinctive local cuisines and wild beaches. Oh, there's also an active volcano, Mt Etna. The Sapienza Refuge (known as the Etna South route) is considered the best for climbing, reaching 1910m and around 12 miles (19km) long, complete with black, volcanic scenery. Each year a mountain bike marathon also takes place on Etna's slopes. But for mortals, it's best to base yourself in a corner of the island and set aside a week to explore. Several tour operators offer self-guided trips with accommodation to Sicily.
**Distances // Various, if touring**
**More info // www.etnamarathonmtb. it/en**

### MAUI, USA

Leave the skinny tyres at home and pack (or rent) a mountain bike for Hawaii. The interiors of the islands offer tropical singletrack trails in dinosaur-movie settings. On Maui, Haleakalā volcano is one of the world's highest at 10,000ft. Rust-red dirt trails snake down its slopes, including the Skyline Ridge Trail, which starts from the summit crater and drops 3000ft in less than seven miles (11km). Expect extraordinary apocalyptic scenes of volcanic cinder cones and the remains of age-old lava flows (Haleakalā is thought to have last erupted in the 17th century). On the way down, as you reach the vegetation line, the Mamane Trail descent to the lavender farms will entertain more experienced cyclists. Crater Cycles in Kahului rent out mountain bikes; they also rent road bikes if you want to try the ascent back up...
**Start // summit of Skyline Ridge Trail**
**End // Kula Lavender Farm**
**Distance // 7 miles (11km)**

# HIGH IN THE HIMALAYA

*Cycling into the foothills of the Indian Himalaya is the best way to meet the people, marvel at the landscape and discover its incredible culture.*

Y ou really had to admire the bus driver: the way he greeted my horror-stricken face, inverted in his windscreen, with such a sweet and engaging smile. Seconds earlier my handlebars had been snared by a low-slung power cable and the bike catapulted from the roof-rack of his bus. Sitting cross-legged on the roof, I'd watched in disbelief as my bike now dangled by power wire above a rutted mountain pass while we continued our descent into the valley.

Hanging from the roof of the bus, I hammered on the windscreen. 'Stop... my bike!' Quite unfazed, he calmly negotiated the narrow mountain pass in reverse until he was positioned under my stranded steed.

I'd cycled up the road to Manikaran three days before in torrential rain and hardly noticed the prayer flags and bunting, the cables and banners that were slung above the road. I was too busy trying to negotiate the landslides, the wheel-sucking mud and covert man-traps masquerading as puddles. The bike was now audibly fizzing with the threat of electrocution.

'Do not worry, I have protective gloves!' said the driver, waving a pair of rubber latex kitchen gloves above his head. He clambered onto the roof of the bus and lifted the bike free from the cabling to a riot of applause from the passengers who had gathered to watch. I had a sneaking suspicion this wasn't his first aerial rescue.

I'd been similarly rescued when I'd arrived at New Delhi's Indira Gandhi Airport four weeks earlier and was startled to find my bike circling the airport carousel with a buckled rear wheel, having been thrown from the aircraft with the rest of the luggage. But in Delhi's cycle market I'd met an incredible artisan who whipped off his sandals and straightened my wheels to perfection with his bare feet.

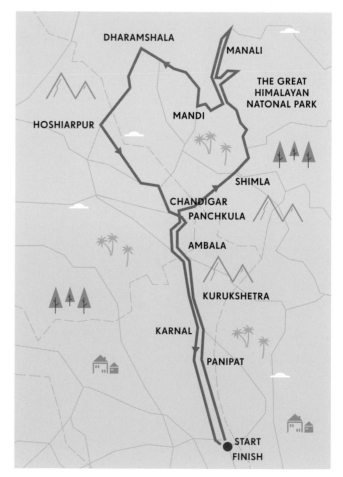

It had taken three days of cycling north out of the capital to catch my first glimpse of snow-crested mountains and feel the cool Himalayan air. It was a welcome relief from the searing heat of the fume-choked plains, where sacred cows ruminated in the slow lane as lorries tore past.

The heat of any day was matched by the warmth of my welcome. Cyclists on single-speed bone shakers would pedal alongside, smile and engage in a light-hearted race. Slamming on my brakes to avoid a wedding party one morning, I was asked to dance with the groom then spent the afternoon as guest of honour. And a few days later, waiting in a lay-by, after a particularly long ascent, I met a motorist holding out a bunch of flowers and inviting me to drink chai and talk cricket.

My first destination was Shimla, the summer home of the British Empire where the government and their families would decamp to escape the heat. And as I rounded a corner one day there was a rather incongruous British church, cast adrift from the age of Empire in the middle of the mountainous green of Himachal Pradesh. After following the narrow gauge train line that leads into Shimla I was confronted with what could almost be, in places, an English market town.

It's 143 miles (230km) from there to Manikaran where the live power cable incident put me off buses for good. By the time I'd hauled my bike another 56 miles (90km) to Manali, I was taking the contours in my stride and was ready for my biggest challenge yet.

The Rohtang Pass on the Manali to Leh highway, takes you to a height of 3978m and is only open during the summer months. The pass separates the Kullu and Lahaul Valleys and its name

## PACKING YOUR BIKE FOR AIR TRAVEL

There are two schools of thought for taking bikes on planes. The first: simply let the air out of your tyres, turn the handlebars round and remove the pedals. You then have to trust the airplane staff to wheel it on and off with care. The second (cheaper) alternative: box it in cardboard with some protection, but some think this simply encourages baggage handlers to throw your bike around.

*Clockwise from top: sunset over Shimla; crossing the Rohtang Pass by bus; wandering musicians in Himachal Pradesh; prayer flags in Dharamsala. Previous page: Manali to Leh highway*

translates as a 'Pile of Corpses', a reference to those who have lost their life trying to cross in bad weather.

But today the road was packed with a convoy of tourist buses, bringing holiday makers from the south high into the mountains to get their first glimpse of snow. They cheerfully alighted at the roadside stalls, to hire outlandish fur coats, walking poles and hats that were clearly essential to tackle isolated patches of dishwater-grey snow. Hundreds of day-trippers, looking like escapees from Narnia, threw obligatory snowballs and attempted to fashion ice and slush into snowmen and igloos.

After a couple of hours' ascent, I found the road blocked by a wall of snow, with no idea of quite how high I was. It certainly wasn't the top of the pass, but it was a genuinely satisfying way to end a climb. I rolled back down the hill, finally overtaking the tourist charabancs, busily returning their arctic gear on the way home.

The day-tripping high jinks were in stark contrast to the spiritual aura that hangs over Dharamsala, home to the Dalai Lama, just a few days' ride away. Its main street is lined with large colourful prayer wheels, and monks making their way to temple, weaving between travellers who've come for meditation, enlightenment and keenly priced banana pancakes.

That week His Holiness would be blessing thousands of pilgrims who queued for a moment in his presence. I joined in for the novelty of meeting a spiritual celebrity, but the warmth of his eyes genuinely moved me. I walked into the nearest barber's and had my head shaved. It may have been a mere fashion statement but the sensation of the wind brushing my scalp on a fast descent out of the Himalayas the following day felt truly spiritual and made the return to Delhi something of a pilgrimage. **MS**

*"The pass separates the Kullu and Lahaul Valleys and its name translates as a 'Pile of Corpses'"*

### TOOLKIT

**Start/End** // Delhi
**Distance** // 994 miles (1600km)
**Getting there** // Fly to New Delhi Indira Gandhi Airport.
**Where to stay** // Camp in parts of Himachal Pradesh or guesthouses are cheap and plentiful.
**When to ride** // During March and April the mountains are getting warmer but tourists are fewer. September and October are also good.
**What to take** // Basic bike parts are plentiful. Opt for a bike that is as simple as possible, take spares of anything that might be harder to source and make sure you can fix it yourself. Carry plenty of water on the road.
**Hot tip** // Himachal Pradesh has great trekking options, so find a guesthouse where you could stash your bike for a few days.

*Opposite: the Raid Pyrenean
passes through St Jean-de-Pied-
Port in the Pyrenees-Atlantique*

# MORE LIKE THIS
## MOUNTAINOUS RIDES

### THE AUVERGNE, FRANCE

In the relatively uninhabited heart of
France, the Parc Naturel Regional des
Volcans d'Auvergne occupies most of the
western Massif Central. About 20 million
years ago this was one of the most active
volcanic areas in Europe. Glaciers then
shaved the tops off the cones, resulting
in this highland of broad-flanked hills,
jade-green valleys, dark-stone villages
and vast panoramas. It's a fabulous spot
for serious bike riding and the summit of
Puy Mary lures many climbing cyclists -
who would be wise to remember to pack
a warm and windproof jacket. A leisurely
three-day, 106-mile (170km) tour starting in
Clermont-Ferrand heads south through the
natural park to Le Mont-Dore then via Puy
de Sancy and the Col de la Croix St-Robert
to Condat. The final day is reserved for
tackling the 1787m-high Puy Mary, joining
the mountain sheep on its alpine pastures.
**Start // Clermont-Ferrand**
**End // Murat**
**Distance // 106 miles (170km)**

### THE HIGH ATLAS, MOROCCO

A route from Marrakech, Morocco to
Zagora on the edge of the Sahara desert
can take you over the High Atlas in the
shadow of the mighty Mt Toubkal. At 4167m
this is the highest mountain in Morocco and
a serious undertaking, but with a guide in
summer it is one worth considering, so pack
a pair of hiking boots in your panniers. Your
bike route heads out of the mountains via
Agdz and on through the Drâa Valley and
some of the most incredibly arid scenery
imaginable. With travel to Morocco very
affordable from anywhere in Europe, this
is a route that could give you your first
taste of cycling in a more remote and
adventurous destination. Zagora is a great
place to take a tour of the desert, by 4x4
rather than by bike, if you want to see the
best of it.
**Start // Marrakech**
**End // Zagora**
**Distance // 342 miles (550km)**

### RAID PYRENEAN, FRANCE

One of Europe's greatest cycling
adventures takes you from the
Mediterranean Sea to the Atlantic,
throwing in some of the most iconic
Pyrenean climbs in the process. This route
includes such Tour de France classic
ascents as the Tourmalet, Aubisque and
Aspin, and if you want official Cyclo Club
Béarnais recognition for your achievement
you'll need to complete the 447 miles
(720km, with 11,000m of ascent) within the
100-hour time frame, getting your carnet
stamped along the way. The entry fee is
pretty modest (currently €14) and includes
your carnet and a finisher's medal. The
route can be ridden in either direction,
although the west-to-east route, starting
in Hendaye and finishing at Cèrbere, is
the preferred direction. There is also the
option of an alternative 10-day route that
is slightly longer at 491 miles (790km) for
cycle tourists, giving you plenty of time to
really soak up the scenery and wildlife of
the Pyrenees.
**Start // Hendaye**
**End // Cèrbere**
**Distance // 447 miles (720km)**

# BHUTANESE DRAGON RIDE

*Traverse the Land of the Thunder Dragon, crossing breathlessly high passes to discover ancient Buddhist fortress-monasteries in the long-hidden Himalayan kingdom of Bhutan.*

If there's one thing more uplifting than watching red-robed Buddhist boy-monks playing soccer, I discovered, it's watching red-robed Buddhist boy-monks learning to ride a bike. It wasn't as if Chimi Lhakhang had a Zen-like air of serenity anyway – perhaps unsurprising, given the heritage of this shrine to the 'Divine Madman'. The temple was founded to honour Bhutan's favourite saint, Drukpa Kunley, the most unlikely of medieval mystics: his wine-and-sex-loving antics are revered as much now as in his 15th-century heyday, and his legacy is evident in huge phalluses painted on many houses to ward off evil.

With two fellow cyclists, I'd halted at the end of a challenging

but thrilling day's ride for a brief rest at this compact temple perched on a rounded hillock (which was reputedly compared to a woman's breast by the lascivious lama). We'd hoped to peek inside, and perhaps receive a blessing with the lama's bone-carved phallus. Instead, we watched a dozen vermillion-robed boys kick a semi-round football between posts that presumably once sported prayer flags. Within seconds, they abandoned their game and crowded round our bikes. Tying robes around waists, they took it in turns to attempt pedalling, and were soon whizzing circles around the temple, giggling and yelling in a most un-meditative way.

These junior holy rollers proved an unexpected highlight of my

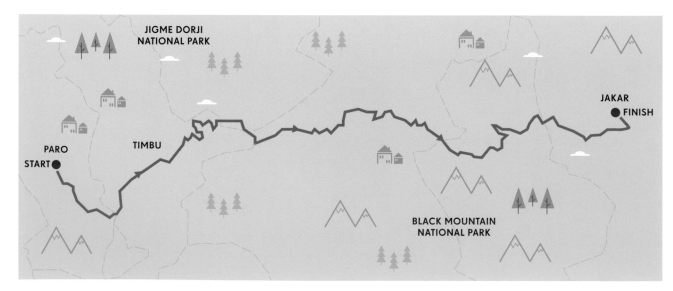

trans-Bhutan bike odyssey. This small Himalayan kingdom, long off-limits to foreigners, even now welcomes only small numbers of visitors to admire its mighty *dzongs* (fortress-monasteries) and tackle its dramatic trekking trails among peaks including Gangkhar Puensum (7541m) – reputedly the world's highest unclimbed summit.

Even fewer take to the saddle – though that's changing. The Bhutanese royal family is evangelical about bikes, promoting the sport through tax breaks, new cycle lanes and events – notably the Tour of the Dragon. This annual one-day race sees iron-calved road riders pedal halfway across the country, covering 166.5 miles (268km) and tackling nearly 4000m of ascent and descent between Bumthang and the capital, Thimphu.

Fortunately, it's easy enough to tackle the route and its four lofty passes, maxing out at Yotong-La (3425m), over several days. Reversing the direction and starting at Paro, site of the country's only international airport west of Thimphu, adds another 31 miles (50km) to the journey, but also offers the chance to visit yet more photogenic spots, including Taktshang, the famed 'Tiger's Nest' monastery. You'll recognise the image, if not the name – almost universally used to promote Bhutan, it's the country's Taj Mahal, its Machu Picchu. And it's just as spectacular, clinging at 3000m to the sheer side of a vertiginous cliff in the upper Paro Valley.

Our ride began with a flattish section on the country's busiest road between Paro and Thimphu, finishing at the capital's huge Trashi Chhoe Dzong. There we happened on a noisy festival

### "Tigers and leopards lurked in the shadows, ready to snack on unwary cyclists – at least so my guide told me"

thronged with monks honking horns and devotees whirling prayer wheels, as the Sakyamuni Buddha peered down from a vast *thondrol* (embroidered image). I span a row of wheels myself, praying for heavenly help the next day, when we'd face our first real challenge: the 3140m Dochu La pass – not the highest on the route, but involving a punishing climb of almost 1000m. That evening we fuelled up on *ema datse* – hot chillies in cheese sauce, Bhutan's ubiquitous national dish – in anticipation of the Big One.

In practice, the winding road was never get-off-and-push sheer; the increasingly verdant surroundings distracted me from the effort, mountainsides carpeted with blue pine and rhododendron forests bustling with spotted nutcrackers. After three hours or so, the rustle and snap of dozens of fluttering prayer flags signalled our arrival at the pass, crowned with no fewer than 108 stupas. What really took the breath away – apart from the altitude – were the sweeping views ahead: an emerald patchwork of forested hillsides and rice terraces stretching towards distant peaks lining the northern horizon. And beneath me the road snaked in endless coils towards the valley floor.

## FESTIVAL FEVER

Visiting a *dzong* (fortress-monastery) during one of the annual *tsechus* – dance festivals – is an electrifying experience. Buddhist monks garbed in rainbow-hued robes don carved masks and perform whirling *cham* dances to the thud of drums and honk of long horns, and devotees throng around a *thondrol* – a huge sacred wall hanging unfurled only at these events. The most popular *tsechus* are at Paro (March/April), Thimphu (September/October) and Punakha (February/March).

*Left to right: masked dancers; terraced fields at Thimphu; leopards lie in wait in Bhutan's forests; young monks at Chimi Lahkhang monastery, which dates from the 15th century. Previous page: Bhutan's Taktshang monastery*

We flew. We whooped. We giggled like those boy-monks. For nearly three hours we hurtled along 25 miles (40km) of pretty much continuous downhill. First we traversed stands of hemlock, cypress and glorious rhododendron; then, as the valley opened out and the temperature rose, we rode alongside terraced rice paddies and hilltop monasteries. Wispy clouds clung to the trees; hawk-eagles soared and laughing thrushes fluttered overhead; and tigers and leopards lurked in the shadows ready to snack on unwary cyclists – at least, so my local guide told me. And eventually we found ourselves at the bottom, watching those holy young footballers grab the handlebars.

That day set the pattern for each one that followed: explore monastery or mighty *dzong*, admire the scenery on long ascent to mountain pass, then thrill to the downhill rush before a feast of *ema datse*. Repeat till ecstatic.

There were other highlights, of course – a farmstay in the Phobjikha Valley, where hundreds of rare black-necked cranes overwinter, and the views from spectacular Trongsa Dzong, guarding the gateway between east and west Bhutan. But it was the daily repetition of action and edification that stuck in the memory.

In this staunchly Buddhist land, the cyclical nature of existence is always evident; prayer wheels whirl, devotees circumambulate stupas, and the wheel of life adorns every temple. So when my time comes to be judged, perhaps those countless revolutions of pedals will see me nudge just a fraction closer to nirvana. **PB**

## TOOLKIT

**Start //** Paro
**End //** Jakar, Bumthang
**Distance //** 197.5 miles (318km)
**Getting there //** Paro, Bhutan's international airport, is served by Druk Air (www.drukair.com.bt) from Delhi, Singapore, Kolkata and Kathmandu, and by Bhutan Airlines (www.bhutanairlines.bt) from Kolkata and Kathmandu. The flight from Kathmandu to Paro provides views of Mt Everest.
**Tour //** Independent travel in Bhutan is not permitted. Book individual or group tours through an approved operator, which will arrange visas, accommodation and transport. Mountain Kingdoms (www.mountainkingdoms.com) offers a cycling tour.
**When to ride //** Autumn (late September–November) is driest with clear mountain views. Spring (March–May) is cloudier but still a good time to cycle.

*Opposite: descending Muktinath Valley*
*on the Annapurna Circuit, Nepal*

# MORE LIKE THIS
## MOUNTAINOUS RIDES

### LHASA (TIBET) TO KATHMANDU (NEPAL)

Arguably the world's longest downhill ride, this snakes some 1150km from the 'Roof of the World', over the barren, breathless Tibetan plateau to the Nepalese capital. You can't rush it – aside from the altitude, often over 5000m (there are six lofty passes to tackle), you'll enjoy countless photo stops, from Lhasa's Potala Palace and Jokhang temple complex to yak-grazed mountainsides fluttering with multihued prayer flags, lofty lakes and fortified Buddhist monasteries at Gyantse and Shigatse. Oh, and the sight of Everest's north face gleaming from Rongbuk monastery. Note: the Tibet–Nepal border was closed for months following the earthquake that struck the region in April 2015. Check the current situation when planning your trip.
**Start // Lhasa, Tibet**
**End // Kathmandu, Nepal**
**Distance // 714.5 miles (1150km)**
**Tour // Only rides on an authorised tour are allowed to cover this route – operators including World Expeditions can organise visas and permits**

### ANNAPURNA CIRCUIT, NEPAL

Scenic variety suffuses one of the world's classic trekking – and now biking – trails. Gawp at verdant rice terraces and the peaks of the Annapurna massif, dominated by the triple peak of Annapurna I (8091m); the stark expanses of Mustang; the plunging gorge of the Kali Gandaki river; and bustling Hindu temples, including Muktinath, one of Nepal's holiest sites. Few tackle the circuit on two wheels, yet it's a spectacular challenge, with 5000m-plus passes, soothing hot springs at Tatopani and a friendly welcome (often accompanied with a side-order of cake or apple pie) at villages and teahouses en route.
**Start/End // Besisahar**
**Distance // 186 miles (300km)**
**Tour // KE Adventure is a respected international operator offering supported trips around the circuit**

### THE COLOMBIAN ANDES

There's a long tradition of Colombian professional cyclists – the latest being Nairo Quintano – who can climb mountains as if unencumbered by gravity. The reason for that lies in Colombia's cloud-covered topography: this is a place where the human body adapts to lower oxygen levels by producing more red blood cells – which is a distinct advantage when racing bicycles. After acclimatising to the altitude, you might wish for a little assistance on what is reputed to be the road cycling world's longest climb, the Alto de Letras in the Colombian Andes. It ascends for 50 miles (82km) from 500m above sea level to 3692m. But cycling in Colombia isn't just about riding tarmac – there are lots of places where a mountain bike is a more appropriate mount, for example bike-packing along jeep tracks in the volcanic Parque Nacional Natural Los Nevados, between Bogotá and Medellín. On or off road, Colombia is an emerging destination for bike riders.
**Start // Bogotá**
**Tour // Saddle Skedaddle offers a guided tour that includes Alto de Letras**

# MAE HONG
# SON CIRCUIT

*Tackle the Mae Hong Son loop through the misty mountains of northern Thailand, beginning a week long journey of challenges and self-discovery.*

When I first visited Chiang Mai in 2011, I nearly didn't leave – a week exploring the surrounding mountains on a rented motorcycle had seduced me. Alas, life came first, and I reluctantly returned to Australia – but a desire to return remained. When my friend Oscar's tenure as a fly-in-fly-out worker came to an end, he suggested we go on a cycling trip. It seemed the perfect opportunity to tackle the famous motorcycle loop through Mae Hong Son, a mountainous region west of Chiang Mai, but on bicycles.

The Mae Hong Son loop totals about 410 miles (660km), with 13,000m of climbing and 4000 bends. We planned to ride it in six stages, with two days off.

But our trip didn't start as hoped. While dining out in Chiang Mai, we overheard the forecast for the next few days and both tensed up – five days of rain during what was meant to be the dry season? We woke at 6am to the confirmation: a steady patter of raindrops on the roof.

Not even the excitement of first-day riding was enough to get the spirits up, as we set off, grimacing in the rain. This changed dramatically when we turned off the main highway on to the small road to Pai, our first destination. We were immediately jolted into rural Thailand, riding on a smooth road lined with dense foliage, interspersed with paddy fields and small villages. Rolling hills got the legs warmed up and we started to smile again, despite the relentless rain. Then the road pitched upwards, straight into the clouds. I gave Oscar a nod and rode off ahead, leaving us both in solitude, walled in by fog on all sides.

At the top of the first peak we sheltered from the rain with some people selling bananas at the roadside, who invited us to share their fire. We loaded up on fresh fruit and continued upwards. Eventually, after a puncture, some hot noodles, and countless false summits, we finally crested the pass and began the descent into Pai. Leaving the clouds behind us, we had clear views of the valley for the first time all day. We stopped to take a photo as a truck carrying an elephant trundled past.

Rolling into Pai, legs weary, we stopped at the first guesthouse we came across that could guarantee a hot shower, and crashed. We spent the following day exploring Pai on our bikes. There's something very genteel about having a rest day after only one day of riding. We visited the local hot springs, got massages, and practised our Chinese at the Kuomintang village, which was settled by fleeing Chinese after the Chinese Civil War. The

*"I was riding gently, tiptoeing up the mountain as though it were a sleeping dog I was trying not to wake"*

following morning we awoke to glorious sunshine. Never trust a weather forecast in the mountains.

The road to the town of Mae Hong Son began with a long, sustained climb that we both took easy. 'It's mostly downhill from here,' I reassured Oscar. 'Gentle rolling hills all the way.'

The next 37 miles (60km) nearly killed him. Straight after lunch the road pitched up with a vengeance – we had encountered the first of about six short but brutally steep climbs that we'd have to overcome before reaching our destination. Each was about 0.5–1.2 miles (1–2km) long with gradients pushing 30% at their steepest. And each climb would be followed by an equally precipitous descent – thrilling roads that seemed to drop away before your eyes, forcing you back off the saddle and onto the brakes so you could bring the speed down enough to throw the bike into another tight corkscrew bend.

Fortunately, the next day's riding to Khun Yuam wasn't too challenging. Our hotel, up a rutted track over a steep hill, was perfect, with the feel of those grand European hotels that are about a century past their best, but still full of character. The trials of the past 24 hours evaporated, as we sat on our balcony

## THE CITY OF THREE MISTS

Mae Hong Son translates as 'the City of Three Mists', named for the heavy fog which engulfs much of the region year-round. When viewed from higher ground — the balcony of a well-located guesthouse for instance — the cloud drifts below, making islands of the mountaintops. It can make for a suspenseful early-morning ride: as the sun's rays take the edge off the nippy morning air, the fog rises to reveal dew-dressed greenery and terraced farmland.

*Left to right: refuelling on Thai food; Mae Hong Son; riding past rice fields; praying for divine assistance at Buddhist temples. Previous page: the wide roads of Mae Hong Son*

and watched the golden light of the setting sun dance across the mosaic of rice terraces.

After another day, only the highest mountain in Thailand stood between us and the end. Doi Inthanon is a monster. It stands barely 2500m tall yet its prominence puts it in the realm of the toughest ascents tackled by the famous races of Europe. From Mae Chaem, it climbs for 17.5 miles (28.3km) at an average of 7% for a total elevation gain of more than 2000m.

We ate breakfast together near the base, wished each other luck, and set off, each at our own pace. It was very quiet, and my breath made clouds of fog as I ticked off the first few miles. I was riding very gently, tiptoeing up the mountain as though it were a sleeping dog I was trying not to wake. Oscar was also riding well, largely thanks to the serious doping program of Ibuprofen he'd engaged in since his under-trained knees began hurting days earlier.

It's incredible what you can do when the end is in sight. The way pain dissolves is something magical. At the top of Doi Inthanon dozens of monks were among the many tourists who'd travelled in taxis to the summit. I couldn't help but feel they were missing out on something intensely spiritual, transcendental even, by being driven up this magnificent mountain. After recovering, I rolled slowly down again, looking for Oscar. I met him 1 mile (2km) from the top, turned back up the road and pedalled up beside him, reaching my arm around his shoulder to give him encouragement. Side by side, we rode the final stretch together. **LP**

## TOOLKIT

**Start/End** // Chiang Mai
**Distance** // 410 miles (660km)
**Getting there** // There are regular flights into Chiang Mai.
**When to ride** // During the dry season: December to March.
**How to ride** // Both directions have pros and cons, but there's no escaping the climbing.
**Where to stay** // Each town on the route has a number of cheap, quirky guesthouses. Look for the ones with the best views, or ask the locals for their tips.
**What to take** // The bare essentials in a light backpack. A light riding jacket should keep you warm on misty mornings and serve as insurance if a storm rolls through. Bring plenty of cash, as ATMs are sparse.

*Opposite: the road to Mt Batur,*
*a volcano in Bali*

# MORE LIKE THIS
## ASIAN CLIMBS

### DOI SUTHEP, THAILAND

A visit to Chiang Mai wouldn't be complete without tackling the imposing Doi Suthep, located right on the city's outskirts. The road snakes through dense green foliage as it climbs steeply up the 1600m high mountain, famous for the sacred 13th-century Buddhist temple near its peak known as Wat Phra That. As you climb, the panoramic views of bustling Chiang Mai are replaced by the tiny hill-tribe villages, which peek from the luscious greenery. The road alternates between steep switchbacks carved into the mountainside, and long, sweeping bends traversing the contours of the land. Upon reaching the glistening golden temple the road narrows, leaving the tourist buses behind and sneaking into the shadows of the deciduous forest that guards the mountain's upper reaches. Away from the tourists, you're left alone to pedal in cool silence to the peak.
**Start // Chiang Mai**
**End // Doi Suthep**
**Distance // 11 miles (18km)**

### TAROKO GORGE RD, TAIWAN

In terms of sheer magnitude, few roads can match Taiwan's trans-island highway. Rising out of the imposing marble cliffs of the Taroko Gorge, this climb elevates daring riders from sea level to 3200m over a relentless, awe-inspiring 54 miles (80km). The climb, famed as the host of the annual King of the Mountain challenge race, begins near Hualian on Taiwan's east coast before entering the unspoilt Taroko Gorge National Park. The narrow, winding road is carved precariously into the sheer marble walls, high above the thundering river below, occasionally leaping across stunning red steel arch bridges and delving into long, dark tunnels. Leaving behind the river, the road soars high into Taiwan's central mountain range, offering expansive views of the surrounding peaks. Fittingly, for a climb of this scale, it saves its toughest grades till last, with the final 6 miles (10km) testing weary legs with an average grade above 10%.
**Start // Hualian**
**End // Taroko Gorge**
**Distance // 54 miles (87km)**

### MT BATUR, BALI

Formed by a massive volcanic eruption, Batur has a number of routes to its 1400m-high caldera rim. In keeping with the island's way of life, most of the routes offer gentle climbs, allowing you to relax, take in the view and enjoy the journey. The mountainside is home to hundreds of orchards, with fresh fruit for sale on every corner, which means you'll never have to worry about the bonk. The last few miles before the summit see the gradient begin to bite, if only to make you appreciate the spectacular view from the top that little bit more. For full effect, climb Batur early in the morning for a chance to catch the caldera flooded with mist.
**Start // Ubud**
**End // Mt Batur**
**Distance // 17 miles (28km)**

# SRI LANKAN SIGHTSEEING

*Monkeys, ancient ruins, very big Buddhas and some of the best tea you'll ever taste are the highlights of this two-week cycle tour of Sri Lanka.*

Dinner-plate sized footprints? Check. Warm, basketball-sized lumps of dung? Check. 'Yep, we're definitely on an elephant's trail,' confirms my guide Pete. Many people go to Sri Lanka specifically to see elephants; there are about 3000 in the wild. But when you're cycling around the island's interior, a 3m-tall *Elephas maximus* – 5000kg of unpredictability – is not something you really want to encounter. We've had an elephant-alert drill for what to do if we cross paths with one: stand stock still and avoiding meeting its eye, while Pete digs around in the pockets of his combat shorts for some firecrackers. These go off with a bang and, theoretically, scare the beast away – if Pete can find them in time.

While we're not here for the elephants on this 14-day tour, many of the wonders of Sri Lanka's archaeological Golden Triangle are on our itinerary: Sigiriya's citadel; Polonnaruwa, the ruins of a 12th-century city; the Buddhas of Dambulla; Kandy's Temple of the Tooth; and the tea plantations of Nuwara Eliya.

I'm part of a guided cycling tour – seven strangers, one guide, 10 days of riding, around 310 miles (500km) in total. There are pros and cons of joining a guided cycling trip. The advantage is that a lot of the organisational effort is avoided: your luggage is taken from one overnight stop to the next, and your guide will know the tried and tested cycling routes. The downside is that you don't get to select all your companions and the experience is fairly prescriptive. You can't stay an extra day somewhere on a whim, or divert too far from the day's plan.

That might seem contrary to the cyclist's instinctive need for freewheeling independence but it does mean that you can take off with your bike to any number of countries around the world with minimal planning. And on this tour of Sri Lanka's backroads, Pete is happy to fit in some extra mountain biking for those who need more of a fix, which is how I find myself on an elephant's trail while my companions are climbing Sigiriya, a 200m- (650ft) high rock pillar rising out of the jungle with a fortress on top.

Our trip began on a riverside path of the northern central lowlands near Lake Giritale, as we acclimatised to the humidity. Like the changing rooms at a communal swimming pool, the river is divided into sections. In one languid stretch women are washing their long dark hair. In the next, young men, waist-deep in water, are in discussion. In another section, parents are washing children,

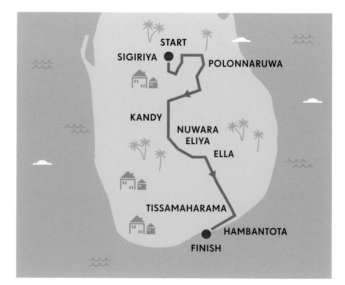

the sudsy youngsters springing like frogs from the riverbank into the water as we pass. Downstream is the tractor and water buffalo washing area.

After my excursion with Pete ends not with a bang but a beer, and we catch up on tales of skulduggery from Sigiriya (see right), our group rides onward to Polonnaruwa, fuelled by lemony, finger-sized bananas. Here the ruins of the 12th-century city are being reclaimed from the jungle, although monkeys – shy grey langurs and bolder macaques – still gambol on bulbous stupas (funerary domes made from millions of bricks). It's worth hiring a local guide to explain the buildings and temples since signposting is thin on the ground; they'll likely have a bicycle, which is the best way to get around the vast site.

Stonework of a spiritual nature is found in Dambulla's mountainside caves, which contain colossal statues of Buddha dating from the 2nd century.

But I've been waiting to get into hill country, south of the Triangle, where the world's finest Ceylon teas are harvested, and the climate is cooler. Our first stop in Sri Lanka's highlands is the city Kandy, and to get to Kandy means, for those who wish, descending 14 miles (23km) down the Knuckles mountain range into the island's cultural hub. Again, there's just one volunteer: me. The first portion of the ride runs through tea plantations, peppered by tea pickers wearing technicolour saris. It was an old tea planter who first showed Pete some routes through the plantations – this is the value of local knowledge.

## SIGIRIYA'S HISTORY

In the 5th century, King Dhatusena's first son, Kasyapa, threatened by the arrival of a legitimate heir, bricked up his father alive in his own palace. Kasyapa's half-brother, Mogallan, fled to India, while King Kasyapa built a fortress on Sigiriya's rock pillar. After seven years, Mogallon returned from exile with an army and, in the ensuing battle, Kasyapa's elephant ran amok, causing confusion in his own ranks and allowing Mogallon to triumph.

*Clockwise from top: the Knuckles mountain range of central Sri Lanka; fresh fruit; riding the dirt roads past Sigiriya; a Buddha at Dambulla. Previous page: descending through tea plantations to Kandy*

Soon the trail rejoins the road and we race against the setting sun around forested mountainsides and through one-street villages, bunny-hopping over 3ft-wide potholes, speeding past fume-belching buses and tuk-tuks. Bats as large as tea towels flap along the valley beside us. We make the final climb into Kandy in the smoggy orange glow of twilight.

Kandy is famous for its Temple of the Tooth. The 18th-century building houses one of Buddhism's most sacred relics, a canine tooth of Buddha, which arrived in Sri Lanka for safekeeping in the 3rd century. Every year, in July, the tooth is paraded through Kandy on an elaborately decorated elephant, but there are three *pujas* (blessings) daily at the temple.

The ride continues south to Nuwara Eliya, a colonial hill station at 6500ft. The rose beds, mist, post office and Hill Club (jackets and ties please, gentlemen) could be an English village circa 1930. English names abound: Horton Plains, Elgin Falls, Gregory's Lake. And then we descend from the highlands all the way to the south coast, hitting the beach after 310 miles (500km) and 238 bottles of water (and uncounted Three Coins beers at the end of each day).

I never did see a wild elephant but being on a bicycle got us close to Sri Lanka's local culture, even if that included the group of children waiting at the top of a pass with homemade bows and arrows, picking off the stragglers. **RB**

## TOOLKIT

**Start //** Sigiriya
**End //** Anhangma
**Distance //** 310 miles (500km)
**Tour //** Depending on the tour operator, the terms of each cycling tour may vary – most include accommodation, some food, but not any extras. Flights may or may not be included. Group sizes typically vary from 5 to 15 – generally, the more the people, the lower the cost. An alternative is to get a group of friends and book a recommended local guide independently.
**When to ride //** December to March.
**What to take //** A visa is required for most nationalities, which will need to be organised in advance.
**Health tips //** Some vaccinations are advisable (tetanus, typhoid, hepatitis A) and it's best to avoid bites from mosquitoes.

*Opposite: terraces slope down
to the sea from the Tramuntana
range, near Sóller in Mallorca*

# MORE LIKE THIS
## SPIRITUAL RIDES

### BALI, INDONESIA

Bali is at its best in the out-of-the-way places. A guided cycle tour here can take in remote beaches, small villages, Hindu temples, markets and rural (and hilly) countryside. Although most cycle tourists arrive via the international airport at Denpasar, Ubud, the culture-rich town in the centre of the island, is the hub for most tours. Set out from here to explore the mountains of the north, coffee plantations, rice paddies, and become absorbed by the ebb and flow of life in villages that never see a coach tour. Some operators offer an optional add-on of a trip to neighbouring Lombok by ferry – the island is far less frequented than Bali and the local people are very welcoming of cycle tourists.
**Start // Base yourself in Ubud**
**Distance //  Variable**

### NEW MEXICO, USA

The Enchanted Circle is an 83-mile (133km) road circuit that revolves around the town of Taos in New Mexico. This part of the American Southwest has long attracted artists, from Georgia O'Keefe and Ansel Adams to author DH Lawrence, whose ranch just north of Taos is a memorial to the man. The region was once hailed as the 'Most Spiritual Place' in the US, maybe because of its deep Native American associations, or its painted historic churches, or perhaps because the stark desert beauty encourages a certain introspection. Cyclists, however, may seek spiritual help for other reasons: the Enchanted Circle Scenic Byway crosses a pair of 2750m passes as it circles 4000m Wheeler Peak via the Taos Ski Valley. It's a stunning ride through the Sangre de Cristo mountains of New Mexico.
**Start/End // Taos**
**Distance // 83 miles (133km)**

### MALLORCA, SPAIN

Mallorca is a Mediterranean island that answers the cyclist's perennial question of 'I wonder what's over there' with mountaintop roads through fragrant forests; long, winding descents; hidden sandy coves, and hilltop villages with excellent eateries. Measuring just 45 miles (75km) north to south and 60 miles (100km) east to west, it offers the highest concentration of great riding in Europe, which is why it's the go-to winter-training destination for professional racing teams. To the east is Es Pla, a plain punctuated by vineyards and hilltop monasteries. A 70 mile (110km) ride here, starting from Manacor then heading to Felanitx, Llucmajor, Puig de Randa, Petra and Vilafranca de Bonany, takes in not just one, not two but three monasteries. Alternatively, on the west side of the island the terrain ramps up to the Tramuntana range, where the Santuari de Lluc is passed on a long, mountainous loop from Port de Pollença.
**Start // Base yourself in Sóller or Port de Pollença to explore the Tramuntana**

# CHINA'S WILD WEST

*This rollercoaster ride through South West China scales the high passes of Yúnnán and Sìchuān, a region that borders Tibet and shares much of its culture.*

Deep in the west of China, Lǐtáng County really feels like the Wild West – except up on the Tibetan plateau, horses have been traded in for motorbikes adorned with stickers, tassels and speakers that boom out Tibetan pop tunes. It was November and winter was fast approaching. Already men were riding around in full-face balaclavas; only their eyes were visible and their yellowing teeth, which were clamped on cheap Chinese cigarettes that dangled out of mouth holes.

These men were the real deal, and this was what we'd come for: real adventures in the mountainous provinces of Yúnnán and Sìchuān. I was drawn to this remote quarter of China to revisit an area I'd explored a decade before. I can still vividly remember the day I first arrived in Lǐtáng, after a hard week of backcountry riding and camping. A group of Buddhist monks, shooting pool on faded outdoor tables, looked up and called out the traditional Tibetan auspicious greeting: 'Tashi Delek!' From a stack of rattling speakers came a theme tune that took me a moment to place. No, it couldn't be... 'The Good, the Bad and the Ugly'. Such a surreal introduction to a rough and ready cowboy town.

Years later, China felt transformed. Dirt tracks had become tarmac highways and, regrettably, bike lanes in cities were now choked with traffic. Historic buildings had been levelled and towns renamed, while billboards for designer clothes and mobile phones now decorated the streets.

But thankfully this quiet, remote backwater was still as wild and untamed as I remembered, and the journey there no less challenging. Each day we climbed relentlessly, one pass after the next. The clusters of Tibetan houses we passed featured architecture influenced by years of survival: small windows to retain heat, large

rooftops to dry produce for the harsh winter ahead, and central heating that came courtesy of livestock, housed below bedrooms come the coldest months. In stark contrast to the consumer delights of China's cities, here life remained largely unchanged.

Our journey had begun in Lìjiāng, a few hours from Yúnnán's capital of Kūnmíng, the City of Eternal Spring. From there, we'd wound our way up on onto the Tibetan plateau, before crossing into Western Sìchuān to loop back down to the lowlands of Chéngdū. Travelling at the tail end of the season promised frigid conditions; thankfully warmth was provided in abundance by the welcome we received wherever we visited. Indeed, our bikes were

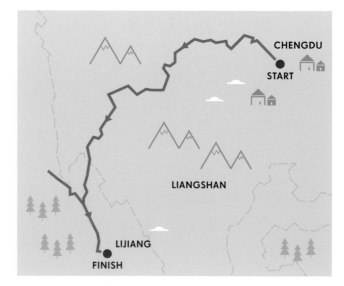

a constant focus of attention and won us instant popularity. Families waved from their houses, fields, even distant hilltops – this could have been The Truman Show.

A few approached to inspect us in closer detail. In the Tagong grasslands, a posse of cowboy bikers pulled over as we were breaking camp. First, they tried on our bike helmets and mitts, to rapturous applause and laughter. Not to be outdone by the music that blasted from their motorbikes, I pulled out the solar panel that powered our own mini speaker and MP3 player. David Bowie seemed to suit the mood, so we sat together and listened to 'Changes', powered by the sun's rays, sharing biscuits and smiling benignly to each other.

Eventually we made it to Lǐtáng, on the southern branch of the Sichuān–Tibet Hwy. A stopping point for travellers on their long journey to Lhasa, and a meeting place for nomads haggling for provisions, its hustle and bustle made a change from the roadside villages we'd been frequenting.

Here, the indigenous Tibetan men were tall and handsome. They sported long and dark hair; either freshly washed and glossy like a shampoo advert, or matted and straggly from the wind, or half hidden under huge fur hats decorated with ornate gold trim. The sleeves on their heavy overcoats were unusually long, out of which they pulled hidden provisions like magicians. Similarly, the women were tall,

## CULINARY CHATTER

China is a gourmet's delight, but making yourself understood can be a linguistic hurdle. I'd suggest striding boldly into the kitchen and indicating the ingredients that take your fancy. Even the unlikeliest roadside eatery never fails to rustle up the most delicious bowl of noodles, or plate of wild mushrooms and ginger pork, washed down with gallons of green tea. Just be very selective about which part of an animal you're pointing at.

*"The jet-black tents of nomads, stitched together with yak hair, stood in stark contrast to the snow"*

austere and reserved. Darting around in high heels, they seemed oblivious to the onset of winter and its ice-encrusted pavement.

From Lǐtáng we rode to the junction town of Yajiang and on to Dānbā, via a series of long and low snowy passes beneath sharp, craggy peaks. Between occasional settlements, the jet-black tents of nomads, stitched together with yak hair, stood in stark contrast to the snow, with guardian Tibetan mastiffs occasionally taking chase. Keen-eyed children scampered down at breakneck speed to meet us when we cycled by, shrieking the obligatory Tibetan welcome, hoping we'd stop and let them run inquisitive fingers over our bikes. One had a large clump of keys jangling importantly around his neck. When I asked to take his photo, he pulled out a pendant of the Dalai Lama, before striking a formal pose.

Ahead lay a massive spiral downwards towards the planes, a 4000m descent to Chéngdū, lying at a balmy 500m in altitude. Eventually, dirt gave way to potholed tarmac, which in turn morphed into a polluted highway that funneled us through a series of long, pitch-black tunnels, before we hit the final stretch of road into this megalopolis.

Soon enough, we'd joined the city's bike lanes, chicaning through a blur of electric bikes, past Western chain restaurants and back into the frenzy of metropolitan life. No doubt about it: we'd left the old world and the quiet majesty of its high plateau far behind, to be thrown rudely back into the hustle and bustle of modern day China.

I know which persona of the country I prefer. Its wild and remote mountainscape had already drawn me back once. Next time, I won't leave it so long before I return. **CG**

*Clockwise from top: switchback passes; homestay accommodation; practical transportation; dumplings for dinner. Previous page: cycling in Yúnnán*

## TOOLKIT

**Start** // Lìjiāng
**End** // Chéngdū
**Distance** // 932 miles (1500km), including a detour to Déqīn, a highlight of the Yúnnán–Tibet Hwy
**Getting there** // Both Lìjiāng and Chéngdū have airports with connections to Běijīng. For a cheaper option, fly to Kūnmíng, from where it's a 6-hour bus ride to Lìjiāng.
**Where to stay** // Your options include wild camping or accommodation in cheap guesthouses and hotels.
**When to ride** // September and October are good months to visit, after the monsoon rains but before the onset of winter.
**What to take** // Pack a full wardrobe of layers, and be prepared for storms at any time. There are mountain passes most days, so make sure you bring your cycling legs.

*Opposite: the Fortress of Tashkurgan*
*on the Karakoram Highway*

# MORE LIKE THIS
## ASIAN HIGHWAY RIDES

### MANALI–LEH HWY

Straddling no fewer than five lofty mountain passes – the highest of which reaches 5350m in altitude – the ride from Manali to Leh is sure to test your mettle. Coursing its way through the Indian Himalayas, this epic road connects green and lush Himachal Pradesh to sparse and desolate Jammu and Kashmir. Road crews work tirelessly to keep the 'highway' surfaced. In reality, it's damaged or broken throughout its length, its condition subject to the vagaries of the elements and regular landslides that wreak havoc across the region, drawing all but cyclists to a standstill. Although the ride is relatively short, a full three weeks are needed in order to reach Manali, acclimatise, and fly back from Leh.
**Start // Manali**
**End // Leh**
**Distance // 297.5 miles (479km)**

### KARAKORAM HWY

The Karakoram Hwy (KKH) is a cyclist's classic. Climbing out of the hot and dusty plains of Pakistan's Punjab, it weaves a path through a knot of 8000m peaks, before crossing the highest paved border in the world – the Khunjerab Pass (4695m). Pushing onwards through China's Xinjiang province, the KKH passes the stunning Karakol Lake (3600m), flanked by mighty Muztagh Ata, part of a mountain range that forms the northern edge of the Tibetan plateau. Skirting the Kyrgyz border, the KKH's final destination, Kashgar, is a melting pot of Central Asian culture, renowned throughout the region for its Sunday market. Allow a full month for this challenging ride. In fact, many choose to start in Gilgit, 373 miles (600km) into the journey. There, cooler temperatures prevail in the Hunza Valley, a region famed for its hospitality, its tasty apricots, and the rich hiking potential that extends within its mountain folds.
**Start // Islamabad, Pakistan**
**End // Kashgar, Xinjiang province, China**
**Distance // 808 miles (1300km)**

### THE PAMIR HWY

The Pamir Hwy crosses Central Asia's Pamir Mountains, connecting Tajikistan's capital of Dushanbe to the city of Osh, in neighbouring Kyrgyzstan. Officially known as the M41, this relic of the Soviet Union has now been usurped by cyclists, who consider it among the most beautiful bike journeys in the world. A strand of the historic Silk Rd, it straddles a series of 4000m+ passes, traversing high plateaux, windswept lakes, and alpine meadows speckled with Kyrgyz yurts. In terms of road quality, the Pamir Hwy is around 70% paved, with plentiful interludes of white-knuckle riding. Most tourers tackle this tough but magnificent ride in 5 weeks. Just make sure you're fully self sufficient, as public transport is limited, and you'll be on your own for much of the time.
**Start // Dushanbe, Tajikistan**
**End // Osh, Kyrgyzstan**
**Distance // 745.5 miles (1200km)**

# BAVARIAN BEER RIDE

*Cycle through the greatest concentration of breweries on Earth — pacing yourself in this corner of Germany is more about quantity of beer than fitness.*

As I pedal through the Aisch Valley in Bavaria, the bars I'm thinking about are not handlebars. In this quiet, seemingly sober valley, things aren't quite as they seem. Beyond the facade of neat villages and cornfields is what's said to be the highest concentration of breweries in the world — the equivalent of about one brewery every 0.6 miles (1km) through the valley. This is one ride in which I'm not being slowed by headwinds or hills, but by temptation.

I'm midway through a three-day cycle trip from Nuremberg to Rothenburg ob der Tauber that's almost entirely defined by liquid: the Main Danube Canal, the Aisch River and, most importantly, the amber stream known as beer. The Aisch Valley is the ride's centrepiece, but in this part of Bavaria, beer is a recurring theme.

I begin my ride in Nuremberg, following the Main Danube Canal north. Hovering high above the water is the canal towpath, peering down onto canal boats as they slip through a series of locks. Flowering canola fields colour the land, and towns betray themselves by the sudden presence of joggers and other cyclists on the unfailingly flat path.

This day I have the pick of around 40 beer gardens that sit beside, or near to, the canal. I choose the town of Forchheim, once part of the Franconian royal court and now a cobblestoned monument to beer. Though there are a couple of breweries at the heart of the town, I pedal to its outskirts and the forested hill of Kellerberg.

Burrowed into the slopes of Kellerberg are more than a dozen caves used over the centuries to store beer at a constant temperature of 6°C to 10°C. Today the cool caves serve as cellar pubs.

Beneath Kellerberg's tall trees, those in search of beer nirvana wander up the slopes to the pubs. I pedal past them all, parking my bike against the wall of one cellar pub. It's fair to say that when I ride back out an hour or so later, I'm a little less steady on the bike than when I arrived.

The Aisch River is a just few miles ahead, pouring into the canal, but this day I ride on past its mouth, continuing beside the canal,

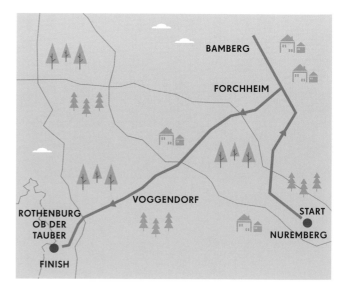

*"The route switches between bike paths and undulating country roads that weave between cornfields and beer gardens"*

which points north like a compass needle to Bamberg. Bike paths lead to the very heart of this beautiful medieval city, where the World Heritage-listed old town is like a Shakespearean stage set.

Bamberg might just as well be called Bambeerg. At the start of the 19th century there were said to be 68 breweries in the city. The city now has the Franconian Brewery Museum, hillsides drilled with cellar caves, and a Bamberg Brewery Trail that guides visitors between the nine remaining breweries and their brewery pubs. I consider it carb loading for my next day of riding.

Cycling is a cure for hangovers, or so I'm claiming, as I return slowly back along the canal the next morning, turning west into the Aisch Valley after about an hour. Here I link into the Aisch Valley Bike Route, a marked 73-mile (117km) ride that will take me all the way to Rothenburg.

For the first time there are roads and hills, as the route switches between bike paths and gently undulating country roads that weave between fields of corn and more brewery beer gardens. Squirrels bounce across the trail, their jaws locked around acorns, and small birds of prey hover over ploughed fields. The Aisch River is my guiding line, though it's rarely in sight.

I stop for lunch in Hochstadt, the largest town I'll pass through this day, but my eye is really ahead to Voggendorf, a tiny village about 6 miles (10km) further down the road. Little more than a cluster of farm buildings, Voggendorf is typical of the Aisch Valley towns I ride through, containing no stores of any kind but possessing a brewery. I feel immediately welcome in the village as I pedal in past a roadside metal sculpture of a cyclist, albeit with its bum being bizarrely bitten by a fish.

On a rise behind the sculpture is Kellerberg Voggendorf, the beer cellar for the Prechtel Brewery in neighbouring Uehlfeld. Cloud has rolled in and the day outside is as damp as the inside of my stein as I sit under cover, staring out over fields and the surrounding towns, each one pierced by church spires.

After a night in a centuries-old brewery turned guesthouse on the banks of the Aisch River in Neustadt an der Aisch, I'm beginning to think that cycling might actually be bad for me. How else to explain this morning headache and dry mouth once again? But I ride on, albeit slowly, for one of Europe's most beautiful medieval towns is my goal this day.

The spread of breweries thins past Neustadt, even as the scene gets more beautiful when I cross from the Aisch to the Tauber Valley. Tiny wooded hills punctuate the horizons, and I'm again winding through fields painted yellow with canola crops. The town of Ipsheim advertises a few wineries – heathens! – but there's barely a beer to be seen.

A wind tows me forward towards my ride's end in the cobbled squares of Rothenburg. As I near the city, beams of sunlight mark the occasion by suddenly breaking through the cloud cover, making Rothenburg's roofs glitter like gold. It feels almost as though I'm riding towards some sort of heavenly welcome at the end of a pilgrimage. But really, there's just another beer ahead. **AB**

## BAMBERG BEER WAR

In 1907 Bamberg breweries upped the price of their beer, pushing the cost of a half-litre from 11 pfennigs to 12. Bamberg drinkers weren't amused. In what became known as the Bamberg Beer War, innkeepers went on strike and patrons boycotted local brews. People power won the day. A week after the price hike, the breweries capitulated – the price remained at 11 pfennigs, as it had been for the previous 10 years.

*Clockwise from left: Rothenburg ob der Tauber, on the Aisch Valley Bike Route; the River Tauber; beer and a bratwurst in Nuremberg. Previous page: Nuremberg, a city of brewers for more than 700 years*

## TOOLKIT

**Start** // Nuremberg
**End** // Rothenburg ob der Tauber
**Distance** // 124 miles (200km)
**Getting there** // The nearest major airport is in Munich; trains run to Nuremberg and Rothenburg
**Ride details** // The ride follows the Main Danube Canal towpath and the Aisch Valley bike route. A 211-mile (340km) circuit can be cycled by following roads and bike paths along the Franconian Rezat River from Rothenburg to Nuremberg.
**Bike hire** // Hire from Partner of Sports (www.pos-nuernberg.de) in Nuremberg.
**Where to stay** // Kohlenmühle Gasthof (www.kohlenmuehle.de) in Neustadt an der Aisch has a guesthouse attached to a working brewery.

*Opposite: Beechworth Mountain Bike Park and Beechworth's historic main street where Bridge Road Brewery serves excellent beer and pizza*

# MORE LIKE THIS
## BEER-LOVERS RIDES

### BEECHWORTH & BRIGHT, VICTORIA, AUSTRALIA

Connected by a section of Australia's no.1 rail trail, the Murray to the Mountains, these two handsome Victorian towns boast excellent craft breweries: Bridge Road Brewers in Beechworth and Bright Brewery in, well, Bright. And both towns are surrounded by some of Australia's best cycling. Beechworth Mountain Bike Park lies on the edge of town and offers some entertainingly rocky trails. Off-road trails also lace the hills behind Bright – ask for a trail map in the Cyclepath bike shop. For road riders, there are hills (Mt Buffalo on the road into Bright) and flatter routes along the goldfield trails around Beechworth. Both breweries also serve food: a pint of Bridge Road's zingy Bling IPA and one of its superlative pizzas is a mouth-watering end to any ride.
**Start/End // Beechworth/Bright**
**Distance // 37 miles (60km)**
**More info // www.bridgeroadbrewers. com.au; www.brightbrewery.com.au**

### BRUGES, BELGIUM

From Belgium's medieval city of Bruges, in the west of Flanders, it's possible to tailor a multiday cycle route that takes in some of the world's best breweries. Start in Bruges, if you can tear yourself away from the variety of strong tripels in the beer bars (and a visit to the Fort Lapin microbrewery in the north of the city centre will include a taste of its '8' tripel), and head southwest for a couple of hours to Diksmuide and the De Dolle brewery. Continue a similar distance across the flatlands of Flanders to the Abbey of St Sixtus, where Trappist monks brew the world's most sought after beer, Westvleteren 12, which can only be bought a case at a time from the door of the monastery. Sleep it off at the B&B at the St Bernadus brewery in nearby Watou (yes, really, a brewery with beds...).
**Start // Bruges**
**End // Watou**
**Distance // around 55 miles (89km)**
**More info // www.fortlapin.com/en, www.sintsixtus.be, www.dedollebrouwers.be, www.sintbernardus.be**

### PORTLAND, OREGON, USA

In this cycle-friendly city of more than 60 craft breweries the union of beer and bike is closer than anywhere. Travel Oregon has outlined a tour of Portland that samples the breweries of the east side of the city, starting at the Burnside Brewing Company on Burnside St, before heading southwest to the Hair of the Dog Brewing Company, a Portland pioneer. From here, turn eastward and ride to the Green Dragon, which has 62 beers on tap, including many of the Pacific Northwest's signature hop-rich pale ales. Next up is Coalition Brewing in the residential Buckman neighbourhood. The final stop is the beer bar Apex to the south.
**Start // E Burnside St**
**End // SE Division St**
**Distance // varies according to route**
**More info // www.traveloregon.com**

# DOWN THE
# DANUBE

*The mighty Danube is the longest river in Europe. The Austrian section of the Danube cycle path, or Donauradweg, is fast, efficient and almost always picturesque.*

My husband and I chose Linz as our starting point, as we headed out along the Danube River, although many cyclists start the Donauradweg upstream in Passau, a German city on the Austrian border. But since we are both amateurs, and reaching our destination of Vienna inside a week would mean covering 43 miles (70km) a day, we jumped to Linz, ensuring our daily cycle was closer to a more leisurely 30 miles (45km).

We lingered in Linz, enjoying ice creams in Hauptplatz, the elegant central square surrounded by baroque buildings painted the colours of strawberry and pistachio. But the river soon tugged us onwards, and as the city's industrial suburbs gave way to verges of nodding daisies, and fields of clover and campion, I realised for the first time, but certainly not the last, that the joy of this holiday lay in the journey.

The Danube was strategically important to the Romans, since it provided a watery barrier against invading barbarian hordes.

But where the waters were later used to shift salt barges along this trade route, now the cargo you're more likely to spot will be gleaming new cars, or excited tourists.

The river is a reassuring travelling companion and covers some of the defining ages in Austria's history, from its Celtic roots, which we found at Mitterkirchen Celtic village, to the castles of the mighty Habsburg Empire, to a more difficult, recent past, which we sensed most keenly in Mauthausen, where 120,000 people died in a concentration camp.

The route was flat, our main obstacles not hills but Lycra-clad cyclists who bombed along the path, head down, like sleek bullets, or in jovial groups, shouting encouragement to us amateurs, easily distinguishable from the pros in our denim shorts and Converse trainers.

By dusk, we were cycling through the sticky scent of poplar trees, with all stages of life parading along the river's banks. We passed a teenage couple, eating pizza between drags on shared cigarettes. Further up, a young family paddled, their picnic of rolls and broken biscuits left behind them. Later, a group of men with beards and paunches cradled bottles of beer while cooking foil-wrapped potatoes on a campfire, their fishing rods momentarily forgotten. And in the twilight, as the 16th-century castle of Wallsee rose ahead, an elderly couple, four walking sticks between them, tottered along, swans on the water escorting them home. That night, after cycling 30 miles (45km), the Austrian diet of fried meat and piles of carbohydrates suddenly made great sense.

From Wallsee we cycled through the orchards of the Mostviertel,

*"We were cycling through the sticky scent of poplar trees, with all stages of life parading along the river's banks"*

where apples and pears are harvested for flat local cider called most. An hour later, flagging before lunch, we were rewarded with the silhouette of Greinburg castle on the northern bank. Loading our bikes onto a tiny wooden ferry, which wouldn't look out of place chugging up the Amazon, we joined tourists bussed into this Disney-like Habsburg town for the castle and kitsch curiosities of Austrian's oldest theatre, built in a granary in 1563.

That evening in Persenbeug, apricots played a starring role on the menu, cooked with pork and used to stuff sweet pancakes, reminding us we were entering the jewel in the fruit-growing necklace of the Danube, the Wachau, or wine district of Lower Austria.

The next day, we saw vines criss-crossing the banks, and the cycle route left the river to meander through orchards, passing gardens ripe with huge courgettes, shiny tomatoes and lines of elegant runner beans. We stopped to stuff a few euros into an honesty box selling bags of apricots, while tumbling pear trees created moments of shade in the 40°C heat, and our bike wheels slipped on the plums and greengages littering the track.

Before Spitz we wiggled through Willendorf, famous for its voluptuous Paleolithic Venus found in 1908, and then Schwallenbach, where a honey-coloured tower, crimson roses and

## SNACK STOPS

There are very few cafes or snack bars en route, so be sure to pack a picnic every morning. But there are some small stalls selling whole mackerel grilled over an open fire. There's a particularly nice one at a bar called Piratenknetpe, just beyond Grein on the southern bank, opposite St Nikola. The mackerel is delicious, served with thick slices of rye bread and butter: very welcome after a long cycle ride.

*Left to right: riding the Danube cycle path; Austrian energy food; Linz; the town of Spitz in the Wachau Valley. Previous page: the 'Danube Loop', an oxbow bend opposite Schlögen in Austria, near Passau*

## TOOLKIT

**Start** // Linz
**End** // Vienna
**Distance** // 150 miles (241km)
**Getting there** // International flights arrive at both Linz and Vienna.
**Tour** // Macs Adventure (www.macsadventure.com) offers a Danube Family Cycling package. Cycle hire costs £60 for adults and children.
**When to ride** // April until October is the best time of year, but check ahead with the Austrian Tourist Board (www.austria.info) about flooding.
**What to take** // Mosquitos are rife during wet and warm months, so pack plenty of repellant.
**Where to eat** // Weinhotel Wachau (www.weinhotel-wachau.at) or Restaurant Hellas (www.hellas-tulln.at).

fluttering white doves transported me to Provence.

In Spitz, our resting place for two nights, we stretched out by the pool, but we soon became restless, hungry for the unexpected adventures we were sharing on the journey. We found these in the medieval castle at Dürnstein, where Richard the Lionheart was imprisoned in 1192. Krems an der Donau, 12 miles (20km) on, was less appealing, heaving with tourists gorging on chips and knocking back gigantic beers at 10am.

The bucolic beauty of the Wachau vanished as we cycled on past gas power stations. It wasn't pretty, but we spotted real, local Austrian life in the mothers gossiping as their children paddled along scraps of beaches, and the excitable teenagers on waterskis showing off to leggy girls on Rollerblades who sliced down the cycle path, futuristic in goggles and knee pads.

At Tulln we raced around the Egon Schiele Museum, posing for pictures beside the elegant, surprising sculpture of Attila the Hun greeting his bride Kriemhild on the waterfront. But there was little time for sightseeing, and when we hit the fringes of the Vienna forest, we passed Russian boats from the Black Sea lining the river as the skyscrapers grew taller, and huge city bridges loomed above us.

Suddenly we lost the familiar Donauradweg as we left the river, instead joining evening commuters and ladies walking their dogs after a day in the office. I missed the bobbing ducks who seemed to have accompanied us all the way from Linz, and the rattle of trams and taxis startled me. I didn't want the journey to end. I wanted the river to flow on beside my spinning wheels forever. **CS**

*Opposite: riding the flat and
traffic-free Tissington Trail*

# MORE LIKE THIS
# TRAFFIC-FREE TRAILS

### CAMEL TRAIL, CORNWALL, UK

Once the railway track that linked the
South West to London, carrying sand and
fish inland, and immortalised in Betjeman's
Cornwall as 'the most beautiful train journey
I know', the Camel Trail is now a super
family-friendly cycle path. It cuts through
some of Cornwall's prettiest countryside.
From Rick Stein's famous fishing port of
Padstow to Wadebridge, it hugs the vast
Camel Estuary before heading through the
woodland of the Camel Valley and onto
Bodmin. The trail then heads inland to the
foot of Bodmin Moor, finishing up at the
moorland village of Blisland. The route is
mostly traffic-free and includes both a Site
of Special Scientific Interest and a Special
Area of Conservation. The estuary section
is especially great for birdwatchers, look out
for peregrines, ospreys and mute swans.
**Start // Padstow**
**End // Blisland**
**Distance // 18 miles (29km)**
**More info // www.sustrans.org.uk/ncn/
map/route/camel-trail**

### TISSINGTON TRAIL, DERBYSHIRE, UK

Following the route of the former Buxton
to Ashbourne Railway, which closed in
1966 and in its heyday carried passengers
and milk from Manchester to London,
the Tissington Trail passes through the
breathtakingly beautiful Peak District.
Highlights include the often elevated views
of Derbyshire's green undulating dales, the
dramatic limestone ravine at Dovedale, the
calcareous ash woods, the stepping stones
over the river Dove, and the wildlife in and
around there, including trout, kingfishers,
grey herons and dippers. Tissington is an
essential detour, as it's frequently cited
as one of the prettiest and most unspoilt
villages in the country.
**Start // Ashbourne**
**End // Parsley Hay**
**Distance // 13 miles (21km)**
**More info // www.sustrans.org.uk/ncn/
map/route/tissington-trail**

### MANIFOLD TRACK, STAFFORDSHIRE, UK

The ride follows the route of the narrow
gauge Leek and Manifold Light Railway,
which ran along the river gorges between
Hulme End and Waterhouses. The railway
opened in 1904 to serve the small farming
communities and carry milk and cheese
from the remote dairy at Ecton. It was
famously known as 'a line starting nowhere
and ending up at the same place,' so
perhaps, unsurprisingly, it closed in 1934.
But it was one of the first train routes to
have its track lifted out and resurfaced
as a path for walkers, cyclists and horse
riders. Now running at 8½ miles (13½km),
it's mostly car-free and flat and there are
two bike hire places in Waterhouses. Thor's
Cave is a worthwhile detour about 76m up
from the track. It's a former home to Stone
Age dwellers dating back at least 50,000
years. Mammoth and giant bear bones
have been discovered there.
**Start // Hulme End**
**End // Waterhouses**
**Distance // 8½ miles (13½km)**

# MONTE AMIATA

*Italy's most rideable former volcano is in Tuscany. Clad in flora and fauna-rich forest, it is known to both local riders and leading chefs: an enviable epic-ride combination.*

M onte Amiata is a welcoming mountain, tree-clad with gentle winds whispering sweet things about the good life. It's a local secret – occasionally grazed by the Giro d'Italia, but mostly a store of cycling routes that the Tuscan riders keep for themselves. Topped by a tiny and delightfully old-fashioned ski station, the most southerly in Tuscany, it doubles up as a summer resort for walkers and nature lovers, or people just visiting the excellent small restaurant at the top.

Covered in thick old-growth forest to the very summit – beech, chestnut and larch – Amiata is rich in flora and fauna, and human anthropology. It presents the cyclist with endless possible deviations in thought and deed to ease the task of grinding up the climb. You can spin up in a low gear on one of the gentler ascents, taking time out for refreshment at the mid-point and the three-quarter points. Or you can pause the journey to join the fungi hunters or picnickers under the chestnut trees. Top chefs, such as Giorgio Locatelli have acclaimed the natural produce from Amiata,

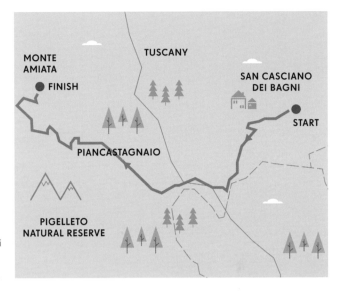

and there is even a brand of upmarket produce named after Seggiano, one of the towns on the slopes.

But if it is a tough workout you want, then you can snap your legs on 15% gradient plus ramps by tackling the shortest, fastest and hardest path to the top. It can be a two-hour-plus climb from the very bottom, 22 miles (35km) steadily upwards with about 1500m of vertical ascent, or park up closer and ascend nearly 900m in just 6 miles (10km) through tackling one of the more brutal direct routes.

After 15 years of climbing Monte Amiata, on road bike and mountain bike, I have yet to exhaust its infinite variety. This is an unusual mountain in that you can customise the kind of ride you want, improvising along the way. There are routes with tempting cafe stops and signs of humanity or paths that allow you to pant away without seeing a soul.

But, for all the choice, there is a classic climb for me that runs from near the border with Lazio. This gives options on passing through two fascinating towns on the southern slopes. The medieval centre of Piancastagnaio comes after a deceptively rolling road through open countryside, which actually rises quite sharply at times. Olive trees thin out as the altitude increases and big views open up across the Paglia valley to the tower atop the rocky massif above the historic town of Radicofani.

As you approach Piancastagnaio, the road rears up with a roughly half-mile (1km) stretch of 12% to 18% gradient that passes through an unsightly mass of rusting giant pipework and

*"Olive trees thin out as the altitude increases and big views open up across the Paglia valley to the tower atop the massif"*

industrial sheds. This may seem a rude interruption in the Tuscan idyll but is actually a remarkable structure and a clue to the whole environment.

Amiata is a long extinct volcano, the second highest volcanic mountain in Italy after Etna, last active around 200,000 years ago. Deep down there is still seismic activity, and since the 1960s this strange installation has pioneered the harnessing of geothermal power as a sustainable resource. You can just about imagine the distinctive landscape around as once a sea of bubbling lava domes and collapsing caldera.

Anyway, the thought of all that natural energy just might inspire you to get over one of the steepest parts of the climb and up into the old centre of Piancastagnaio. Here you have a choice: take the direct route up or deviate via Abbadia San Salvatore, a richly historic town that takes its name from an 8th-century religious foundation, built upon as a staging post along the Via Francigena, one of the great pilgrimage routes to Rome. Abbadia is also known for a tough mining past, now captured in a small museum. Through cinnabar mining, a deadly toxic job, Amiata was the single largest

## THERMAL BATHS

The volcanic history of Amiata delivers an attractive side-offering for the tired bodies of cyclists – a visit to a thermal bath. Around the foothills of the mountain are several natural spas, with various levels of scalding water that are rich in minerals, and much valued by bathers for their health properties since Roman times. Film buffs may remember Bagno Vignoni as a fog-filled place of alienation in Tarkovsky's *Nostalgia*.

*Left to right: riding past Radicofani; local wines include Montepulciano. Previous page: a Tuscan panorama with Monte Amiata in the distance*

source of mercury in the world at the start of the 20th century but the industry collapsed by the time of the WWII.

I usually press on via the less-travelled direct route to the top, the Strada Provinciale Vetta dell'Amiata, where the miles click by while you scan across the woodland to spot strange boulders and volcanic rock formations, or even rare fauna. The wild boar and deer of the valleys will be unlikely up here, but I have seen a porcupine on the road and there is bird life aplenty. There is even, whisper it well away from any farmer's ears, that most precarious of Italian wild mammals, a wolf-pack, somewhere not far away.

About 5 miles (8km) up from Piancastagnaio, the first signs of the ski resort become apparent at the 1200m elevation. You pass the Contessa Hotel on the left at the base of a ski run. The air cools as the trees give shade while there are also gentle breezes filtered by the forest. Now a final push, just 2 miles (3km) to go before the road finishes at around the 1600m elevation, with the peak another 100m higher up a grassy – or snowy – slope. Time your arrival around lunchtime and enjoy a fine plate of polenta con funghi at Bar La Vetta (aka Gigi's, the name of the affable owner), with the boletus picked fresh from the forest floor around you, accompanied by a glass of excellent local wine (Montalcino and Montepulciano are not far away). There may be a fantastic pudding on offer, *torta ricciolina*, a chocolate confection particular to this area. You've earned it – perhaps even two slices, and a grappa. It's all downhill from here. **LB**

## TOOLKIT

**Start //** San Casciano dei Bagni, 12.5 miles (20km) south of Amiata
**End //** The top of Monte Amiata
**Distance //** 22 miles (35km) one way or 46.5 miles (75km) for a full loop, with deviation back through Abbadia
**Getting there //** The closest airport, Rome Fiumicino, is just over two hours away, driving south. A car is fairly essential.
**Where to stay //** San Casciano dei Bagni has good hotels, such as Sette Querce (www.settequerce.it/en/). Alternatively, find an agriturismo (a kind of B&B) in the countryside around the mountain.
**When to ride //** Between March and October (although check there isn't a late spring snowfall).
**What to take //** Bike shops are surprisingly thin on the ground, so bring spare tubes and tools.

*Opposite : cyclists taking part in L'Eroica, an annual ride on Tuscany's strade bianche*

# MORE LIKE THIS
# ITALIAN RIDES

### MONTE BONDONE

For a similarly epic sylvan ride in the north of Italy, Monte Bondone in the Trentino is a great experience. It is an easy ride to the base from Trento, where there are lots of hotels and restaurants. Tackle it as part of the annual Granfondo Charly Gaul in July, which honours one of the great breakaway race wins of all time, the 1956 Giro triumph by the Belgian climber Gaul who crawled in eight-minutes ahead of the next rider in the middle of a blizzard atop Bondone. He needed to be carried off his bike. Better to ride it mid-summer, when it provides a delightful relief from the heat further south. But be prepared for surprise showers, which can lead to a slippery descent.
**Start // The cathedral square of Trento
End // Località Vason, Monte Bondone
Distance // 14 miles (23km)**

### STRADE BIANCHE, SOUTH OF SIENA

The 'white' dirt roads of Tuscany are a distinctive and now protected feature. Dusty with loose surface in summer, in the winter they can rattle the bones with their frozen corrugated ridges. In the wet, they are lethally slippery. But they are a lot of fun, opening up a very traditional experience that takes you back in time. The roads are widespread but those that form part of the spring pro-race, called the Strade Bianche, have been partly marked out as a trail that you can do any time of the year. Start from Montalcino, taking the road towards San Giovanni d'Asso, then take a left on to Strada Provincale 75 and 103, two white-road routes.
**Start/End // Montalcino (fortezza) via Buonconvento and Bibbiano
Distance // 37 miles (60km)**

### HILL TOWNS OF THE FIORA VALLEY

In the very south of Tuscany lie a set of hill towns that sit atop striking outcrops of rock where the Fiora river has cut through the soft tufa rock. This is a landscape unlike any other, in part born out of the volcanic origins. Each of these towns – Sorano, Sovana, Pitigliano – give the rider a chance of good climbing and descending and together they can make a great day's riding. The thermal spa of Saturnia is also just a few hills further away. Every town has its own distinctive attractions – near Sovana are some of the best Etruscan tombs, while Pitigliano has a fascinating history involving an ancient Jewish community, which grew out of the border country trading traditions. You can eat, drink and rest up in extremely pleasant ways for modest sums.
**Start/End // Pitigliano via Sorano and Sovana
Distance // 17 miles (28km)**

# THE BRYAN CHAPMAN MEMORIAL

*Cycling Wales end-to-end and back in a weekend is the best way to discover its mountainous beauty, incredible wildlife and potential for adventure.*

The bright lights of Menai Bridge appeared out of the gloom like the scene from a Christmas card, and after almost 199 miles (320km) in the saddle it was like being thrown into solstice festivities after months of winter. I'd been marking all the significant milestones, like opening doors on an excruciating advent calendar.

It was gone midnight, we had cycled from Chepstow in South Wales, to Anglesea on its northern tip in 18 hours. Now all we had to do was to turn around and retrace our steps home.

It was too much for Dan. After a 40-minute food-stop we crossed the bridge for the homeward leg and the need for sleep soon kicked in. Hanging onto the back of a bleary peloton, he drifted across the empty road and was still pedalling as he guided his front wheel into a ditch.

'I think I'm going to have a little snooze,' he said, waking momentarily in a tangle of brambles and bike frame.

People like to tell you that cycling is the new golf – a magnet

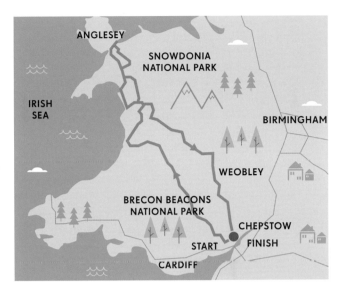

for middle-age chaps who dress like Chris Froome to test their competitive mettle in sportive events.

Audax rides are very different. There's no medal or commemorative T-shirt and the entry fees are a fraction of the cost. And while a carbon fibre bike might get admiring glances at a sportive, it's an eccentric three-wheeler that attracted an appreciative crowd at the 6am start of the Bryan Chapman Memorial, a 373 mile- (600km) ride from South to North Wales and back.

The classic Audax bike is made of steel, hand-built, often with a weathered canvas Carradice bag hanging from a leather saddle. It's not a race: getting round the course within the time limit (40 hours in this case) is the only challenge. So you constantly find yourself in the company of different riders on the road, and you'll meet plenty more as you stop at tea houses along the way.

There's enormous camaraderie, which is good news because after the most glorious day of navigating the hills of mid-Wales in blistering sunshine, crossing Barmouth Bridge in the warmth of the afternoon and marvelling at the mountainous scenery of Snowdonia in the honey-rich glow of early evening, I find myself stranded, in the dark, 30 miles (48km) from our overnight stop at Dolgellau.

It started with a twang that became a repetitive clunk that evolved into the nagging 'vrrrrmm' of a buckled wheel rubbing against the brake blocks. I reluctantly said goodbye to the group of riders I was with and watched their rear lights disappear into the gloom. It was 2am, I was alone and in the shadow of Snowdon, Wales's highest peak, with no idea of how to fix my wheel.

'I've got a spare spoke,' said one rider who appeared like a fairy godmother out of the gloom. It got me back on the road.

This is a route I've wanted to ride for many years. You can feel the topography of the country bristle into life as you head north across the Brecon Beacons and climb over the Cambrian Mountains. The official ride happens in May, when quiet, tree-lined country roads are bustling with wildlife. White-bibbed

## GET INTO AUDAX RIDING

Audax (www.aukweb. net) rides run through the year across the UK, typically from 62 miles to 124 miles (100km to 200km), up to 746-mile (1200km) events, such as the Paris–Brest–Paris or London–Edinburgh–London. You need to be a self-reliant cyclist, able to mend mechanical problems and get yourself out of trouble. Start on a 124-mile (100km) event and learn how to follow route cards before building up to bigger rides.

*Clockwise from top: Llanberis Pass; the suspension bridge over the Menai Strait; book-loving Hay-on-Wye; a red kite. Previous page: Harlech beach*

*"Red kites soar above, long-tailed tits flit through woodland canopy and flocks of goldfinch flash across country lanes"*

dippers stand on rocky islands of mountain streams, red kites soar above, long-tailed tits flit through woodland canopy and flocks of goldfinch flash across the car-free country lanes.

I think I see the eyes of a badger flash in the dark as I finally climb to the Dolgellau YHA at 4am, and the promise of two hours of sleep. I'm too nauseous to eat and when I find someone already sleeping in my nominated bunk, I haven't the heart to turf them out, so I put on everything I own and curl up on the floor.

Two hours later I'm somehow back on bike with its wonky back wheel, climbing through the early morning drizzle, taking stock of every ailment. I'm drenched, my backside is raw, my shoulders ache and an Achilles heel has ballooned preposterously. I'm overtaken by a man in a knitted cycling top in his late 60s and I am filled with the deepest of admiration. Audax rides are open to anyone: youthful racing snake, middle-age Lycra devotee, or vintage cyclist. You meet them all on this ride.

The sun finally comes out as I pass Llanbrynmair and reminds me of just how green and beautiful this overlooked part of Wales is. I fall in with a group of riders and we cheerfully count down the miles together, working in unison on the climbs and stopping to refuel at village halls and corner shops.

I'm on my own for the final 12 miles (20km) that takes me along the Wye Valley, following the river that springs up in the Cambrian Mountains. I watch as a pair of exhausted tandem riders cheerfully tumble from their bike on a steep ascent and then, with just a few miles to go, I curl up by the river and sleep for 20 blissful minutes. There's a monster of an ascent from the ruins of Tintern Abbey back to Chepstow and I summon every ounce of energy left to grind to the top, only to come to a halt a mile (1.6km) later on a slight incline on the outskirts of Chepstow. And finally, there it is... the Severn Bridge. I freewheel home, having cycled over 373 miles (600km) for the first time in my life and discovered the real beauty of Wales. **MS**

## TOOLKIT

**Start/End** // Chepstow, Wales
**Distance** // 373 miles (600km)
**Getting there** // Trains to Chepstow or, alternatively, there is a cycle path over the old Severn Bridge. Many riders stay in the Travelodge (www.travelodge.co.uk/hotels/97/Bristol-Severn-View-M48-hotel) on the English side of the bridge.
**Where to stay** // The actual route uses the YHA Kings (www.yha.org.uk/hostel/kings) at Dolgellau as an overnight stop.
**When to ride** // The official route runs in May but longer summer months offer scope to do it yourself.
**More info** // If you want to follow the route independently but break it over more days, the YHA Snowdon Pen-y-Pass (www.yha.org.uk/hostel/snowdon-pen-y-pass) is another possible stopover. There are no 24-hour garages in Snowdonia, so you need to carry all the food and equipment required.
**What to take** // Full lights if you're going to be riding through the night, plus a complete bike repair kit with spare inner tubes and a tyre sleeve or spare tyre. Spare spokes and tools (and the knowledge to use them) also a good idea.

*Opposite: crossing the Scottish
borders near Moffat on the
London-Edinburgh-London audax*

# MORE LIKE THIS
# AUDAX RIDES

### PARIS-BREST-PARIS

First ridden in 1891, this is the world's
oldest long-distance cycling event and the
inspiration for the Tour de France, which
launched 12 years later. Entry is open
to anyone who can complete qualifying
rides of 124.3 miles (200km), 186.4 miles
(300km), 248.5 miles (400km) and 372.8
miles (600km) in the year of the event, and
the emphasis is on self-reliance. PBP, as it
is known, runs every four years, taking you
across northern France, where whole towns
spill onto the streets to wave riders on. The
atmosphere of this blue riband event is just
as important as the gruelling challenge of
completing the 745.5 miles (1200km) within
the 90-hour limit (the strongest riders will
complete in half that time).
**Start/End //** Paris
**Distance //** 745.5 miles (1200km)
**More info //** www.paris-brest-paris.org

### LONDON-EDINBURGH-LONDON

Like the Paris-Brest-Paris, this ride runs
every four years (the next event is 2017)
and gives you 100 hours to complete one
of Britain's toughest cycling challenges
at around 870 miles (1400km). You set
off from The Mall in central London and
head north across the flats of Cambridge
and Lincolnshire, over the Humber Bridge,
before tackling the Pennines, and skirting
the Yorkshire Moors. The route then takes
you through countless small villages and
into the Scottish Lowlands. From Edinburgh
your return journey provides a bit of
variety, but exhaustion and fatigue will be
keeping your mind firmly fixed on getting
back to London. There's no qualification
requirements and the entry fee (over £320
for 2017) covers all your sleep stops, bike
repair support and bag drops, so you can
be assured of a fresh pair of bike shorts
somewhere along the route.
**Start/End //** London
**Distance //** 870 miles (1400km)
**More info //** www.
londonedinburghlondon.com/route

### BOSTON-MONTREAL-BOSTON

This 745.6-mile (1200km) ride from New
England, US, to Canada and back used to
run every year as an organised randonée
event and was considered to be North
America's answer to the Paris-Brest-Paris.
It was only on PBP years that this event
would take a break. Since 2006, it no
longer operates as an organised randonée,
but lives on as a 'permanent': a route that
riders can follow, at any time of the year,
completing within the time limit. The ride
takes you through Massachusetts and then
north through Vermont, riding through the
beautiful landscape of New England. You
clip the corner of New York State before
heading over the border into Canada for
a short foray to Huntingdon, Quebec, your
turnaround point, before the journey home.
**Start/End //** Boston, USA
**Distance //** 745.6 miles (1200km)
**More info //** www.bmb2011permanent.
wordpress.com

# PEDALLING THE SPANISH PICOS

*The Picos de Europa of north Spain are popular with walkers but these mountains also offer fantastic cycling and great wildlife, worthy reasons for a two-wheeled expedition.*

Quite what the three of us were doing on Justin's honeymoon was the question on everyone's lips as we cycled onto the ferry in Portsmouth to set out across the Bay of Biscay.

This had been billed as a two-wheeled stag do, but events had overtaken us. An illness in the family had brought the date of the wedding forward, and two days before the ceremony Justin's wife-to-be agreed that since he had bought the tickets already he might as well put them to good use. So the groom, Muddy and I all disembarked at Bilbao on Spain's northern coast, full of trepidation at the thought of our first honeymoon together.

Spain's Picos had seemed the obvious location for a pre-wedding bike ride. It's an impressive mountain range of muscular-looking peaks with incredible wildlife, fresh air, big climbs and superb walks. They would provide challenge and purpose; a wholesome five-day pilgrimage to Oviedo where our Lonely Planet guide promised us Celtic music, late night parties and 'no-frills drinking'.

And as we pedalled away from the ferry, past Torrelavega and towards the sun-bathed seaside town of San Vincente de la Barquera, we congratulated ourselves on an excellent choice of route. But the following day, with the mountains in our sights, we were hit by a Cantabrian storm: a wild paso doble of hail,

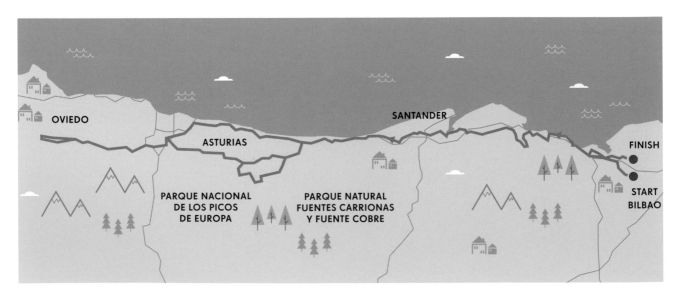

OVIEDO

SANTANDER

ASTURIAS

FINISH

PARQUE NACIONAL
DE LOS PICOS
DE EUROPA

PARQUE NATURAL
FUENTES CARRIONAS
Y FUENTE COBRE

START
BILBAO

gusts and torrential rain.

'I thought Spain was supposed to be sunny,' cried Muddy as he pulled on a waterproof in a lay-by just outside of Panes, where the mountains spring into life.

As the gradient steepened, our progress was slowed not just by gravity, but by a distinct lack of focus. Wildlife was half the problem. We'd often look over our shoulder to see Justin's silhouette a few hundred metres behind with binoculars glued to his face. Black kites, buzzards and white storks; griffon vultures, red-backed shrike, alpine chough and egrets were good reasons for this committed birder to stop and scan the skies.

As a structural engineer, Muddy's main distraction were the bridges. Ornate steel structures required an admiring explanation of their tensile loading, weight bearing coefficient and the socio-economic influence behind their design. As long as we could make regular stops at roadside bars to sample the wine and test out my rusty Spanish, I was happy with our progress.

We'd spend half the day hauling heavily loaded bikes to the top of a demoralising switchback, legs heavy with lactic acid, and then what seemed just minutes careering down the other side. Suddenly we'd turn a corner and find ourselves shaded from the heat of the day and cycling through a narrow, steep-sided gorge. Then we'd round another and be treated to a snow-capped peak rising in the distance, while we baked in the heat of the day.

*"We stopped to celebrate with a group of dairy farmers who'd won a trophy for their prize herd"*

The Picos rise to over 2600m and run the full gamut of mountain architecture, from broad table-top plateaux and long knife-edged ridges to sharply symmetrical peaks that stand proud and solitary. The higher we went the further the gap between settlements, and the more removed each one felt from modern life.

Our target was Sotres, at 1045m one of the highest villages in the Picos. It was only linked by road to the rest of Spain in 1968; it got electricity in 1981 and telephones in 1989. A slightly eccentric air hangs over the village and the best way to experience it is with a meal in Casa Gallega, a tiny restaurant with legendary hospitality. We tucked into the local delicacy of *fabada* (a heavy ham and bean stew) while the owners, the Moradiellos family, treated us to the full story of how their Jewish ancestors fled to the Picos to escape persecution in Spain.

From here we knew the majority of our route would be gravity assisted, and over the next few days we flew back down through the mountain, stopping to celebrate with a group of dairy farmers who'd won a trophy for their prize herd, or to hang out with football

## HIKE
## THESE HILLS

From the village of Sotres there is an excellent adventurous add-on to a bike trip: hike up to El Naranjo de Bulnes, a beautiful limestone peak where you can overnight in the Refugio de Urriellu. Walk over lush meadows with a constellation of alpine flora, then high into rugged mountain terrain with an easy-to-follow path. Find somewhere safe to leave your bike and take plenty of water, as sources are scare.

*Left to right: the Basilica of Covadonga in Asturias; pouring cider the local way; an Alpine chough, a mountain resident; San Vicente de la Barquera on the coast. Previous page: the Picos de Europa mountain range*

fans in small village bars. We raced through Cangas de Onís, once the capital of Asturias, site of the first post-conquest Iberian church and known for its beautiful humpbacked Roman bridge. And before we knew it we were cruising into Oviedo, with its promise of dive bars and raucous music.

It did not disappoint and just 36 hours later, after making friends with possibly the entire population of the city, we were heading back towards our ferry, all nursing very sore heads. We decided to rest in the town of Laredo, which would leave us with an easy 37-mile (60km) ride back to the ferry. We would eat well and recover that night, then arrive for our 4.30pm departure and head back to the UK for a hero's welcome.

It was early the following morning that someone decided to check our tickets and the departure time, which actually turned out to be four hours earlier than we had thought. We leapt on our bikes and tried to summon every ounce of athletic ability in a dishevelled peloton that tore along the undulating road. After three exhausting hours we were rewarded with the sight of the Bilbao–Portsmouth ferry slipping its moorings and setting sail without us. For the man who had promised to return to his new marital home, all seemed lost. Salvation came in the form of the Santander to Plymouth ferry two days later. It was the long way home but it could save a marriage from floundering before it had celebrated its first fortnight in the saddle. **MS**

## TOOLKIT

**Start/End** // Bilbao
**Distance** // 419 miles (675km)
**Getting there** // Ferry from Portsmouth to Bilbao
**Where to stay** // Plenty of *pensións* (basic accommodation), campsites, and scope to camp wild in the mountains, as long as you have the right kit.
**When to ride** // Anytime from May to October.
**What to take** // Warm sleeping bags are a must if you're camping out, but you might prefer to eschew this flexibility, shed the weight and pay for accommodation if you're planning to tackle some of the bigger mountain passes.
**What to spot** // You'll see lots of griffon vultures, but also look out for golden eagles and Egyptian vultures. There are also populations of wolves and brown bears in these mountains.

*Opposite: horse racing on All Saints
Day in Todos Santos, Guatemala*

# MORE LIKE THIS
## CELEBRATORY RIDES

### LONDON, UK TO MUNICH, GERMANY

Oktoberfest is one of the biggest parties
in Europe: a time when hordes gather to
drink beer from outrageously large glasses
and slip into lederhosen. There are a range
of routes that will take you from London to
Munich, and the best of these is Euro Velo
Route 15, which follows the Rhine until it hits
Stuttgart. From here you can hang a left
and complete the final 168 miles (270km)
to Munich. There is a case for following EV
15 down to the beautiful Lake Constance
(see p220) and riding to Munich from
here, but that adds a significant amount
to your total distance. Do remember that
the Oktoberfest lasts a whole month so you
don't need to rush!
**Start // London**
**End // Munich**
**Distance // 168 miles (270km)**

### MELBOURNE TO ADELAIDE, AUSTRALIA

Depending on what kind of a party you
want waiting for you at the end, you could
either choose to ride from Melbourne
to Adelaide for WOMADelaide world
music festival in March or in reverse from
Adelaide to Melbourne for the Australian
Rules Football Grand Final in September.
Either way you get to ride along the Great
Ocean Rd, one of the most stunning
coastal bike rides in the world. If you're
tackling this in spring there is a high
chance of seeing whales from locations
around Warrnambool, koalas around the
Great Otway National Park, and you can
stop off and marvel at The Twelve Apostles
(limestone sea stacks) and the tales of
shipwrecks and rescue. For the ultimate
outdoor adventure, pack in a spot of
surfing at Anglesea and Bells Beach.
**Start // Melbourne**
**End // Adelaide**
**Distance // 1118 miles (1800km)**

### ANTIGUA TO TODOS SANTOS, GUATEMALA

On 1 November the village of Todos
Santos, Guatemala, turns into a wildly
colourful horse race, with traditionally
dressed villagers competing to see who
can stay on their horses the longest,
as they ride up and down while getting
progressively drunker. It's a riotous
festival of xylophone playing, Merengue
dancing and *aguardiente* (cane alcohol)
and the perfect finale to a celebratory
bike ride. Start in the Unesco heritage
city of Antigua and then make your
way via Chichicastenango, Panajachel,
Quetzaltenango and on to Todos Santos.
You'll pass incredible smouldering
volcanoes and the beautiful Lake Atitlán as
you tackle some very demanding ascents.
It's a route that leads you through beautiful
towns, each with their own distinctive
dress and language. There are 21 Mayan
languages spoken in a country the size of
Wales, but Spanish is widely used.
**Start // Antigua**
**End // Todos Santos**
**Distance // 243.5 miles (392km)**

# CLIMBING MONT VENTOUX

*The Beast of Provence is, with good reason, the most notorious ascent of the Tour de France, and a serious challenge for any road cyclist.*

Mont Ventoux is such a totemic climb in the annals of the Tour de France, its flanks littered with so many broken reputations and bodies, its peak clouded by so much history, that it's perhaps better to approach it askance. After some good wine, even. Let me explain. It was at a Norfolk wedding a few years ago that I got talking to an Irishman: the wine we were all drinking was not only excellent, it was in fact from his own vineyard in Provence, a few miles to the south of Mont Ventoux. Had I heard of Ventoux, he asked. Had I ever.

A year and a summer holiday invitation later, I found myself cycling away from my new best friend's vineyard while my family still slept. In the early morning May sunshine I did my best to ignore the monstrous Ventoux, a volcanic bully squatting nearly 1.2 miles (2km) over the famously appealing hills of Provence.

I wasn't hammering towards a summit finish on a sportive ride let alone a Tour de France stage, I was merely sidling up to it from a few miles away, wasn't I? If only. My jersey told its own story: out of one pocket spilled sandwiches, bananas, gel packs and energy bars for the 13-mile (21km) ascent; from another, factor 50 sunscreen for my lily skin on the broiling lower slopes, and a wind jacket for the descent of the bald, wind-lashed upper approaches. My fragile mind also needed help: the previous day a bike mechanic in Bédoin had sorted out a nagging chain rub in my road bike's lowest gear – the only gear I'd be using for most of the morning.

At 1912m, Mont Ventoux is head and shoulders above the surrounding hills. No strategic col or picturesque alp lies at its summit, only a 1960s telecommunications tower and a few tourist concessions. So the route up Ventoux is a road to nowhere, really,

which is somehow fitting, given its notorious status as the most demanding climb in the Tour de France.

In the 1955 edition, four years after the climb's first inclusion, the 1950 Tour winner Ferdi Kübler set the tone: he attacked maniacally 6 miles (10km) from the summit, crashed several times on the descent, before pulling out of the race at the stage's conclusion, never to race the Tour again. Twelve years later came Ventoux's darkest day: the British rider Tom Simpson, overheating in the high temperatures pulsing off the bare limestone, drugs in his system, falling behind the leaders, refusing to acknowledge the toll the mountain had taken on him, collapsed and died half a mile (1km) from the top.

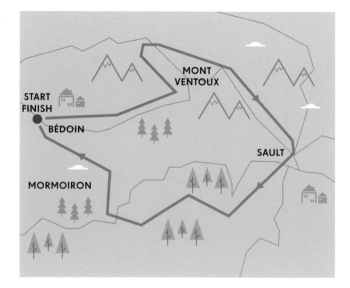

"Il faut rallentir un peu, monsieur..." I looked to my left, to see a fellow road cyclist, a Frenchman, offering me some friendly advice. Slow down? I was hanging on for dear life! Nothing can quite prepare you for the left turn at St Estève – the 13-mile (21km) climb of Ventoux officially begins at the eastern exit of the town of Bédoin but after three gently inclining miles (5km), it's here that the road rears up. And how.

The 6 miles (10km) from St Estève is a ramp that deviates little, the surrounding cedar trees and their scent enveloping you in an airless, green tunnel. There were few cars, thankfully, but also few other cyclists; I decided to try to get this over with as quickly as possible. Which is when Philippe offered his wise words. He was down from Grenoble, about my age and had ridden up Ventoux before – we chatted, trying to ignore the gradient. Philippe was there largely to support a friend who was running up Ventoux (we later passed the friend; he looked like hell; I felt better).

At the Chalet Reynard the road ascends beyond the tree line, and turns west through the unearthly white limestone landscape of the mountain's upper reaches. Here, the average 10% gradient

## "The road that snakes along the north of the canyon climbs to the day's second highlight, the Belvedere du Castellas"

eases off and the main challenge is wind; though we were fortunate, just the occasional sigh from the valley, as we ground on, past the Simpson memorial, decorated with club water bottles and other cycling trinkets, to the summit.

Then, more quickly than I imagined, there I was, clattering about beneath the observatory tower on my cleats, looking for a water refill, with Bédoin, a vertical 0.6 miles (1km) and 100 minutes beneath me. The Mediterranean lay in the distance; my legs were still working; I was happy, and in awe of the Tour riders who knock the climb off in half my time (at the time of writing, anti-doping campaigners have yet to demand data records of my power output).

I swapped email addresses with Philippe, and began the exhilarating descent to Sault on the eastern flank of the Ventoux massif. Sandwich time. Map check. And then on to the outrageously dramatic gorge created by the Nesque river.

The road that snakes along the north of the canyon climbs gently to the day's second highlight, the Belvedere du Castellas and its astonishing view of the high crumbling limestone edifice the Rocher du Cire opposite, falling several hundred metres to the narrow valley floor. All that remained was to enjoy spinning through the shady gorge-side tunnels on the descent to Villes sur Auzon, and through the vines of the Auzon valley to my friend's vineyard on the ridge above. Now, finally, I could gaze upon Ventoux squarely. I looked up. The mountain-top was shrouded in low cloud. I turned and wondered what the vineyard might offer me by way of compensation. **MH**

## MONT VENTOUX BY FOOT?

Around 1350, the Italian poet Petrarch wrote a letter reflecting on an apparently successful ascent (on foot) of Ventoux from Malaucène on 26 April 1336. He mentions the view of the Mediterranean and the Rhone, and his brother, who accompanied him. Academic debate since appears to vary between citing Petrarch's climb and his thoughts upon it as a key event in the development of the Renaissance mind and whether Petrarch made the whole thing up.

*Clockwise from left: riding through the gorge of the Nesque River; the memorial of cycle racer Tom Simpson on the slopes of Mt Ventoux; cafe stop in Bédoin. Previous page: the telecommunications mast atop Mt Ventoux, a backdrop to triumph*

## TOOLKIT

**Start/End** // Bédoin
**Getting there** // Avignon airport is the nearest.
**Distance** // Around 56 miles (90km)
**Bike hire** // La Route du Ventoux cycles (www.francebikerentals.com/fr; rentals from €45 per day)
**When to ride** // The summit is typically snowbound from December to April, so any other time is ideal, depending on your ability to tolerate the Provençal heat and crowds.
**What to read** // William Fotheringham's admired biography of Tom Simpson, *Put Me Back on My Bike*; Les Woodland's *Yellow Jersey Companion to the Tour de France*
**What to take** // Prepare as you would for a long, warm day's cycling but with a decent wind jacket – it can be howling and many degrees cooler at the summit of Ventoux.

*Opposite: the foreboding approach to
the Colle delle Finestre, Italy*

# MORE LIKE THIS
## GRAND TOUR CLIMBS

### ALTO DE L'ANGLIRU, SPAIN

This cloud-covered peak – remote,
foreboding – is lurking in the limestone
ranges west of the Picos de Europa
National Park in the Asturias region on
Spain's north coast. It's not long but it
is brutally steep, ascending 1266m. The
gradient is an average of 10.2% but it
ramps up to 23.5% near the top. The
Angliru first raised its ugly head in the 1999
Vuelta a Espana, Spain's grand tour. Riders
quickly learned that they would have to
lower their gearing if they wanted to pedal
and not walk to the summit. The fastest
ascent was 41 minutes and 55 seconds.
If you want to take on this monster, the
nearest big city is the capital of Asturias,
Oviedo.
**Start //** La Vega
**End //** Alto de l'Angliru summit
**Distance //** 7.7 miles (12.5km)

### ALPE D'HUEZ, FRANCE

Twenty-one, 20, 19, 18... counting down the
hairpin bends of Alpe d'Huez won't make
them any easier. The dead-end road up to
the summit's ski resort from Bourg d'Oisans
is wide but steep and zigzags relentlessly
up the hill. It has been the backdrop to
drama ever since its first inclusion in the
Tour de France in 1952: Fausto Coppi
sealed his bid for the *maillot jaune*
(yellow jersey) with the first victory here;
teammates (in name only) Greg LeMond
and Bernard Hinault finished neck-and-
neck in 1986; Marco Pantani scorched
up in a barely believable 37 minutes and
35 seconds in 1997; and in 2001 Lance
Armstrong eyeballed rival Jan Ullrich before
accelerating into the distance.
**Start //** Bourg d'Oisans
**End //** Alpe d'Huez summit
**Distance //** 8.5 miles (13.5km)

### COLLE DELLE FINESTRE, ITALY

It's probably not the most famous cycling
climb of the Giro d'Italia – that would
perhaps be the Passo di Mortirolo in
Lombardy. Nor the most photogenic – that
might be the Passo dello Stelvio. But what
it lacks in fame or beauty, the Colle delle
Finestre makes up for with an interesting
personality. It lies in the Cottian Alps in
Piedmont, northwest Italy. The final 5 miles
(8km) are on a gravel track, a feature that
cycle racing fans love, because it adds to
the challenge and uncertainty, and some
of the pros are less comfortable about,
especially with a gradient that hits 14%
in places, up 55 hairpins. As befits this
idiosyncratic star, it makes only infrequent
appearances in the Giro: 2005, 2011 and
2015. Make a day of the Col of Windows
by descending the paved road on the other
side, continuing onward to the climb of
Sestriere and then looping back to Susa:
22 vertiginous miles (35km). Epic? You bet.
**Start/End //** Susa
**Distance //** 11 miles (18km)

# BEATING THE BIRKEBEINERRITTET

*Attracting 17,000 racers, Norway's epic 57-mile (92km) Birkebeinerrittet is the biggest mountain-bike event on the planet, but you can ride the historic route any time.*

Ascending through Åstdalen, a forest-fringed valley, into the wild hills of Hedmark and Oppland, I glance over my shoulder and a rash of goosebumps rushes across my exposed skin – a reaction that has little to do with the sudden bite in the August air.

Stretching back as far as it's possible to see, there are bikes. So very many bikes, rolling through the pine trees and into the mountains like an invading army. It's the most extraordinary sight. A thrilling scene in which to be a bit-part player.

The Birkebeinerrittet is an annual mountain-bike marathon that charges along an historic course in eastern Norway – but that doesn't even begin to describe this race, which is spectacularly splattered in eccentricity.

Let's start with the numbers. Each year, upwards of 20,000 riders attend the weekend-long event, which offers a range of race distances. The Saturday shindig is the big one, with 17,000 riders taking on a 57-mile (92km) course that rolls along dirt roads and double track, from the streets of Rena, through the mountains to Lillehammer.

The field is so huge that riders begin in waves, each containing roughly 250 bikes, with a few minutes' space between each one. It starts at 7am with the fastest non-professional riders going first.

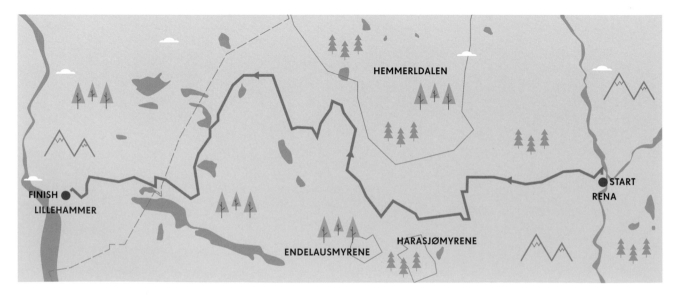

The elites are released last, at 3pm, so there's lots of exciting overtaking action along the course – good crowd-pleasing stuff for the thousands of spectators that line the scenic route, cheering riders on, cooking on barbecues, drinking beer and creating a carnival atmosphere.

Not only is the Birkebeinerrittet the world's largest off-road riding event, it's also the only cycling race I've ever come across that has a history stretching back over 800 years – predating the invention of anything resembling a bicycle by some six centuries.

Because – like its winter equivalent, the Birkebeinerrennet ski race – the event celebrates a pivotal moment in Scandinavian history. In the midst of the 1205–6 winter, when Norway was in the grip of a bitter century-long civil war between the Birkebeiners and the Baglers, an infant prince, Haakon Haakonsson, was smuggled through these mountains by two skiers who were protecting him from assassins. The skiers, Torstein Skevla and Skjervald Skrukka, were Birkebeiners, and Haakon would become Norway's most celebrated king (Haakon IV), ending the war, uniting the country and leading it into a golden age.

The epic journey undertaken by Skevla, Skrukka and the child prince is commemorated by a cross-country trail, Birkebeinerløype, which wends across the mountains and forms the route of the annual ski race (that also attracts 17,000-plus participants). Outside of winter, this well-marked 33½-mile (54km) trail can be hiked, but much of it is too marshy to be biked. Instead, the cycling

*"Thousands of spectators line the route, cooking on barbecues, drinking beer and creating a carnival atmosphere"*

track takes riders on a longer adventure, which criss-crosses the classic trail several times and joins it for certain sections.

The route is waymarked and can be ridden independently as soon as the snow melts. If you do it on race day, however, you must wear the weight of history on your back, because the number one race rule is this: all competitors, even the elites, have to carry an extra 3.5kg of bulk (over and above any food or drink they might consume during the race) to symbolically represent the weight of the baby prince.

Rows of weighing scales surround the starting line, and riders nervously queue to make sure they're carrying enough bulk, with some adding hefty stones to their backpacks to make up the difference. I'm warned that spot checks take place at the end, to ensure that people are still lugging their fair share of regal ballast.

From Rena, the route climbs relentlessly for the first 9 miles (15km), through Skramstadsœtra, before dropping dramatically along a short section of technical trail at Svartåfloen. This stint of steep, loose dirt decisively separates the crowd, with experienced mountain bikers sailing through, while others nervously dismount, and a few in-betweeners are unceremoniously bucked from their steeds.

Another section of tricky terrain greets riders on the other side of

## OFF-PISTE PEDALLING

An 'ultra' version of the Birken takes serious mountain bikers on a more challenging and technical 76-mile (122km) course, with lots more singletrack. The right to roam – known locally as *allemannsretten* – is enshrined in Norwegian law, applying to all non-motorised forms of transport, as well as walkers. You can explore wherever you like on your bike, so long as you don't cause damage to environment or property, making Norway a nirvana for pedal-powered adventurers.

*Clockwise from left: seafood sustenance; a traditional hut; crossing the wild Norwegian backcountry; racing the Birkebeinerrittet (and previous page)*

Djuposet – this one a stern ascent – but for the majority of its 57-mile (92km) length, the route winds along gravel roads and reasonably wide tracks, which allow riders to maintain a fast average speed.

During the race, many of the serious competitors are chasing a much-coveted *merket* – medals awarded to those who finish within a certain time (calculated by averaging the times of the first five riders across the line in a competitor's class, and then adding 25%). Those that nail it, I'm told, often mention *merket* results in their professional CVs.

For most, though, it's simply about taking part in a tradition and the experience of riding through Norway's beautiful backcountry – a wonderfully wild place where wolves and even the occasional bear still roam, and where mountains and pine forests are punctuated by little hamlets, full of huts with hats of grass and flowers.

After starting at 260m and following an undulating but mostly rising route, the trail tops out just before Storåsen, 42 miles (68km) into the course. From this 860m vantage point the dramatic Jotunheimen range looms on the horizon. These moody mountains are home, according to local folklore, to trolls and giants – and not the Disneyfied ones from Frozen either – the tear-you-limb-from-limb variety that populate Norwegian mythology.

But for bikers, the beasting is nearly over by this stage. From the hilltop resort town of Sjusjøen it's a thrilling downhill dash along forest tracks to the end, with one final steep and sketchy descent delivering riders to the doors of Lillehammer's Håkon Hall, where the judgemental weighing scales await. **PK**

## TOOLKIT

**Start //** Rena
**End //** Lillehammer
**Distance //** 57 miles (92km)
**Getting there //** From Oslo's Gardermoen Airport, trains regularly service Lillehammer, a journey of just under two hours. Bus services link Lillehammer and Rena, with extra buses put on to transport bikes and riders for the race.
**When to ride //** The Birkebeinerrittet takes place in August.
**What to take //** The route/race is rideable in one day for anyone with reasonable fitness on a hardtail or dual-suspension mountain bike. The trail passes through a remote region – carry a mobile phone (coverage is good), wear a helmet, take spare tubes and tools, and pack sufficient food and water.
**More info //** Visit www.birkebeiner.no.

*Opposite: riders in the Dolomiti*
*Superbike race, Italy*

# MORE LIKE THIS
## MOUNTAIN BIKE RACES

### THE MOHICAN MTB 100, USA

This annual ultra-endurance 100-mile (160km) mountain-bike race roars through the Mohican State Park in North Central Ohio in early June. The highly technical course is almost entirely (90%) on dirt and the route sends riders around a monster one-lap circuit, passing through four counties and featuring over 11,000ft (3350m) of climbing on singletrack, doubletrack and unsealed roads. The trail wends through trees virtually all the way, and the race forms part of the US National Ultra Endurance Series (www.nuemtb.com), which also includes such epic challenges as the Lumberjack 100 in Michigan (June), the Breckenridge 100 in Colorado (July), the Wilderness 101 in Pennsylvania (late July) and the Shenandoah 100 in central Western Virginia (September).

**Start //** Loudonville
**End //** Mohican Adventures, one mile (1.6km) from downtown
**Distance //** 100 miles (160km). A 62-mile (100km) option is also available.
**When to ride //** June
**More info //** www.mohican.net

### DOLOMITI SUPERBIKE, ITALY

With over 20 years of history behind it, this tough off-road circuit through the Dolomite Mountains in northern Italy is a super scenic challenge for rough riders. Setting off from Villabassa in South Tyrol, the epic 74-mile (119km) course rolls through Prato Piazza, Carbonin, Dobbiaco, San Candido, Monte Baranci, Sesto, Croda Rossa, Prato Drava and Versciaco before finishing back at Villabassa. Like the Birkebeinerrittet, around 80% of the race route travels along gravel roads, so the pace is fast, and there are sections of singletrack and sealed surface in between. But with this race, riders have to contend with 3822m of climbing, and the course tops out at 2014m. If all that sounds too much, there is a half-distance option of 36½ miles (59km).

**Start/End //** Villabassa
**Distance //** 74 miles (119km)
**When to ride //** July

### OTWAY ODYSSEY, AUSTRALIA

Over the past decade the Odyssey has established a reputation as Australia's premier mountain-bike marathon, despite changing its format from a point-to-point race to a loop-based event. The circuit in question passes through the sensational singletrack of Forrest, a trail-rich section of rainforest in the Otway National Park, close to the Great Ocean Rd in the state of Victoria. The 62-mile (100km) race – which is all off-road and is as rewarding as it is demanding – attracts the region's best riders, including Olympians. There are also 31-mile (50km), 18½-mile (30km) and 6-mile (10km) route options, and the whole thing culminates with a big bike-based festival.

**Start/End //** Forrest
**Distance //** The main race is 62-mile (100km).
**When to ride //** February
**More info //** www.rapidascent.com.au/GiantOdyssey (see also www.rideforrest.com)

# WEST CORK'S WILD COAST

*Cycle above cliffs, around peninsulas and beside beaches along West Cork's coastline for big Atlantic seascapes, a maze of country lanes, and whale watching.*

When I'm back home in County Cork and feel like a break I'll often stuff a sleeping bag, a few harmonicas, some rain gear and a pair of sunglasses into my bike's venerable panniers and pedal west for a week or so. I'm prepared for all weathers, ready to join in pub music sessions and able to sleep out if that's the way things go. Navigation? All I have to do is keep the sea on my left. It's an easy approach to cycle touring.

Three times, so far, I've ridden the 186 miles (300km) between Clonakilty and the tip of the Beara Peninsula to the west, following in the tyre tracks of Irish travel writer Peter Somerville-Large. In the

snows, rains and wind of early 1970 Somerville-Large set off on a 3-speed bike, carrying a canvas tent and an umbrella, to research his book The Coast of West Cork. His writing ranges across history, conjuring up cattle raids, sword-'n'-shield battles, pirate fleets and eccentric landowners, as he pedals between ancient ring forts, medieval castles, ruined manor houses and village ports. Cycling nearly half a century ago he describes a rural Ireland still focused on small farms and close-tied villages. Food then was, by his account, far from inspiring.

Cyclists in West Cork today – far better fed – can still enjoy the meandering spirit of Somerville-Large's inspiring trip, not least

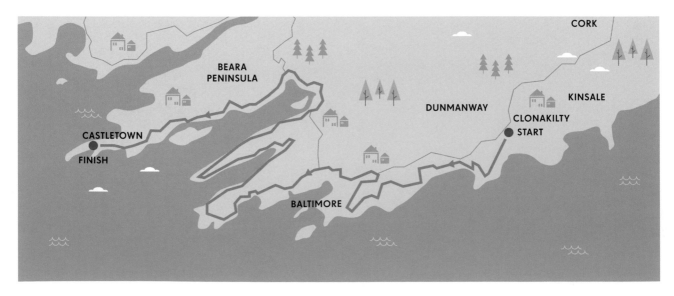

because the small roads of coastal West Cork now form the most southerly section of the Wild Atlantic Way, a 1533-mile (2500km) 'signed route' designed to lure travellers off busy arterial roads and into the quiet veins and capillaries – the country roads and *boreens* (lanes) – that network the 'Next Stop America' seaboard of Ireland's west.

West Cork attracts and rewards cyclists of all stamps. A peloton of hard-cranking English friends raced the route from west to east in miserable summer weather that drove them into one pub after another for shelter; they loved it. At different times I've lent an old single-speed bike, and the Somerville-Large book, to a guitar-toting Frenchman, to an Israeli student and to a German woman. Each disappeared for a week or two and each had totally different adventures; one sitting in with musicians and cycling from gig to gig, another camping out on remote beaches cooking self-caught fish, and the third island-hopping across Roaringwater Bay before ending up in a Buddhist retreat centre on the Beara.

It's all about the quality of the distractions rather than the mileage, I reckon. Will Clonakilty's street music, or guitar- or cycling festivals change your plans? Will you be tempted by country-market day in any one of the towns along the coast, with stalls of local cheeses, home-baked breads, organic vegetables and cakes? Or a day heading out to sea on a whale-watching boat? An evening sea-kayak trip while phosphorescence lights up the waters? A pub lock-in, as accordions, fiddles, pipes and banjos pepper the air with machine-gun-fast riffs? Things happen when moving at pedal-speed in West Cork.

On the most recent of my cycle 'de-tours' – so-called because of their haphazard nature – to the Beara I started by riding through a chill autumn night to watch the dawn sun rise over the eastern seas and light up the miniature Stonehenge of Drombeg Stone Circle. Then I freewheeled – mostly – down to Union Hall for a full-Irish breakfast in The Coffee Shop. Bacon, sausages, eggs, toast, and famed Clonakilty black pudding, as well as apple

## WHALE WATCHING

Harbour porpoise, common and bottlenose dolphin are present year round in West Cork, blue whale and orca are rare sightings, but it's the minke, fin and humpback whales that are the real attraction. Though they can sometimes be seen from high cliffs with binoculars, for the full marine Jurassic Park experience take a specialist boat trip (www. whalewatchwestcork. com) to get out among the whales as they lunge, dive and breach spectacularly while feeding.

*Clockwise from top: Bantry Bay and the town; the Sheep's Head lighthouse; Guinness for strength, in Clonakilty. Previous page: Uragh stone circle near Glengarriff, one of many here; the coastline of West Cork*

tart: the heavy fuel I needed for a day of grinding up hill after hill.

As always, I was making route choices as I rode. If the early morning sun hadn't given way to drizzle, I'd have cycled on to Baltimore to take the ferry across to Cape Clear Island, where Irish is spoken, traditional jigs and reels (Irish folk dancing) played, and I could have pedalled out to the seaward cliffs, where I'd been told there was a good chance of seeing a pod of minke whales feeding close inshore. But with visibility poor I headed around Roaringwater Bay, across the Mizen and onto Sheep's Head instead. By evening I was sitting in a friend's clifftop cabin sipping tea and watching the sunset.

For cyclists, the Sheep's Head is like the whole coast of West Cork, or even the Wild Atlantic Way in miniature. A coast-teasing 50-mile (80km) circuit following small roads, many so little used they have a strip of grass down their centre. Big cliffs and, in storms, even bigger seas. Hidden stone circles, smaller than Drombeg. Pubs where conversation easily sparks into song. The 'needle-to-an-anchor' old-style shop, post office, and sometime wine bar that is J F O'Mahony's in Kilcrohane. Few cars. Perfect riding country.

The next morning from the Sheep's Head I could see the length of the Beara Peninsula far across Bantry Bay. On a big-engined rigid-inflatable boat you'd be across, tip to tip, in 20 minutes, but by bike there's another couple of relaxed days to go, and more distractions. Bantry, with its Friday market. Cafes in touristy Glengarriff. The Caha and Slieve Mishkish mountains inland, Hungry Hill wreathed in cool mist. A pint of Beamish in MacCarthy's in Castletown Berehaven, enjoyed among fishing crews from half a dozen nations' trawlers. Then the long haul to the peninsula's end, cranking out mile after mile, until finally there was only air and water ahead and I'd run out of land. All I had to do now was turn around and head back home. This time keeping the sea on my right. **JW**

*"I'd been told there was a good chance of seeing a pod of minke whales feeding close inshore"*

## TOOLKIT

**Start** // Clonakilty
**End** // The tip of Beara Peninsula
**Distance** // 186 miles (300km)
**Getting there** // Fly to Cork Airport, cycle 12 miles (20km) to Kinsale and you're on the Wild Atlantic Way. Irish buses will usually take one, maximum two, bikes if there's room in hold.
**Bike hire** // Cycle Scene (www.cyclescene.ie/rentals) in Cork City can deliver/pick up; Bike N Beara (www.bikenbeara.ie/hire.php) also do baggage transfer and bike drop/pick up. See also www.ireland.com/what-is-available/cycling/bike-rental/destinations/republic-of-ireland/cork/all.
**When to ride** // Early autumn offers good weather, enough evening light, open restaurants, cafes and accommodation, and less tourist traffic.
**Where to stay** // For hotels, B&Bs and campsites, see www.ireland.com; for independent hostels, see www.independenthostelsireland.com/Munster/munster.htm.
**Where to eat** // See www.westcorkmarkets.com for details on country markets.

*Opposite: the Gap of Dunloe
on the Ring of Kerry*

# MORE LIKE THIS
## IRISH RIDES

### DUBLIN & THE BARROW

This classic three-day journey traces the Grand Canal Way from central Dublin, wending west along the historic waterway to Robertstown in County Kildare. Hang a left here and cycle south along the towpath of the Barrow Navigation, which skirts Ireland's second longest river. Hug the banks of the much-storied and beautiful Barrow as it meanders betwixt several counties, past castles, around woodlands and through ancient towns, including Monasterevin, Athy, Carlow, Borris and Graiguenamanagh, until you reach the last lock in St Mullins, where the river becomes tidal and the towpath evaporates. As you'd expect from a canal-based route, there's no climbing, but there are muddy sections, so a hybrid or mountain bike is recommended.
**Start //** Dublin
**End //** St Mullins, County Carlow
**Distance //** 93 miles (150km)

### CONNACHT CLASSIC

There's been a huge surge in the popularity of cycling in Ireland over the last decade, but nowhere has embraced the bike revolution more than the beautiful and charismatic County Mayo town of Westport, though. Myriad routes meander along the coast and into the Connacht countryside from here, including the popular Greenway, but the loop out towards Connemara and delightful Doolough and back is arguably the perfect cycling circuit, taking in the super scenic Sheeffry Pass, Tawnyard Lough and 585m of climbing en route. The outride is mostly along quiet country lanes, past several tempting pubs, while the return route sidles past Croagh Patrick – a stunning peak where St Pat apparently sat for 40 days of fasting in the 5th century. It's a rapid finish along an R-road and then a cycle path back into the embrace of Westport, where Matt Malloy's legendary bar awaits.
**Start/End //** Westport, County Mayo
**Distance //** 42 miles (67.5km)

### RING OF KERRY

A back-route version of the famous Ring of Kerry starts from Killarney, heading out along the quiet country lanes and ultra-remote roads of the Iveragh Peninsula to the wild west coast. The outbound route rolls past Lough Acoose and Glencar, traverses the Ballaghasheen Pass and hits the Atlantic at Waterville, opposite the Gaeltacht (Irish-speaking) village of Ballinskelligs. If you have the legs for it, return via Castlecove and Sneem, pedalling alongside delightful Derrynane Beach, across the Coomakista Pass (a Ring of Kerry highlight) and through the Gap of Dunloe, a gorgeous glaciated valley, on your way back to the many welcoming pubs of Killarney. Examples of ogham stones (standing pillars engraved with an early Irish alphabet), lay close to this route, as does the Staigue Stone Fort. With over 1500m of climbing, and scenery that refuses to be rushed, this ride is best spread across two or three days.
**Start/End //** Killarney, County Kerry
**Distance //** 95 miles (153km)

# A CORSICAN CHALLENGE

*A sublime cycling journey through the heart of Corsica, the Mediterranean's
'L'île de Beauté', riding part of the route of the 100th Tour de France.*

Corsica is a mighty lump of rock, a chain of mountains protruding proudly from the Mediterranean Sea. With 21 peaks above 2000m and over 150 cols, it is something of a nirvana for cyclists. There are glorious roads winding down through remote hamlets to turquoise coves; medieval villages untouched by the 20th century; chestnut groves, pine forests and canyons; challenging climbs and sweeping descents on well-paved tarmac with few cars; excellent local wines and sensational seafood as well as limestone hills and golden, sandy beaches, all set within a staggeringly lovely coastline. It is hard to think of another place that packs so much into such a small, beautiful space.

My four-day tour started and finished in Bastia, the second largest town, and took in the northern half of the island, known as 'Haute-Corse'. I concentrated on the north and west coastlines, which are more jagged, wild and wondrous.

The ride started humbly enough – on a flat cycle path between

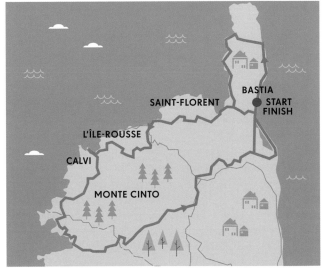

a stagnant lagoon and the sea, with the airport as a backdrop. There was no sense of the grandeur and the glory that awaited me. There was not even a hint of the beauty of Corsica – a level of pulchritude that I have seldom experienced in just a few days on a bicycle. Nor, in the cool air of the young day, was there any suggestion of the cauldron of heat I would encounter in the canyons ahead.

With memories of the airport fading, I pedalled through Bastia and north along the maquis-covered eastern coast of Cap Corse, past a series of tiny ports. Then I headed inland, up and over the spine of mountains that bisects the peninsula, past Cagnano and down to Pino. Riding south down the western side of the cape, you are never far from the sea. There are some breathtaking sections of winding road along the serrated coastline, which is dotted with tiny fishing villages and old Genoese lookout towers.

After a cold glass of Pietra, the local beer, in the Café de la Tour in Nonza, there was a sting in the tail – a 4-mile (6km) climb followed by a fast descent – to return to Bastia.

On the second day, I rode over the granite backbone of the island from east to west, via the highest tarmac col – Col de Vergio (1478m). I don't set off to ride 93 miles (150km) and climb 2750m in a day lightly. When the cycling is this good, though, when it all comes together in a day of spellbinding pedalling, I can't help but feel that every time I've ever been on a bike has been

*"Breathtaking sections of road wind along the coastline, which is dotted with fishing villages and old Genoese lookout towers"*

preparation for this hour, and that all my roads have lead me here.

'Allez, garçon!' two old men shout, over their early morning brandies in the first village. As I started to climb towards the town of Borgo, my legs warmed, the traffic diminished and the roads narrowed.

At the first col, I passed through a notch in the rock and turned my back on the shining sea, heading inland on a beautiful balcony road that contoured the mountains. The villages – Vignale, Scolca, Campitello, Lento, Canavaggia – rolled off the tongue like an Italian football team sheet, reminding me of the island's history – it was part of the Republic of Genoa long before it was purchased by France in 1768. These sleepy villages are dominated by imposing granite churches, which, from a distance, seem to hang off the mountainsides.

After an ice cream and an espresso in Ponte Leccia, I headed south-west for the long climb. The first section is through a gorge carved into granite cliffs beside the dashing waters of the Golo River. It was like a furnace here, in the doggo hours of early afternoon.

## CALANCHES DETOUR

There is a highly recommended 15.5-mile (25km) extension to this route: ride south from Porto, up to Piana via the famous 'Calanches' – a series of weathered, pink granite cliffs and inlets that are now part of a Unesco Nature Reserve. The views, through the rocks and across the Gulf of Porto, are remarkable. The colours in the rocks are richest in the evenings, but it's a stunning ride at any time of day.

*Left to right; alongside the Golo River; Corsican specialities; Calvi's old town. Previous page: swooping past Bastia at sunset*

After a picnic and forty winks beside the lake in Calacuccia, I climbed again, now in the cooler air and the shade of a Laricio pine forest. By the time I reached the top of the col, set beneath the great 2500m-plus peaks of Monte Cinto and Paglia Orba, the heat of the day was finally backing off.

Time stood still on the flowing, serpentine, 18.5 mile- (30km) descent through three climatic zones. It was stunning. The whole way down to Porto, there were glimpses of the Mediterranean and the path of gold on the water, leading west over the sea to the setting sun.

The next day, following the coast road north to Calvi, was easier but no less glorious. In fact, this road ranks among the most beautiful coastal roads in Europe. From Porto, I climbed up to Col de la Croix, for the first in a series of staggering views. Then it was down and up again to the Col de Palmarella, before the descent into the Fango Valley, another lovely area of undisturbed and arresting, natural scenery. The final climb of the day, up to Col de Marsolino, revealed my destination: the fashionable port of Calvi with its lofty citadel perched above the sea.

On the final day, I followed the north coast along the rocky maquis hinterland and then up into the hills again, before a long, gentle descent to the former fishing village of Saint-Florent. After a swim in the sea and lunch, I attacked the tough punch up to the ridge above Bastia, for one final eyeful of the shimmering sea. **RP**

## TOOLKIT

**Start/End** // Bastia
**Distance** // 281 miles (452km)
**Getting there** // There's an airport and ferry port in Basta. Flights to European destinations are more frequent from June to late September. Day and overnight ferries run from several destinations in mainland France and Italy year-round.
**Bike hire** // In Bastia, try Europe Active (http://cycling.europe-active.co.uk).
**When to ride** // April, May, June, September and October: in July and August it's hot and peak holiday season.
**What to eat** // If you're pedalling round Cap Corse and feel like lunch, try L'Auberge du Chat qui Pêche in Canari (www.aubergeduchatquipeche.com).
**What to drink** // Local wines (especially from the Patrimonio area).
**More info** // See www.corsicacyclist.com.

*Opposite: sun-kissed
Matera in southern Italy*

# MORE LIKE THIS
# IDYLLIC EUROPEAN RIDES

### SARDINIA

Another Mediterranean paradise for cyclists: a larger, more arid, but equally captivating version of Corsica, Sardinia, too, offers quiet roads, excellent food, mountains and endless beaches. Avoid the main roads, but you can ride almost anywhere else. Try an east coast route from Olbia, which combines stretches of lovely coastal riding with an excursion up into Barbagia, the remote, mountainous region of central Sardinia. Here, you pass medieval towns, great lakes, rugged limestone peaks, chestnut woods, olive groves and vineyards (including Oliena, the village where Sardinia's prized Cannonau red wine is produced). The ride starts gently, beside the sea. There are then two days in the mountains, before returning to the coast for the final stretch to reach the dynamic port of Cagliari.
**Start // Olbia**
**End // Cagliari**
**Distance // 279.5 miles (450 km)**

### SOUTHERN ITALY

From the Adriatic to the Tyrrhenian, from shining sea to shining sea, and from peasant villages to glamorous beaches, this ride savours some of the least visited and loveliest parts of Italy. Starting with a wheel in the water in Polignano a Mare, near Bari, you'll pedal past hilltop villages, troglodyte cave-towns, UNESCO World Heritage sites and Greek ruins, to reach the lovely Amalfi Coast. The terrain is hilly rather than mountainous, rising over the foot of the Apennines and crossing the mythical mountains of the Cilento National Park. There are a few harder climbs towards the end of the route. The route generally follows lightly trafficked country roads through such intriguing towns as Matera, Castelmezzano and Palinuro, though traffic picks up around the major port of Salerno. Try and ride the Amalfi Coast stretch early in the morning, as it can get busy.
**Start // Bari**
**End // Amalfi**
**Distance // 301 miles (485km)**

### CROATIA & BOSNIA

With 1118 miles (1800km) of coastline and over 1000 islands, Croatia is perfect for anyone who loves to ride beside the sea. Perhaps the best way to soak it up is a two-wheel, island-hopping journey using the local ferry service. From the ancient, buzzing city of Split, you can head south to the wondrously beautiful port of Dubrovnik via the islands of Brač, Jelsa, Korčula and Hvar. There are majestic Roman monuments, Venetian forts, cathedrals, fishing villages, tiny medieval towns, pebble coves and vineyards to explore along the way. The local cuisine, based on olive oil, fresh fish and vegetables, is excellent too. If you're feeling bold, and fit, you can follow an inland route back to Split via the historic town of Mostar and the rich, green hills of Bosnia and Herzegovina.
**Start/end // Split**
**Distance // approx. 248.5 miles (400km)**

# CIRCLING LAKE CONSTANCE

*One bike, two wheels, three countries... This ride bundles Europe's best into one neat package, with history, lakeside loveliness and Alpine views on every corner.*

Morning sunlight bounces off Lake Constance as I pedal along Friedrichshafen's promenade, the mist slowly rising to reveal tantalising glimpses of the Swiss Alps across the water. It's a crisp late-autumn day to kick off a bike tour of Central Europe's third largest lake, which dips into Germany, Austria and Switzerland as it hugs its shores.

As I trundle along the waterfront, I hear snatched conversations in Italian, German, French – a reminder that the lake sits bang in the heart of Europe. And because of its tri-country location, the lake feels like Europe in a nutshell, with Roman forts, Benedictine abbeys and medieval castle-topped villages ripe for a kids' bedtime story, forested mountains tapering down to vineyards and wetlands teeming with birdlife.

You don't need to be a Lycra-clad pro to give it a shot either: bar the odd minor incline, the 168 mile (270km) Bodensee Cycle Path circumnavigating the lake is mostly flat and well-signposted, making it doable for cyclists of every fitness level and age. Then, of course, there is the sheer novelty of it: where else can you freewheel through three countries, enjoy Alpine views without the uphill slog and tick-off multiple Unesco World Heritage sites in the space of a week?

Should time be an issue, ferries make hopping across the lake a breeze, so the trail highlights can be covered in a long weekend. I've allowed myself four days for a loop beginning and ending in Friedrichshafen, a place that has been synonymous with the Zeppelin ever since Count Ferdinand von Zeppelin launched the first of these humungous airship beasts in 1900. They are still used for sightseeing spins to this day – and one floats above me, casting long shadows across the lake, as I pedal out of town.

I ease into my ride as I roll southeast on a trail that weaves

among quiet meadows, skirts the yacht-clogged harbour of Langenargen and passes through fruit orchards and vineyards. Like many of the dinky hamlets on the lakefront, Wasserburg sports an onion-domed church, a castle and a handful of gabled houses. It's a restful place for a breather before continuing to one of Lake Constance's most enticing towns: Lindau.

As medieval towns go, Lindau fits the fairy-tale bill nicely. A bone-shaking ride through its cobbled lanes takes me past gabled houses in a fresco painter's palette of pastels and a town hall ablaze with fancy murals, through a square filled with market bustle and down to the prettiest of harbours. Here

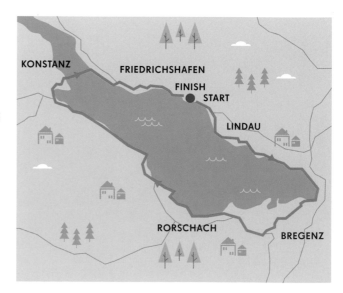

camera-toting day-trippers pose for selfies in front of its two lighthouses and a Bavarian lion sculpture, endeavouring to squeeze the Alps on the horizon into the frame. It's hard to do its beauty justice with a smartphone.

Lindau is just a short pedal from the Austrian border and, on the approach, hills rise steep and wooded above me – the first flush of autumn apparent in their colour-changing foliage. Within no time I reach Bregenz, an affluent town with a couple of striking galleries and a world-famous summer opera festival. I'm particularly drawn, however, to the Pfänder, the 1064m peak that rears above it. I haul my bike into the cable car to the summit. From the top, Bregenz seems toytown tiny and the lake spreads out before me. The Alps feel so much closer here, with views of the already-snow-capped Arlberg and Silvretta ranges, and walking trails leading through a park that's home to ibex, deer and whistling marmots.

After picking up speed downhill, I find the bike path seems remarkably gentle as it threads west of Bregenz, passing pockets of sun-dappled woodland and lakefront beaches now devoid of sunbathers. I pause on the banks of the Bregenzerach, a river that flows swift and glacially cold, pummelling moraine and boulders as it makes its way down from the lush spruce forests of Vorarlberg.

Close by is the Rhine Delta nature reserve, one of the region's most important wetlands for migratory birds. A grey heron darts across the water as my bike casts late-afternoon shadows across the reed-fringed trail. The route heads on into Switzerland from here, where I spend a day happily riding

## EXTEND YOUR TRIP

Tag on an extra couple of days to tour the northeast shore of the lake in Germany – see the exuberant rococo pilgrimage church of Birnau and the prehistoric pile dwellings in Unteruhldingen, which form part of an extensive Unesco World Heritage site. Another worthwhile detour west of Konstanz and on Swiss shores is Stein am Rhein, with its showpiece medieval Rathausplatz, where houses embellished with frescoes and oriel windows vie for attention.

*Clockwise from top: the view from Mt Pfänder; Montfort castle on Lake Constance; Lindau in Germany and the stone lion guarding its harbour. Previous page: Lindau*

*"The route heads into Switzerland where I spend a day happily riding through late-medieval towns, orchards and fields"*

through late-medieval towns, fruit orchards, and fields where wheat ripens come summer.

Hopping back over the Swiss–German border, Konstanz is next on my radar. Once the seat of the 15th-century Council of Constance, the town has kept a tight grip on its history while simultaneously clicking into the groove of a laid-back university town. Presided over by a 1000-year-old cathedral, its alley-woven centre was mercifully spared from the WWII bombings that obliterated other German cities, and its plane-tree-lined promenade is a pleasure to stroll and cycle at leisure.

If I had time to linger, I could easily tag on a detour to the Mediterranean-style botanical gardens of Mainau nearby, or the Unesco-listed island of Reichenau, home to a former Benedictine Abbey founded in 724 by a missionary named Pirmin. But I have a ferry to Meersburg to catch.

I can think of nowhere more fitting to spend the last evening of my tour than this astonishingly lovely lakefront town, crowned by a twinset of castles – one medieval, one baroque – and backed by vine-striped hills. Snug in the interior of a low-beamed wine tavern, I raise a toast of the local Pinot Noir to what has been a terrific few days on the trail. Outside, the water laps against the shore, as the fading light paints the sky pink. It is back to Friedrichshafen tomorrow and I know I will miss this view of the lake. **KC**

### TOOLKIT

**Start/End //** Friedrichshafen
**Distance //** 168 miles (270km) for the Bodensee Cycle Path, but the route can easily be broken down into shorter chunks.
**Getting there //** Regular ferries operate between major towns on the lake, including Konstanz, Friedrichshafen, Meersburg and Bregenz. The main operators are BSB (www.bsb.de) and Vorarlberg Lines (www.vorarlberg-lines.at). The nearest airport is Friedrichshafen, served by airlines including British Airways, Lufthansa and easyJet.
**Bike hire //** Bikes can be hired in towns locally for between €10 and €20 per day.
**When to ride //** Come in spring or autumn for seasonal colour and fewer crowds. The route gets busy in summer and accommodation can be sparse.
**More info //** www.bodensee-radweg.com

*Opposite: riding in Lavaux,*
*Switzerland, near Lake Geneva*

# MORE LIKE THIS
## LAKE RIDES

### LAKE GENEVA, SWITZERLAND

With the French Alps on the horizon, vineyards staggering down to glittering shores and countless petite villages, a spin of Lake Geneva bundles some of Europe's most sensational scenery into one neat package. Largely flat and suitable for most levels – families included – the newly marked, 124-mile (200km) Tour du Léman follows Cycle Route 46. Bidding Geneva au revoir, it weaves largely along country tracks, with views of the lake opening up as you pedal past beaches and hamlets to the Olympic city of Lausanne. From here it gets incredibly scenic, dipping into the Unesco World Heritage vineyards of the Lavaux, before descending to skirt the lake and take in Vevey, Montreux and the turreted romance of medieval Château de Chillon. The route then swings clockwise back to Geneva, via the Rhone delta and small market towns straddling the French-Swiss border.

**Start/End //** Geneva
**Distance //** 124 miles (200km)
**More info //** www.tour-du-leman.ch

### LAKE ANNECY, FRANCE

Even in a land blessed with sublime lake and Alpine scenery, the French have to admit this lake is special – shimmering an extraordinary shade of turquoise (from the minerals in the meltwater that flow into it) and rimmed by oft-snow-capped peaks. A leisurely day's pedal makes a loop of the lake – its western shore has a dedicated bike route, while minor, sometimes busy, roads follow its eastern shore. It's rare to get big Alp views like this without the uphill slog, but if you're hankering after more of a challenge, take a climb up to 1660m Crêt de Châtillon. Otherwise, you'll be passing picture-book pretty harbour towns, sleepy villages and beaches where locals come to swim, row and kayak, such as Sévrier, Talloires, castle-crowned Menthon-Saint-Bernard and Veyrier-du-Lac.

**Start/End //** Annecy
**Distance //** 29 miles (46.5km)
**More info //** en.lac-annecy.com

### LAKE COMO, ITALY

Freewheeling along the shores of Lago di Como on this 99-mile (159km) route is a little slice of Italian heaven. Comprising scenic paths and roads reaching from flat to more demanding, this is a moderate to challenging ride, best avoided on summer weekends when the streets are rammed with traffic. What's the draw? Mountains that rise sheer and wooded above campanile-dotted villages in a fresco painter's palette of colours, lakefront promenades, beaches, gutsy Lombard food – in short, a pinch of everything that makes Italia bella. Go clockwise from Como to stick closest to the lakeshore and you'll pass postcard-worthy Cernobbio, Tremezzo with its waterfront villa and botanical gardens, and Menaggio. On the eastern shore, you'll pass through the tranquil Pian di Spagna Nature Reserve, before dipping into such enchanting villages as Varenna on the return stretch to Como.

**Start/End //** Como
**Distance //** 99 miles (159km)
**More info //** www.lakecomo.it

# SIERRA NEVADA TRAVERSE

*A tour of Andalucía's mighty Sierra Nevada mountains and Las Alpujarras, a quiet and beautiful part of southern Spain, ending in the culturally dynamic Granada.*

From the top of Pico de Veleta – at 3,393m, the second highest peak in mainland Spain – the view was astounding. I could see the entire Sierra Nevada range of mountains rolling out to the south and the east in a series of cappuccino brown peaks. Beyond that were the narrow, green, winding valleys of Las Alpujarras. In the distance, the silvery Mediterranean Sea was illuminated by afternoon sunshine. It was a view to die for – and I felt like I had nearly died for it.

The ascent of Pico de Veleta has to be one of the greatest European cycling challenges. It is an extraordinary climb by any measure: the bare statistics are staggering. I had cycled uphill for 31 miles (50km) from the centre of Granada, clocking over 2700m of vertical ascent. The major part of the ride is on a good paved road, which serves the ski resort in winter; the last half-mile (1km) or so is on gravel; the final 100m is on foot, over rocks.

Climbing to the top of Pico de Veleta was the culmination of a four-day tour of the Sierra Nevada, Spain's highest range of mountains, and Las Alpujarras, the foothills that roll south from the high peaks towards the sea. It is an enchanting, often overlooked part of Spain. Decent roads, plenty of sunshine and minimal traffic (at least until you approach Granada) make it a wonderful place to ride a bicycle.

The whole area remains profoundly rural – a region of whitewashed villages, arid highlands, terraced hillsides, wooded valleys, almond trees and olive groves. The Berbers from North Africa occupied Las Alpujarras for several centuries, before they were expelled with the Moors from Granada in the 15th and 16th centuries. Remarkably, half a millennium later, their legacy remains – in the labyrinthine villages, the flat-roofed houses and the irrigation systems that are still in use today: taking snowmelt water off the mountains to grow vines, oranges, lemons and pomegranates. The pace of life here is slow, almost otherworldly: for the first two days, I wondered where everyone was. Eventually, I stopped caring.

My ride started in the Southern Sierras, known as the Sierra de la Contraviesa. It is a long ride up from the shores of the Mediterranean: I cheated, and got a lift halfway, to the village of Albondón. After a coffee and a sandwich in a sleepy cafe, I set off along even sleepier roads, winding through vineyards, down to the small town of Ugíjar. After the scalding, white heat of midday, it was a delight to climb up to the village of Laujar de Andarax in the soft, golden light of early evening. In the small square, locals were busy constructing a stage and bars for the annual fiesta.

Because the coast of Spain has been such a magnet for tourists in the last half century, areas like Las Alpujarras have been slow to develop. The region only really began to emerge from the Middle Ages with the demise of the Franco regime and the enactment of a democratic constitution in the 1970s. As a consequence, places to stay are still few and far between and I had to put in a long ride to get over the Sierra Nevada range twice the next day, to reach a delightful hotel, La Alquería de Morayma, near the town of Cádiar.

The road gently rose and fell to the pretty village of Ohanes, before climbing through arid countryside and, higher up, holm

## ALHAMBRA ARCHITECTURE

The Alhambra was rebuilt and added to by successive Moorish rulers of Granada from the 11th to the 15th centuries, as it grew from a simple fort to the grand citadel of the Nasrid sultans, rulers of the last Muslim kingdom in Spain. The complex of stately and military buildings set in beautiful gardens represents the glorious climax of Moorish art and culture in Europe. Allow several hours for a visit and book tickets in advance.

*Clockwise from top: riding in Andalucía; the Albaicín district of Granada; the whitewashed town of Laujar de Andarax in the Alpujarras, where hams cure beside the road. Previous page: the Alhambra overlooking Granada, Andalucía*

oak forests, to reach the first col of the day, Puerto de Santillana (1337m). It was deserted and the descent to the town of Abla was fast, open and memorable.

The main climb of the day, up and over Puerto de la Ragua – 10.5 miles (17km) with 920m of ascent – is a Category 1 climb, which has featured in the Vuelta, Spain's great pro-cycling stage race. The climb starts just outside the picturesque village of La Calahorra. The first few miles wind gently through a sweet-smelling pine forest. At each bend, there are panoramic views down to the 16th century Renaissance Castillo de La Calahorra, one of Andalucía's emblematic fortresses, with its huge, squat turrets. Beyond, the great reddish-brown plain of Marquesado stretches away to the north.

At the top of the col, there is a picnic area and a spring-fed fountain. After a snooze in the shade of the trees and a head bath in the water trough, I sped down on a well-tarmacked road, easing through the bends, savouring the views south over Las Alpujarras. The final part of the day was up and down a beautiful winding road through the villages of Valor, Yegen and Mecina Bombaron to reach Cádiar, as the sun began to sink.

The following day, the sky was a luxurious cobalt blue again. Before the sun rose over the high peaks, I pedalled down through the Guadalfeo valley. After the wild country at the eastern end of the Sierra Nevada, the towns of Órgiva and Lanjarón felt cosmopolitan. The heat and the traffic intensified as I snaked through canyons and over rivers to reach the Puerto del Suspiro del Moro, the 'Pass of the Sigh of the Moor'. From there, it was a gentle run downhill into Granada; to the mighty palace-fortress, the Alhambra, one of the most intriguing monuments in Europe; to the tapas bars and the riverside cafes; and to my bed, for a long sleep before the gruelling ascent of Pico de Veleta. **RP**

*"Decent roads, plenty of sunshine and minimal traffic make Las Alpujarras a wonderful place to ride a bicycle"*

## TOOLKIT

**Start** // Sierra de la Contraviesa
**End** // Granada
**Distance** // 239 miles (385km), with a total vertical ascent of some 8500m
**Getting there** // Airports in Málaga and Granada provide plenty of options to get to and from this part of Andalucía.
**Bike hire** // Rent A Bici (www.rent-a-bici.com; €25 per day, minimum of two days) in Granada.
**When to ride** // May, early June, late September and October are the best times to cycle the Sierra Nevada: in July and August it's too hot, and busy with holidaymakers.
**Where to stay** // In Cádiar, La Alquería de Morayma (www.alqueriamorayma.com/en/) is a good option.
**What to eat** // Thick, meaty stews, charcuterie and black pudding are popular – but the locally grown fruit and vegetables are excellent too.

*Opposite: Roquebrune-Cap-Martin,*
*near cycling hotspot Menton, on the*
*Cote d'Azur, France*

# MORE LIKE THIS
# CROSSING RANGES

### SIERRA NEVADA, US

If you like the look of the Andalucían Sierra Nevada mountains, then you'll love the American range of the same name. Roughly straddling the California–Nevada border for some 398 miles (640km), the Sierra Nevada mountains are the highest and longest range in the contiguous United States. Gems in the landscape include the turquoise-coloured Lake Tahoe and the mighty Mt Whitney (4421m), but the natural beauty of the range just rolls on and on, through granite peaks, pine forests, waterfalls and alpine hot springs. This is the place, after all, that inspired two of America's great naturalists, John Muir and Ansel Adams. A loop starting in Placerville and taking in Lake Tahoe, Sierraville and Nevada City would be a great way to start exploring.
**Start/end // Placerville**
**Distance // 261 miles (420km)**

### ATLAS MOUNTAINS, MOROCCO

Twenty years ago, the Atlas Mountains were the exclusive domain of mountain bikers, but the expanding network of tarmac roads means the region has more recently opened up to road cyclists. There are snow-capped mountains, fertile valleys, cauldron-like gorges and great deserts to observe from the saddle, but there is just as much to enthral off the bike. Morocco is a fascinating blend of Africa, southern Europe and the Middle East: the kasbahs, souks, hammams, food and architecture make for a captivating, two-wheel journey. Heading south from the regional capital, Marrakech, you have to cross the high passes of the Atlas; go on further south, and you reach the Anti Atlas before you encounter the northern edge of the Sahara; head west and all roads lead to the Atlantic Ocean, from where it is easy to loop back round to Marrakech.
**Start/end // Marrakech**
**Distance // approx. 373 miles (600km)**

### PROVENCE, FRANCE

This undulating ride, from the elegant, medieval town of Avignon to the city of Nice on the glamorous and gleaming Cote d'Azur, crosses archetypal Provençal countryside. Along the way you will pass ochre, hilltop villages unblemished by the late 20th century, bustling farmers markets shaded by plane trees, fields of poppies and church spires protruding from row upon row of lavender. There are climbs but they are never back-breaking, while the descents are laid-back, winding and glorious. You'll ride down into the Gorges du Verdon, perhaps the most beautiful river canyon in Europe, and round the Lac de Sainte-Croix, before crossing the oak-covered, red volcanic hills of the Massif de L'Estérel for your first view of the Cote d'Azur. Following the Boulevard du Midi along the coast via Antibes, you can roll lazily past beaches, glamorous hotels and ritzy yachts to Nice.
**Start // Avignon**
**End // Nice**
**Distance // 217.5 miles (350km)**

# THE SOUTH DOWNS WAY

*Bucolic views over England's south coast, Iron Age settlements, country pubs, history and lots of hills: this is the South Downs Way, the easy way.*

'Did you call them?'

'No,' I admitted. And now my phone had no signal. Mike was normally the most mild-mannered of men, so it was a shock to sense his exasperation. I began to panic.

We continued, Mike riding ahead of me as usual. After a few more minutes, I noticed the signal-strength bars on my phone increase again; I stopped and dialled.

'Hello, can I help you?'

I explained our desperate predicament. There was a pause, then a reply:

'So, that's one roast beef with potatoes and veg and one roast lamb with potatoes and veg?'

'Yes, that's right,' I replied, with relief. 'We'll be there just after nine o'clock. Thank you.'

I relayed the news to Mike, that the kitchen at the Fox Goes Free pub in Charlton, our overnight stop on the South Downs Way, would start cooking our supper before they closed for the evening. The tension dissipated immediately.

It was now around 8pm on a balmy summer's evening and we were cycling on a narrow chalk path through the middle of a field of barley, the bristles swaying in a light breeze. A skylark sang high

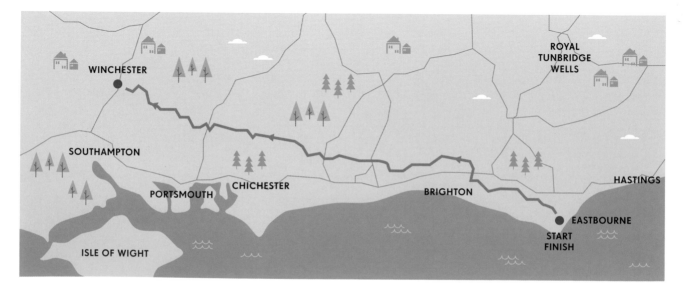

above us. Golden light from the setting sun suffused the scene.

The South Downs Way runs diagonally across England's southern counties of Hampshire and Sussex, from Winchester in the northwest to the coastal town of Eastbourne in the southeast. It's an ancient, and still unpaved right of way, running up and down the spine of low hills that make up England's newest national park, the South Downs. The route is popular with hikers, horse riders and mountain bikers – and one Easter I even encountered a man dragging an enormous wooden cross over his shoulder along it.

Central to the appeal of the South Downs Way is that both ends (and several towns along the route) are served by railways with fast connections to London, with journeys of around an hour. Most cyclists spend at least a couple of days riding the route, or part of it, but there is a big South-Downs-Way-in-a-Day scene: 100 miles (161km) starting at dawn on the longer summer days, finishing around 13 hours later. There are also people who take on the Double – there and back, nonstop. Mike and I preferred the South Downs Way the easy way: 60 miles (97km), a pub dinner and a comfortable bed, then another 40 miles (64km) to finish.

Cyclists typically ride from Winchester towards Eastbourne, in the direction of the prevailing wind. To be contrary, we started from Eastbourne train station and we started late, after midday, hence the rush to beat the setting sun and last orders at the pub's kitchen. In hindsight, the Eastbourne start was a good decision. It

*"As dusk fell, we rolled into the pub to find our meals ready, pints pulled, and a starlit garden beckoning"*

meant that we got the only section that was difficult navigate – the confusing network of route options and roads behind Brighton – out of the way early on. And we also dispatched the bigger hills of the Eastbourne end of the Way first, with fresh legs, starting with the pearly white cliffs of Beachy Head (the trail veers behind them but it's easy to detour up to the cliff edge). These crumbly cliffs are the exposed edge of a chalk layer that extends across the Channel and resumes in France. It was pushed up, ruptured, to form this undulating ridge more than 70 million years ago. England's early settlers, from Iron Age people (500BC) to the Romans, found the hilltops made perfect vantage points.

Riding from Eastbourne, we had already conquered our first Iron Age hill fort at Chanctonbury Ring. The place has a long history of pagan worship, including sacrifices. Our only sacrifice was not stopping to explore. We also whizzed past the chalk outline of the Long Man of Wilmington, which is now thought to be not quite as old as believed, dating from the 16th or 17th century.

As the sun inched down the sky, we left the sea to our left and angled inland towards our overnight pit-stop. The Fox Goes Free sits at the foot of the Downs. It's just a couple of miles from the

## RIDGEWAYS

In prehistoric times, travelling by foot along ridgeways was often preferable to hiking along the valley floor. Ridgeways, such as the SDW, were well-drained and offered great visibility – the penalty being that they were also exposed to the weather and were rarely flat. For these reasons, ridgeways often became ancient roads, used by drovers to drive livestock to market (and soldiers attacking settlements). Today, the traffic is of bikers and hikers but evidence of the importance of these ridgeways remains all around.

*Left to right: near Firle Beacon at the east end of the South Downs Way; the Fox Goes Free pub midway; sunrise over the Downs. Previous page: near Bignor Hill, halfway along the route*

Weald and Downland Open-Air Museum at Singleton, where buildings from the 13th century and onwards are restored. As dusk fell, we rolled into the pub to find our meals ready, pints pulled, and a silent, starlit garden backing onto the hills.

Rejoining the South Downs Way the next morning, we had perhaps the prettiest section of the route ahead. This central part of the route passes through east Hampshire, with views over green fields and villages, and is punctuated by chalk sculptures by Andy Goldsworthy. The trail, as well signposted as ever, darted through woodland, including the beech forest of the Queen Elizabeth Country Park where we tackled the mountain bike trails before climbing the highest point of the South Downs Way, Butser Hill. Here too there is an Iron Age (300BC) farm and fort.

But for fort aficionados, the best was yet to come: the Iron Age fort of Old Winchester hill. This would have been the guardian of the fertile Meon valley. It remains unexcavated but you can easily see the earthworks – ditches and ramparts – that would have protected the site. There's also a Bronze Age cemetery here (look out for tumuli the whole length of the South Downs).

From Old Winchester Hill, we knew we were on the home stretch, heading towards Winchester, an ancient capital of England. We passed the statue of Alfred the Great in the city, then one of Europe's largest Gothic cathedrals, before arriving at the railway station for our afternoon train to London. But we would have happily turned the clock back one day to that hour of magical light and the fields of gold. **RB**

## TOOLKIT

**Start/end** // Eastbourne or Winchester
**Distance** // 100 miles (161km)
**Where to stay** // The Fox Goes Free (www.thefoxgoesfree. com) in Charlton offers bed and breakfast (and dinner). There are several other options around halfway on the route, including youth hostels.
**What to take** // A mountain bike is best, the fist-sized flint stones won't be a comfortable experience on a cyclo-cross bike. Use a saddle bag to carry overnight gear. Stay hydrated by filling up water bottles or hydration packs at the public taps along the route, detailed on the National Trails website (www.nationaltrail.co.uk/south-downs-way).
**When to ride** // Weather is an important factor. Check the wind direction before deciding where to start. Summer days are best; in the wet the chalk becomes treacherously slippery.

# MORE LIKE THIS
## ANCIENT WAYS RIDES

### THE RIDGEWAY, ENGLAND

Running through the Chilterns and along
the Wessex Downs in central southern
England, the Ridgeway links several
important prehistoric sites, including
Avebury stone circle and Silbury Hill, a
manmade mound dating from 2300BC. All
are part of Wiltshire's Neolithic collection
of sites around Stonehenge. Originally, the
5000-year-old route, used by travellers,
soldiers and merchants, extended between
the coasts of Dorset and Norfolk but
now it meets the Icknield Way in the
Home Counties (where it also becomes
a footpath towards its eastern end). The
whole route, like the South Downs Way, is
thoroughly signposted and treacherous to
ride in winter. In summer, however, such
sights as the Bronze Age white horse of
Uffington in Oxfordshire are marvellous.
Look up to spot resurgent red kites,
England's once-almost-extinct graceful
birds of prey.
**Start // Ivinghoe Beacon,
Buckinghamshire
End // West Kennett, Avebury, Wiltshire
Distance // 87 miles (140km)**

### ICKNIELD WAY TRAIL, ENGLAND

Arguably the oldest long-distance path in
England, the Icknield Way begins in South
Norfolk, at the foot of the Peddars Way
(also bikeable) and follows veins of chalk
to Ivinghoe Beacon in Buckinghamshire,
where it meets the Ridgeway. English poet
Edward Thomas walked the Icknield Way
in 1911 and his journal still inspires hikers
to travel the 150 miles (241km) along it.
Thomas describes the Icknield Way as a
'white snake on a green hillside'; while it's
true that rural sections remain unspoiled,
other parts of the route now pass through
industrial areas and towns. But that's part
of the experience, with layers of history
overlapping each other. Cyclists have to
take the Icknield Way Trail, following the
Neolithic axe emblem; the multi-user trail
follows most but not all of the route of the
ancient footpath, starting and ending in
different locations.
**Start // Ashridge Estate, Hertfordshire
End // Knettishall Heath Country
Park, Suffolk
Distance // 170 miles (274km)**

### RENNSTEIG CYCLE PATH, GERMANY

Germany's oldest ridgeway trail is the
Rennsteig, which traverses the deep, dark
Thuringian Forest in central Germany's
green heart. Much of the route lies along
a ridge, above the treeline, affording
outstanding views across the countryside.
The Rennsteig was first used by messengers
in the Middle Ages but it's now Germany's
most popular hiking trail. There's a parallel
shared-use track for cyclists (mostly
mountain bikers). It passes the spa town
of Masserberg, the winter sports resort of
Oberhof, and the birthplace of Johann
Sebastian Bach in Eisenach, also home to
Wartburg Castle. At Blankenstein the trail
ends at the Saale River. There are plenty of
places to stay along the Rennsteig; refuel
on sausages and beer. Mind the wild boar.
**Start // Horschel
End // Blankenstein
Distance // 120 miles (193km)**

*Scenes from the Icknield Way*
*Trail as it passes from Norfolk*
*to Buckinghamshire*

# ARTY COPENHAGEN CRUISE

*Be a Dane for a day on this leisurely coastal cruise from the world's most bike-friendly city to Denmark's must-see Louisiana Museum of Modern Art.*

Riding over Knippelsbro bridge, with views of copper-roofed Christiansborg Palace, the Danish parliament, from the island of Christianshavn in central Copenhagen, it seemed as if I had slipped into a parallel universe; a City of the Cyclists, in which bicycles ruled the roads and unhurried riders glided like shoals of fish through the city. And this little fish, relishing the freedom, couldn't wipe the grin from his face.

Laid out over a series of islands, Denmark's capital is the most bike-friendly place I have pedalled. Some streets see 30,000 cyclists per day; and dedicated traffic signals and junctions, cycle lanes separated by kerbs from cars, and supersized bikeways all help to keep them moving safely. Indeed, in 2015 the city opened an aerial bikeway, the *cykelslangen*, swooping above the harbour and a shopping mall.

Here, a bicycle is the best way to encounter the fun-loving side of Copenhagen, from the cafe-backed beach park at Amager to the parks and gardens of Frederiksberg. Architecture fans can pedal down Ørestads Blvd for Jean Nouvel's blue-clad concert hall, food-lovers can tootle along the canals of Christianshavn, home to the famed restaurant Noma (and its newest little sister, 108). Danes cycle to work, they cycle to school and they cycle to bars, restaurants and parties.

But, irresistible though the city is on two wheels, I have an out-of-town trip in mind: a 25-mile (40km) or two-hour jaunt north along the Danish Riviera to the Louisiana Museum of Modern Art, near Helsingør (Elsinore), where castle Kronborg was the setting for Shakespeare's Hamlet.

Before I plan my route, though, I have a coffee with photographer-turned-bicycle-ambassador Mikael Colville-

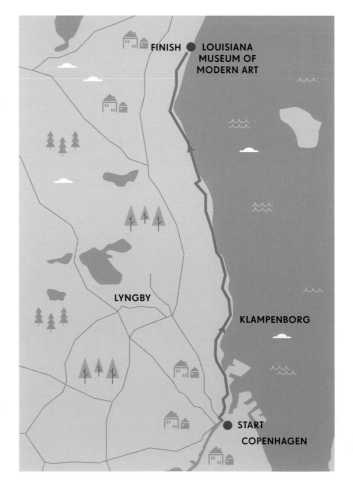

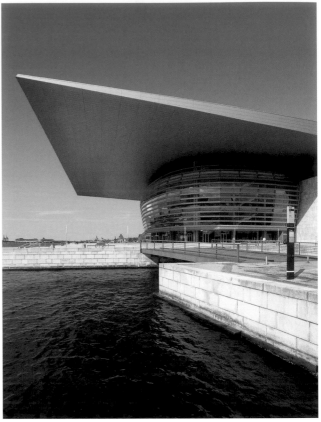

Andersen, who agrees cycling is a quick entry point into a country's culture. 'If you're standing shoulder to shoulder with 100 cyclists at a red light, smelling the perfume of the person next to you, that contributes to a sense of community.'

Danes pedal with panache: women wear heels and skirts, men sport suits. 'Anything you can walk in, you can cycle in,' says Mikael. Few wear helmets, feeling as safe on their bikes as they do on foot or in a car, and none break the rules – I spy not a single red-light jumper. Danes ride all year round ('Viking biking' Mikael calls it), easily navigating the city, in wind, rain or sun, on robust town bikes.

'Bicycles are like vacuum cleaners in Denmark', Mikael tells me, 'we all have one and we all use them every day but we don't think about them all day, we don't have ten of them, and we don't polish them; it's a tool.'

The next day I borrow one of these tools from a friend in Frederiksberg and set off on my Danish Riviera trip, starting with a big breakfast. Lying at the end of a cobbled lane next to a canal and embodying the Danish concept of *hygge* (warmth and wellbeing), Parterre satiates with avocado on rye toast, skyr with muesli, and fresh-baked pastries.

At the far end of Christianshavn and its colourful canal-side buildings is Copenhagen's landmark opera house. Once you've taken a spin around the island and some photos, head back

*"It was no longer unusual to see somebody pedalling a cargo bike with their dog in the front"*

onto Torvegade, Christianshavn's main road, and over the Knippelsbro bridge.

From here, I jump onto Bredgade and turned north through the city, cruising past the star-shaped Kastellet fort.

The roads are busy but cyclists have a segregated path to themselves. I remember Mikael's most important point of etiquette and keep to the right side of the lane so faster cyclists, or at least those who know where they are going, pass me to the left. Young or old, male or female, it seemed that everybody was on a bicycle and moving along with an elegant efficiency. It was no longer unusual to see somebody pedalling a cargo bike with their dog in the front, or breeze around a corner, head up, skirt billowing.

Eventually the city's industrial zone peters out, to be replaced by a marina. This is where navigation becomes a cinch: just keep the sea to your right. Soon, the bike path runs alongside the waterfront: on the other side of the stretch of sea lies Sweden.

This is the start of the Danish Riviera. When the sun is out, the

## CHRISTIANIA

Christianshavn is also home to Christiania, the alternative enclave and self-proclaimed 'free state', known over the years as a marketplace for cannabis (and police raids). Epic Rides readers will, naturally, be more interested to learn the place has lent its name to a range of practical cargo bikes, in which Danes ferry their groceries and families. Christiania is also the only place where unusual upright Pedersen bicycles are made (and can be bought at www. pedersen-bike.dk).

*Left to right: cycling Danish-style; Copenhagen's Opera House; beaches and maritime weathervanes on the way to Louisiana. Previous page: Nyhavn waterfront in Copenhagen*

clear blue water is speckled with white sails and slowly turning wind turbines. But in overcast weather, the view can be as gloomy as a Scandinavian detective drama. I pedal on, my heavy town bike dictating the sedate pace, though unimpeded by any hills. I roll through Klampenborg, a low-rise village with yachts moored just beyond the sea wall, then through Taarbæk and Skodsborg, the sea always just a few metres off my right shoulder. Bike Route 9 seeks out more traffic-free paths and lanes.

The signposts suggest that I'm nearing my destination, the Louisiana Museum of Modern Art, a long and low white building best known for its collection of works by Alberto Giacometti. Louisiana was founded by Knud Jensen in 1958 – his original intention was to display Danish art, but he soon changed direction and decided to promote international art in Denmark.

I park my bike outside – I'm not the only person to have cycled here – and go exploring. Louisiana's best feature is a seafront sculpture garden, featuring works by Henry Moore and Joan Miró. It's a sunny day and families picnic on the lawns, dabbling in the sea and running around the sculptures.

As the afternoon passes, I begin to think about getting back to Copenhagen. I cycle to the local railway station and jump on a S-Train from Humlebæk to Nørreport station in central Copenhagen with my bicycle – simple, sensible, practical. So very Danish. **RB**

## TOOLKIT

**Start** // Copenhagen
**End** // Louisiana Museum of Modern Art, Humlebæk
**Distance** // About 25 miles (40km) one-way
**Getting there** // Fly to Copenhagen international airport; there are easy-to-navigate rail services into the city centre.
**Where to stay** // City-centre hotels, hostels and B&Bs.
**Bike share** // From 125 bike-sharing stations and also rail stations, such as Osterport (www.rentabike.dk). Bycyklen bikes (www. bycyklen.dk/en; from 25kr per hour) with GPS screens are available. For cargo bikes (and normal bikes) try www.christianiacykler.dk in Christiania.
**What to take** // Wet weather gear.
**More info** // Maps of cycle routes from tourist information offices: www.visitcopenhagen.com. Louisiana (www.louisiana. dk) is open from 11am-10pm Tue-Fri, to 6pm Sat and Sun.

*Opposite: riding the Yarra Trail
into Melbourne, Australia*

# MORE LIKE THIS
## BIKE-SHARE RIDES

### PARIS, FRANCE

In France, the bicycle is known as *la petite reine* (the little queen). It might not rule the French capital but it's a great way of getting around. Paris' Vélib (*velo liberte*, bicycle freedom) bike-share scheme was one of the first and there are now more than 1800 street side stations for 20,000 bikes and more than 273 miles (440km) of bike lanes. Additionally, roads along the Seine and elsewhere are closed to traffic during Sunday; yes, that includes the Louvre and Jardin des Tuileries. And the Eiffel Tower. One great route is to follow the 3-mile (4.5km) Canal St-Martin from République to Quai de Valmy pausing at cafes for *ravitaillement* (refreshment) as required. You can continue to follow canals, such as Canal de l'Ourcq for as far as you want.
**Start // République**
**End // Quai de Valmy**
**Distance // 3 miles (4.5km)**

### MELBOURNE, AUSTRALIA

As a bike-friendly city, Melbourne stands head and (compulsory) helmet above its Australian counterparts. This is not just due to the influence of Jan Gehl, the Danish urban designer and consultant to cities around the world on how they can be more like Copenhagen, who spent several years in the 1990s advising Melbourne. The city's topography plays its part too: the Yarra River runs from the northeast down to the bay; and running beside it is the mixed-use Yarra Trail. It's a tranquil, green corridor; as it passes through Yarra Bend Park try to spot the flying fox bats roosting in the trees beside the river during the day. When the trail reaches the city, it's possible to connect with the Bay Trail that follows Melbourne's bay south to Seaford, via St Kilda.
**Start // Eltham railway station**
**End // Melbourne CBD**
**Distance // Yarra Trail is about 20 miles (32km) in total.**

### PORTLAND, USA

If any American city can be said to emulate Copenhagen, it's Portland, Oregon: the city in the Pacific Northwest is no stranger to cargo bikes or rain. It's an eclectic, sustainable, independent sort of place, famed for its coffee and craft beer – what more could a cyclist want? In 2015, Portland announced a bike-share scheme, called Biketown, consisting of 600 bicycles and stations across the city. There are already more than 350 miles (563km) of bike lanes in the city, including the 11-mile (18km) Waterfront Loop along the Willamette River. To get out of town, the 125-mile (201km) Willamette Valley Scenic Bikeway starts south of the city and flows into Oregon's world-class wine-making country.
**Start/End // Start the Waterfront Loop from the Salmon Springs Fountain and head north.**
**Distance // 11 miles (18km)**
**More info // There's a downloadable map at www.portlandoregon.gov/ transportation/article/348454**

# AROUND THE ÎLE DE RÉ

*This pretty island off France's Atlantic Coast is flat with a network of well-maintained bike paths: the closest you'll get to family holiday cycling nirvana.*

The hardest thing about cycling around Île de Ré? With each turn of the pedal, a new sight: a salt pan, birds over marshland, a fort, wooden fishing boats in a harbour, a pine forest, whitewashed houses with red flowers in window boxes, pristine wooden shutters in bright aquamarine hues...I wanted to stop and take pictures of it all on this most Instagrammable of islands. But we were riding bikes so I contented myself with drinking in the views as they blurred past instead, and pointing things out to my five-year-old son, who was joined to the back of my bike on a tagalong.

Riding with tagalongs for the first time in such a photogenic setting was a revelation, as we could cover longer distances than my newly cycling son could manage, while giving him a safe on-bike experience. He was also just near enough so that I could chat comfortably to him and answer all his 'whys' as best I could. My husband pulled our three-year-old along in a trailer, while our friends with similarly aged kids had the same set up: eldest on tagalong, youngest in a trailer.

Many parents had recommended Île de Ré to me as the perfect family cycling destination. And these weren't just hard-core city cyclists, it was often mums with young kids who wouldn't dream of pulling them along in a trailer back home. Yet within three minutes

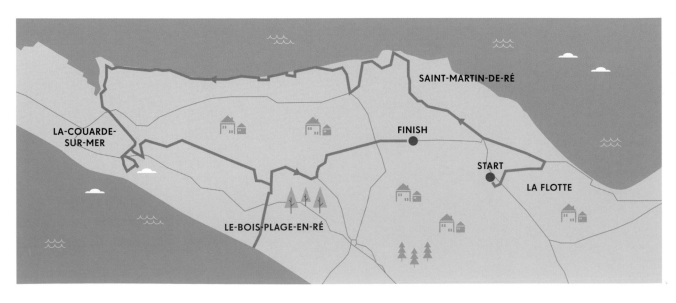

of riding away from our bike hire shop in La Flotte, a lovely old port on the north of the island, I understood why.

Our bikes, like most of the hired ones we passed on our route, were robust and surprisingly fast with efficient gears, but they were also stylish with relaxed Dutch-style handlebars and baskets. The latter were very handy for our first stop at the half-covered market in La Flotte. We loaded up on delicious bread, olives, charcuterie, cheeses and fruit, and then rode west along the clearly signposted cycle paths towards the island's capital and Unesco Heritage site, Saint-Martin-de-Ré.

Once one of the favourite targets of the English navy, centuries ago, the fort walls were now breached by the bike path. Though I found myself half hoping a drawbridge might rise up and trap us here forever.

We paused for a picnic in the Parc de la Barbette and gave the kids a ride on the famous and somewhat bemused-looking *ânes en culotte* (donkeys in short trousers). We then rode into the centre of Saint-Martin and parked up by the harbour to visit the most celebrated ice cream parlour on the island. With flavours such as mango, blueberry, lychee, banana flame and intense chocolate, it didn't disappoint.

Once out of Saint-Martin we found ourselves cycling along one of the most picturesque bike paths imaginable, right next to the deep blue sea. The sun was glinting off the water, moored fishing boats bobbed about, the setting really was dreamy, so we didn't mind at all when one of our party realised he'd left his phone in a bag by the ice cream shop and he had to go back. He found the bag exactly where he'd left it, which further added to our good impression of the place.

We passed salt marshes and oyster farms and though we barely had room for any more food, friends had told us we had to stop

### OYSTERS & ÎLE DE RÉ

Île de Ré produces 6000 to 8000 tonnes of oysters a year and *cabanes* (oyster shacks) are scattered all over the island, many right next to the bike paths. As with wine, an oyster's taste will be determined by where it was produced, and those reared in Île de Ré are considered some of the tastiest in France.

*Clockwise from top: riding the traffic-free paths of the Île de Ré; buying provisions at La Flotte en Ré; shopping in Le Bois-Plage-en-Ré; local oysters. Previous page: La Couarde-sur-Mer*

and try the oysters and prawns at Cabanajam just off the bike path, so we duly obliged. The kids played hide-and-seek at the edge of a vineyard, coming over to dip the odd prawn in aioli but scrunching their faces up dramatically at the suggestion of oysters.

Back on the path, we continued to hug the island's edge by marshland, salt pans and oyster farms, then we broke inland and headed south towards La Couarde-sur-Mer, a cute seaside resort village. We cycled around it but decided to push on to our final stop: the long, sandy coastline at Le Bois-Plage-en-Ré, the biggest resort on the island, though in truth it still had a mellow small-town feel. Like the rest of the island it was – refreshingly – full of independent shops, consistent with Île de Ré's classy seaside aesthetic.

After all that time in trailers and on tagalongs, the kids loved letting off steam at the funfair, then the playground by the beach, and then the actual beach for hours, and we enjoyed watching them. We had to drag them away at the end of the day, and then we sped back to La Flotte, through vineyards and fields, and to the start of our loop.

Cycling on Île de Ré really is like riding in an alternate bike-led universe. The island is only 19 miles by 3 miles (30km by 5km) yet it has 62 miles (100km) of cycle paths, which are often off-road or segregated. But even when they aren't, it's fine, as the cars were definitely in the minority and, to my mind at least, were driven less aggressively as a result.

We passed many families riding around with young kids in trailers, or slightly older ones on tagalongs or riding bikes themselves. And it was all very civilised: people rode in normal clothes, at regular speeds, though we couldn't resist the odd blast when we got to a clear bit of path. If only they could bottle Île de Ré's approach to cycling then all holidays could be as active yet as easy-going as this. **SH**

*"We loaded up our baskets with bread, olives, charcuterie, cheeses and fruit and then rode west along the cycle path"*

## TOOLKIT

**Start/End** // La Flotte
**Distance** // 14 miles (22km) via Saint-Martin-de-Ré, La Couarde-sur-Mer and Le Bois-Plage-en-Ré.
**Getting there** // Brittany Ferries (www.brittany-ferries.co.uk) depart the UK from Portsmouth to Caen, with a drive time of approx. 5 hours across France to Île de Ré. The nearest airport is La Rochelle, a 30-minute drive from the island.
**Bike hire** // There are hire places in La Flotte and all over the island, including at many campsites. Rhea Velo (www.rhea-velo.fr/laflotte) rents bikes from €8 per day and have great tagalong and trailer options.
**Where to stay** // La Grainetiere (www.la-grainetiere.com) offers well located camping at La Flotte and has an excellent kids' pool.
**What to eat** // La Martiniere (www.la-martiniere.fr) for ice cream, Cabanajam (www.cabanajam.com) for oysters.

*Opposite: Gimsøystraumen Bridge links Austvagoy with Gimsoy in the Lofoten islands*

# MORE LIKE THIS
# FAMILY ISLAND RIDES

### SARK, CHANNEL ISLANDS, UK

On Sark all motor vehicles are banned, except tractors, so the only way to get about is by horse and cart, walking or cycling. Which goes a long way to explaining the island's bike-friendly credentials. As does the fact it's virtually flat, super mellow and only 3 miles (5km) by 1.5 miles (2.5km). It has 9 miles (14.5km) of coastline, which you can ride around enjoying views of the other Channel Islands and France. Kids will enjoy a detour to see the secret garden at La Seigneurie and the Window in the Rock, which is exactly what it sounds like and a great spot for a picnic. Older children can give coasteering and sea kayaking a go. Sark was the first designated Dark Sky Island so, if it's not cloudy, a night cycle should guarantee an awesome starry sky backdrop.
**Start/End // The Avenue**
**Distance // 9 miles (15km)**
**More info // See www.sark.co.uk/getting-around**

### CAPE BRETON ISLAND, CANADA

The stunning Celtic Shores Coastal Trail on Cape Breton Island in Canada's Nova Scotia is 57 miles (92km) long, with some lovely off-road family-friendly sections. A good place to start is Creignish. Go past Christy's Look-off trailhead, enjoying the wonderful views of St George's Bay then head north towards Michael's Landing. The trail here is mostly flat and on hard-packed dirt, which is freshly levelled each year. Cycle past lobster boats, small fishing harbours and, if you're lucky, there may even be some whale-sightings. There are plenty of rest spots for a picnic, and just north of Michael's Landing is Judique, which has a Celtic Music Interpretative Centre, a nod to the region's Scottish settler pioneers. The town is also a good place to sample the famous local cream chowder and fish cakes.
**Start // Creignish**
**End // Judique**
**Distance // 11 miles (17.6km)**
**More info // See www.celticshores.ca**

### LOFOTEN ISLANDS, NORWAY

Not one for winter, when the islands will be covered in snow and ice, but a dreamy summer trip, where families can enjoy cycling in the magical Arctic light, never-ending days, and even take a ride under the midnight sun. This narrow chain of islands has more mountains than the rest of Norway put together, which makes for a dramatic panorama, yet, surprisingly, much of the cycling is on flat, easy terrain. Enjoy a landscape of jagged peaks, moorlands, lakes and fjords, while sea birds and eagles soar all around. You'll find plenty of beaches to relax on and, if you're feeling hardy, you can have an extremely refreshing dip in the icy sea.
**Start // Svolvær**
**End // Henningsvær**
**Distance // 16 miles (25.9km)**
**More info // See www.lofoten.info/en/Bike**

# THE TOUR OF FLANDERS

*Hardy hordes of amateur riders grab the chance to cycle Belgium's legendary cobbled climbs, just 24 hours before the famous Spring Classic professional race.*

I s the Tour of Flanders the biggest one-day cycling party on the planet? Flandrians, who refer to the event in Flemish as the Ronde van Vlaanderen, usually just shortened to De Ronde, certainly think so. And when you're sipping your fourth or fifth Belgian beer in the medieval surroundings of Oudenaarde main square or at a canal-side bar in nearby Ghent, still in your Lycra after an unforgettable day's riding, arguing will seem as futile as resisting another brew.

In one cycling-mad corner of the continent local riders and their feverish supporters count down the days until their local Spring Classics. Summer in Europe may be all about the Tour de France, but this season of one-day rides sees the professional peloton searching for early form on punchy climbs, bone-jarring cobbles and fiercely contested sprints.

Best of all, amateur cyclists can get in on the fun. Races, including the E3 Harelbeke (a one-day race named after a motorway, no less) and Liège-Bastogne-Liège, have a challenge ride open to all and sundry. These are usually held the day before the professional rides and many draw thousands of entrants.

None, however, is quite like the Ronde van Vlaanderen. This race, up steep, cobbled hills and over a pacy course crossing rolling farmland and through festooned towns, is a symbol of regional pride. It's where Belgium celebrates Flemish history and culture. International winners, and celebrated local winners, are feted and their bravery lauded.

The sportive, like the professional ride, has acquired mythical status. Sixteen thousand riders set off on their own tour of the region. Most start from Oudenaarde, approx. 20 miles (approx. 32km) south of Ghent, but a sizeable number begin in Bruges if

they opt for extra miles to ride a similar distance to the pros. What follows is a mix of testing ride, rolling celebration of the European cycling spirit and a Flandrian party like no other. Everyone taking part leaves as an honorary Flandrian, having tested themselves as generations of locals have done.

One-day cycling events, especially those involving riding a few miles, tend to start early, and many riders are on the road before dawn, either to tick off some of the distance or to get down the road before things get too clogged up on the main climbs. These climbs are what makes the Tour so famous. De Ronde was to be my first taste of cycling in Belgium, and I opted for the medium

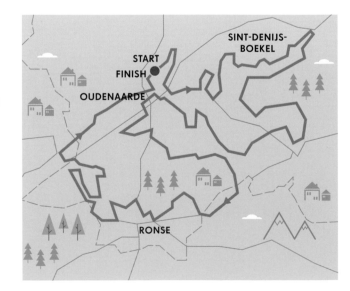

distance of approx. 79 miles (approx. 127km). I wanted to try my luck on the *hellingen*, mostly short, narrow climbs of less than 1 mile (approx. 2km) but some with fearful gradients and many with bumpy cobbles to handle as well.

The cobbles of Paris-Roubaix may be more famous, and those who have ridden both say the size and roughness of the bumpy stones of northern France pose more problems to riders, but the experience of attempting to get up the Koppenberg with dozens of other riders is nonetheless one of the great cycling challenges.

I soon found that you need to be lucky to make it up these 0.5 miles (approx. 700m) of cobbles, with a maximum gradient of 22%, not because I couldn't ride up it, but because if one rider ahead puts their foot down then there's nowhere to find space. Happily I only fell victim to this on one hill and made it up all the others without walking.

As other riders warned me, it's best not to stress. I was both providing the spectacle the fans have come to see, and learning another lesson about mass participation sportives: it's about taking part. If you simply must make it to the top of the narrower climbs, come back on a quieter day when you can have as many goes as you like. The best chance of success, counter-intuitively for a British rider, comes from sticking to the left side, the continental overtaking lane.

*"Not many pros will cross the finish line and tuck into those twin pillars of the Belgian diet: frites and beer"*

## FAMOUS RIDERS

The sense of history that shadows each De Ronde is enriched by the thought of riding in the wheel ruts of such local heroes as Eddy Merckx, Eric Leman and Roger de Vlaeminck. Banners and murals depicting their feats can be spotted on the route. More recent celebrated riders, such as Tom Boonen and Greg Van Avermaet, can be seen trying to add to their *palmarès* (list of races won) the day after the amateur ride.

*Clockwise from top: cycling fans in Flanders; the old town of Ghent; put a foot down on the Koppenberg and you'll stall; Belgian beer is the recovery drink of choice. Previous page: racing under the Flandrian lion*

All these short, sharp hills can make a cyclist hungry, and the organisers of the Ronde van Vlaanderen have thought of that too. Refuelling stations on one-day rides can be famously variable, with some especially cruel organisers running low on stocks of sugary and salty fill-ups for slower riders. Not here. These pit stops on the Tour are places where large bunches of Flandrians wait for stragglers who have been strung out on climbs. The ones on the latter parts of the ride served as impromptu outdoor raves, where loud music and very sugary waffles produced a unique kind of fever. I was surprised at just how many waffles I could eat on one ride. It may or may not have helped me over the latter climbs but they tasted very, very good.

As I ticked off the hills one by one, the ride rolled back towards Oudenaarde and the finish line. Crowds built on the last few hills, especially the Paterberg and Oude Kwaaremont, a favoured spot for VIPs to gather to watch the professionals the following day. Many fans stake out their spot the day before. Riding past lines of motorhomes added to the feeling of getting a taste of big-time cycling. That said, not many professionals will ride across the line and find themselves within minutes tucking into those pillars of the Belgian diet: frites and beer. That privilege is reserved for those of us who tackle the day-before sportive, a must-do on the list of any cyclist looking to have ridden the great rides of the world. **TH**

## TOOLKIT

**Start/End** // The Centre Ronde van Vlaanderen (www.crvv. be/en) in Oudenaarde. As well as being the museum of the ride, its website has details of signed routes that can be ridden at any time.

**Distance** // Around 79 miles (around 127km) for my medium-distance route.

**Where to stay** // Ghent has plenty of accommodation and is closer to Oudenaarde, where the short and medium routes run from. It makes for a beautiful base and is an easy drive from the start.

**What to take** // Most riders will be on road bikes, with some high calibre machines in evidence. Regular tyres should, in theory, cope with the cobbles. Mitts help prevent blisters from the bumps. Arm and knee warmers will help with riding through the chilly spring dawn.

*Opposite: whether dusty or muddy, the cobbles of Paris-Roubaix are a brutal test of skill and endurance*

# MORE LIKE THIS
## THE CLASSICS

### PARIS-ROUBAIX, FRANCE

'The Hell of the North'. That's Paris-Roubaix. This moniker has been attached to the race since organisers visited the scarred landscape of northern France after WWI and were shocked at what they saw. Things are more pleasant now, but the race has kept its name based on the challenge it offers: long sections of jagged cobbles that rattle speeding riders to their bones. This combined with no-win weather – mud when wet, dust when dry – means slips, punctures and all-out pile-ups are common. Once the worst is over, the prospect of lapping the famous Roubaix velodrome offers sweet relief.
**Start // Paris**
**End // Roubaix**
**Distance // The challenge ride offers three options: approx 43 miles (approx. 70km), approx. 86 miles (approx. 139km) and approx. 101 miles (163km). All take in the famed bumpy bits.**

### LIÈGE-BASTOGNE-LIÈGE, BELGIUM

There may not be many cobbles on offer in this other famed Belgian classic but there are hills. Lots of them. From Liège, the ride snakes its way out into the Ardennes, biting off climbs that range from long, shallow grinds, such as the Col du Rosier, to the steep slopes of La Redoute: sure to get riders out of the saddle. The mass-entry sportive of La Doyenne (The Oldest) offers three routes, but only the longest visits Bastogne, the others taking shorter loops that still offer thousands of metres of climbing. The hills keep coming right to the suburbs of Liège. Like the Tour of Flanders, thousands of riders converge on Belgium to follow in the footsteps of such riders as French legend Bernard Hinault, who in 1980 won the race in blizzard conditions. To this day, Hinault blames that race for damaging circulation in his hands. All you have to worry about is being able to hold a beer in Liège's marketplace afterwards.
**Start/End // Liège**
**Distance // 169 miles (273km)**

### TOUR OF THE BATTENKILL, USA

Billing itself as 'America's Queen of the Classics' and the country's largest pro-am race, the Tour of the Battenkill aims to offer some of the judders and skids of Europe's cobbles scene in upstate New York. Riders come from across America to take on the Battenkill. The test takes place each June and starts 35 miles (approx. 56km) north of state capital Albany. Both the superfast pro-am race and the Gran Fondo event run on a 68-mile (approx. 109km) course, with 15 miles (approx. 24km) on seven sections of bone-shaking gravel tracks. There's 1219m (approx. 4000ft) of climbing for the *grimpeurs* (climbing-specialist cyclists).
**Start/End // Greenwich, New York**
**Distance // 68 miles (approx. 109km)**

# FROM SEA TO SEA

*A rite of passage for active Brits (and inquisitive foreign riders) through
the dramatic landscape and history of the north of England.*

Great Britain's best-known challenge ride is attempted by thousands of people every year but it still has plenty of bite. Some come away scarred by the steep gradient of some climbs, especially on the Pennine sections, or vow never again to tackle the longer ascents. Others mutter curses about the northern English weather, which can throw tempests at you any time of year. Known also as the Coast to Coast (C2C on signage along the route) by many who ride it, this is a journey undertaken by all kinds of cyclists, from touring couples to older families to groups raising money for charity.

This is a fabulously open ride: anyone with a bike in decent condition with a long weekend to spare can dip their back wheel in the Irish Sea and a few days later victoriously place the front wheel in the North Sea. Some riders take longer, while others manage the whole thing in one (very) long day.

The route can be travelled in either direction. We headed west to east, getting the major climbs out of the way earlier and – in theory at least – leaving the rainier side of Britain behind. Our party of three mustered at various points on the train ride north, then swung south from Carlisle to Whitehaven, overnighting in the first of three B&Bs en route.

Whitehaven's rich history and lovely marina made for a

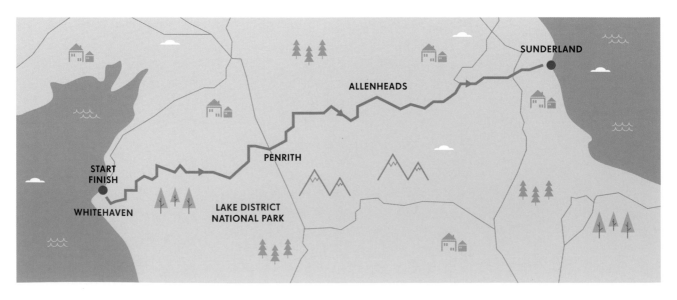

surprising start to the journey. Once we'd left the town behind – you can also start the signed route from nearby Workington – the path passed sculptures and quickly entered classic Lakeland scenery. On one hand this meant we were riding through deep beauty. On the other, the road was certain to soon go up. A lot. The first major landmark is the long haul over the Whinlatter Pass followed by the off-road descent into Keswick. Whinlatter is, happily, not as severe as most other Lake District passes, and ascending riders are kept on a quiet road away from the main road. Care must be taken on the descent. The tight curves are easy to skid over, and new Lycra shorts are not cheap.

Beyond Keswick, the mountains begin to peter out and, once past the looming summit of Blencathra, the scenery becomes more rolling and less rocky. If it felt odd to be effectively leaving the Lakes so soon, it was also heartening that we were making real progress. Castlerigg stone circle is a must-stop, with stellar 360-degree views that suggest a pre-bicycle civilisation that knew a thing about the value of round things. From here the path twisted and turned alongside and away from the busy A66 to Penrith. This underrated market town offered a welcoming place to pause and, like many other places en route, had excellent facilities for cyclists, which was just as well, as my front wheel wasn't happy at being asked to work hard and needed replacing at short notice. A bike service before setting out is essential.

The most memorable challenge of the route for me was the ascent of Hartside, the dramatic behemoth emerging from the Eden Valley a few miles/km after leaving Penrith. On busy summer weekends there's a steady stream of cyclists on the C2C – and Pennine Cycleway that also uses the route – puffing up the switchback climb to the 583m summit. It's a steady not steep climb, but feels like the defining moment of the journey, possibly because you get to look at dozens of other riders making their way to the

## WIGGO'S WAY

The popularity of the C2C has led to the establishment of several alternative sections, including the unofficial Wiggo's Way, a route dedicated to British cycling legend Bradley Wiggins, and various off-road sections that can be tackled by those with fatter, knobblier tyres. You may not feel like Wiggo when riding some of the more challenging sections, but you will have taken on an iconic British ride that's been often imitated but never bettered.

*Clockwise from top: crossing Hounsgill Viaduct in County Durham; dip a toe in at Tynemouth; Penrith; setting off from Whitehaven. Previous page: Castlerigg stone circle near Keswick*

top from the cafe once you're at the top.

The middle section of the ride is the toughest, and includes a beast of an incline out of Garrigill, steep climbs out of former lead-mining villages, such as Allenheads and Rookhope, and the highest point on the entire ride at Black Hill, where Cumbria and Northumberland meet. Take a breather, and a photo opportunity. Yes, parts of this route hurt a lot, but it felt like honest toil, with the reward of one incredible view after another, and a sense of achievement at the end of each day.

The C2C shows off northern England at its most green and pleasant, with a landscape that varies from mighty mountains to rolling hills descending to the sea. This being England, many villages and towns have a fine selection of local shops and pubs. In fact, cyclists make a significant contribution to the regional economy: for bonus points, go for local produce where you can. Given that each night will see you collapse into a B&B in need of extra-large refuelling for the coming days' efforts, this probably won't be a problem.

The final stretch, with no significant climbs and few sights after the dramatic crossing of the Hownsgill Viaduct outside Consett, inevitably became focused on the finish. After several days aiming at Tynemouth, getting here was always going to be sweet, with front wheels duly dunked, and ice cream beside salty sea air as a reward. We knew we had to ride back to Newcastle, but those final miles/km flew by, or at least seemed to in the fog of the celebratory beers that followed. The alternative finish at Sunderland, with a lovely beachside setting, competes with Tynemouth for the best possible ending, and both have merits.

The C2C isn't an exclusive club for elite cyclists, more a ticket to smile more times than you may expect and say 'I did that', all for the price of one long weekend of unbeatable riding. **TH**

*"The C2C isn't an exclusive club for elite cyclists, more a ticket to smile more times than you may expect"*

## TOOLKIT

**Start/End** // Whitehaven/Workington or Tynemouth/Sunderland
**Distance** // 140 miles (230km), Whitehaven to Sunderland
**Getting there** // Trains can get you to the start of the ride then home again, but bike space should be reserved (via railway booking office or phoning the relevant train company). There's no charge but space is limited. Failing that, a (moral) support car can help with transport.
**What to take** // You don't need a full-spec mountain bike to cover the route, but a road bike won't be up to off-road sections. A hybrid or cyclo-cross bike offers the right compromise (or follow signs to avoid unpaved sections).
**More info** // See www.c2c-guide.co.uk. The printed Sustrans route map (www.sustrans.org.uk) is an essential companion.

*Opposite: tackling the Taff Trail across
the Brecon Beacons in Wales*

# MORE LIKE THIS
## COAST-TO-COAST RIDES

### DEVON C2C, ENGLAND

As riders puffing through the early stages of Land's End to John O'Groats will testify, the south-west of England offers hills without the hype. Happily, the Devon C2C running from Ilfracombe to Plymouth has almost flat railway paths, including the start and finish. One section of the ride follows part of the Tarka Trail. Named after the eponymous otter of Henry Williamson's influential novel, this path was one of the earliest reclamations of disused railway for walking and cycling in the UK. The hills on the middle section are few enough in number to mean that moderately fit beginners can safely tackle this 100-mile (161km), two- to three-day ride. The middle section, when not on similar paths, traverses undulating country lanes as it skirts Dartmoor, with the Meldon Viaduct, located just outside Okehampton, providing both a scenic highlight and the highest point on the route. And just as Devon isn't flat, its southerly latitude does not guarantee clement conditions, so come prepared for all conditions.
**Start // Ilfracombe**
**End // Plymouth**
**Distance // 100 miles (approx. 161km)**

### LÔN LAS CYMRU, WALES

The Lôn Las Cymru (Welsh Green Lane) is the perfect way to discover Wales' wonderfully hilly hinterland. This 253-mile (approx. 407km) route runs from Cardiff in the south to Holyhead in the north. The route follows the Taff Trail railway path, then crosses the Brecon Beacons, the Wye Valley and over to the sea at Machynlleth. From here Snowdonia offers tough climbs and wonderful seaside views before crossing onto Anglesey via the magnificent Menai Bridge. This is one of the toughest routes on the National Cycle Network, even if you start in Chepstow rather than the Welsh capital and stay on tarmac for most of the ride. The reward for traversing hundreds of miles/km of mountains is a special insight into the great beauty of Wales, and a sense of satisfaction for having travelled across it from one wonderful corner to another.
**Start // Cardiff/Chepstow**
**End // Holyhead**
**Distance // 253 miles (approx. 407km)**

### SCOTTISH C2C, SCOTLAND

Completing the UK coast-to-coast quartet is the Scottish C2C, running from Annan to the Forth Bridge across the Southern Uplands of Scotland. Given Scotland's rightly rugged reputation, this is a surprisingly easier and marginally shorter ride than the English C2C, but that doesn't mean it should be taken lightly. There are some testing sections and the odd lengthy climb as the route winds through the borders on a mix of lightly trafficked country lanes and railway paths. The C2C reaches its climax passing through Edinburgh before reaching the Firth of Forth.
**Start // Annan**
**End // Forth Bridge, Firth of Forth**
**Distance // 122 miles (196km)**

# THE CÉVENNES: RIDING THE RIDER

*Tim Krabbé's 1978 novel The Rider remains the best account of how it feels to race a bike. This is the route that inspired it.*

I n the mid '70s Dutchman Tim Krabbé discovered road bikes, and trained hard to turn himself into a pretty handy rider; *The Rider* is the fruit of those experiences.

It recounts the fortunes of a rider (called Tim Krabbé) in the Tour du Mont Aigoual, a fictional race in the dense hills of the Cévennes in southern France. The *parcours* (course) is a figure-of-eight with the pretty town of Meyrueis at its centre, and it takes the reader down river gorges, then up and over the Causse Méjean, one of the region's high limestone plateaus deeply incised by rivers, and back down to Meyrueis. It sidles up Mont Aigoual (at 1507m the highest point) obliquely as if trying to take it unawares, then down the other side to the Col de Perjuret and a mad downhill rush to Meyrueis again.

The route is 85 miles (137km) long and ascends around 2400 vertical metres in three proper climbs, though it is of course altitude-neutral. Nothing won, nothing lost, a zero-sum game. A non-cyclist might wonder why expend all that effort just to come back on

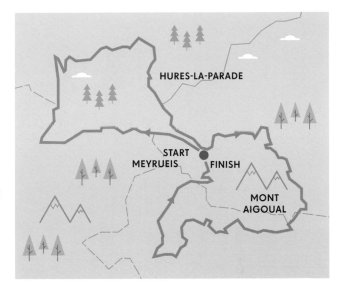

yourself; to climb only to descend again. But non-cyclists are not really the point: and it is this kind of cycle-obsessive psychology that Krabbé taps into so brilliantly. He maps the emotions and thoughts flowing like an underground river beneath the moves that animate the race. And, in so doing, *The Rider* articulates a lot of truths about cycling, life and everything else. The syntax and grammar of racing; alliances, attacking and getting dropped; the glamour of cycling history and the suffering it takes to aspire to race and race well.

I've ridden the Tour du Mont Aigoual in howling wind and blazing sun, abandoned it three-quarters of the way up the main climb when the pouring rain turned to snow, and the route is rich, always revealing something new.

Leave Meyrueis, with vultures circling overhead, and freewheel down the Jonte, turn gently up the Tarn, and then, after around 18.5 miles (30km), the race begins in earnest, with a crazy zigzagging attack up the steep gorge wall to the flatlands above.

'The cols here are made of air and lie upside down in the landscape,' Krabbé wrote. 'Climbing from plateau to plateau is particularly tiring.' And it's true that if you're used to normal riding in the mountains the rhythm is unfamiliar: a big effort on the climb followed by a sustained ride over the causse; then a long descent and climb again straight away, just when your legs have been resting long enough to have forgotten what you're asking of them. But that's for later: each uphill is long enough to settle

*"The rest of the descent passes in an adrenaline rush, the invisible stopwatch and Krabbé in hot pursuit, urging you on"*

into. Concentrate on the wheel in front of you and focus the mind, or stare at the view and let it wander; count your breaths, count sheep or work out if the gear you're riding comes close to Krabbé's magic ratio of 43/19 (his 20-tooth cog was, as aficionados of the book will know, as clean as a whistle).

The *causses* can be capricious, and you may get a fierce headwind over the blasted heath, persistent rain and the smell of wet pines and cows, or a gentle breeze that ruffles the wild flowers in the roadside meadows. Whatever greets you, it's a slog to the other side, where a giant crack in the landscape opens up and you fly down to Meyrueis again to take on the second – and longer, and higher – loop to Mont Aigoual.

Exiting Meyrueis, you'll immediately climb again, cross another causse to reach Trèves, a sleepy, picturesque village caught at the bottom of another great fissure in the rocks. Beware of the sign on the left turn – 'Mont Aigoual, 28km' (17 miles) – it can be depressing! The road up from Trèves is barely a car's width, with a precipice on one side where a small stream flows, and the 17 miles

## MONT AIGOUAL

Mont Aigoual is the second highest mountain in the Cévennes. It is said that, on a clear day, you can see the Mediterranean Sea, the Pyrenees and Mont Blanc, thanks to the 360-degree views. But consider yourself lucky if you stumble upon such a day: the weather station at the mountaintop records that it is one of the rainiest places in France, with an average of 240 days of cloud each year.

*Left to right: the road out of Meyrueis as it was in the 1970s; griffon vultures soar above; Trèves; gorges and ruines crease the causses. Previous page: cycling the Cévennes*

(28km) are an awful grind. The road averages 3.5% but it dips and rears, making it difficult to get a rhythm on the steeps or take advantage of the nearly-flats. After what will probably be an hour's climbing, Krabbé's race takes him left, on a lower road, but it's advisable to take a 3-mile (5km) detour to the top. That's not how a racer would think – but your long-cut will give you the fantastic views and a sense of achievement, and afterwards there's only downhill all the way to the finish line.

The top of the descent is windswept and open but, further on, it curves and bucks to negotiate the steep-sided cliffs that fall away on all sides before the Col de Perjuret. That was where in 1960 Roger Rivière, a great hope of French cycling, fell into a ravine. 'Le Terrible Accident de Roger Rivière' announced the newspaper that week, but despite visits from some of the biggest stars of the era, Roger would never walk again. OK, so there's a tiny bit of uphill before Perjuret (never trust anyone who tells you it's downhill all the way home) but the rest of the descent will pass in an adrenaline rush, the invisible stopwatch and the sound of Krabbé's breath in hot pursuit urging you on, chasing you down the hill.

Cross the bridges, sprint the final straight, and sit with an Orangina on a sunny cafe terrace as the other racers trail in behind you. In the book Krabbé narrowly loses first place, but in a pretty competitive time of four hours, thirty minutes. How will you measure up? **ML**

## TOOLKIT

**Start/End** Meyrueis
**Distance** // 85 miles (137km)
**Getting there** // Meyrueis is deep in the Cévennes National Park and quite isolated. Montpellier and Nîmes are around 2.5 hours' drive, and both have international airports, and TGV railway stations.
**Where to eat & stay** // Meyrueis is full of modestly priced hotels and restaurants serving local specialities. Stop at Jeff Bar on the main street for a coffee before you set off.
**When to ride** // Mont Aigoual can be windy – and, thanks to its altitude, cold – in any season, but you'll have a chance of a fine day any time between May and October.
**More info** // There is a tourist office in Meyrueis, and you can download a route GPS here: www.bikely.com/maps/bike-path/Ronde-van-de-Mont-Aigoual.

# MORE LIKE THIS
## LITERARY RIDES

### ROBERT LOUIS STEVENSON'S DONKEY TRAIL, CÉVENNES, FRANCE

Towards the end of 1878, Treasure Island author Robert Louis Stevenson set out on a voyage of discovery. Travels with a Donkey in the Cévennes is his account of the trip that is now considered a pioneering work of travel literature. As the title suggests, Stevenson did not walk alone: he had Modestine, a grumpy and uncooperative donkey who provides a lot of the book's humour. Stevenson walked around 120 miles (193km) south from Le Monastier in the Haute Loire to Saint Jean du Gard. Le Chemin de Stevenson is now the GR70 hiking trail that can be followed on mountain bikes (hire locally); or it's easy to piece together a road ride of a similar length taking in the towns and mountains Stevenson passed.
**Start // Le Monastier**
**End // Saint Jean du Gard**
**Distance // 120 miles (193km)**

### EDWARD THOMAS' RIDE, LONDON TO QUANTOCK HILLS, UK

Follow in the wheel-tracks of English poet and nature writer Edward Thomas, who in 1913 left London one cold and blowy Easter morning and rode his bike to the Quantock Hills in the West Country 'in pursuit of spring'. It was a poetic pilgrimage to where Samuel Taylor Coleridge, a hero of his, had once lived for a year and written The Rime of the Ancient Mariner. It's easy to piece together a route from his account, which was published the following year. Leaving London now takes you through endless suburbs, but by the time you reach Hampshire, and Jane Austen's house, you'll be travelling along green lanes, cart tracks and bridleways that won't have changed much in 100 years, and you can spend the night in inns Thomas himself frequented.
**Start // London**
**End // The Quantock Hills, Somerset**
**Distance // 250 miles (402km)**

### LANCE ARMSTRONG'S FAVOURITE CLIMB, CÔTE D'AZUR, FRANCE

Lance Armstrong got plenty of things wrong, but he was right that Nice, on the Côte d'Azur, is a cycling haven. His autobiography, *It's Not About the Bike* details his life there as a pro and, in particular, his favourite climb, the Col de la Madone. Roughly surfaced, sinuous and narrow, it climbs almost from the seafront in Menton, on the Italian border, to 925m in around 8 miles (13km), and Armstrong knew that if he went well on the Madone he'd be ready for the Tour de France. Start your day in Nice at the Café du Cycliste, and staff will give you directions for a stunning 50-mile (80km) ride that also takes in the Col d'Èze climb made famous by the Paris-Nice stage race.
**Start/End // Café du Cycliste (www. cafeducycliste.com/the-cafe/), Nice**
**Distance // 50 miles (80km)**

*Edward Thomas lived near Steep, in Hampshire, where the Harrow Inn is a pretty pitstop for cyclists*

# INTO THE OUTER HEBRIDES

*This other-worldly odyssey by road and water through Scotland's Atlantic archipelago offers stark beauty and unforgettable, windswept cycling.*

The Western Isles tempt those of us who plan journeys by tracing fingers along roads on maps. An easy-to-follow line of land and sea runs all the way from Vatersay (Bhatarsaigh), at the southern tail of the chain to the Butt of Lewis (Rubha Robhanais), at the northern end of the chain. The individual islands are linked by causeways and ferries and seem, from afar, a very mysterious prospect. What is to be found on what are, by definition, the furthest flung islands in the archipelago off Scotland's north-west coast? And what better way to find out than by taking advantage of the island-hopping ferry service and the endless liberties offered by a bicycle, a pair of panniers and brimming overenthusiasm?

The Western Isles are a very long way from the bright lights of the UK. To best make the trip by public transport, you must first get to Glasgow, then an onward train to Oban, one of the west coast's great transport hubs. Ferries buzz to Mull and various smaller islands from here, but the ferry to Barra (Barraigh) still feels like a big deal. The thrill of walking my steel tourer into the body of the boat added to the excitement. Over the next few days I would board several more boats in this fashion and each time I felt the same thrill.

It takes just under five hours to cruise through the Sound of Mull, passing the Summer Isles and other green, rocky specks of land before Castlebay (Bàgh a' Chaisteil) looms into view. By Scottish standards, this is a very long journey indeed.

My own schedule didn't allow for too much dawdling on Barra, so I was grateful that the late summer's evening sun gave me time to catch a little of Vatersay's beautiful beach before bed, with hardly a glimpse at the weather forecast. The next day dawned drizzly and progressively got worse until things were resolutely

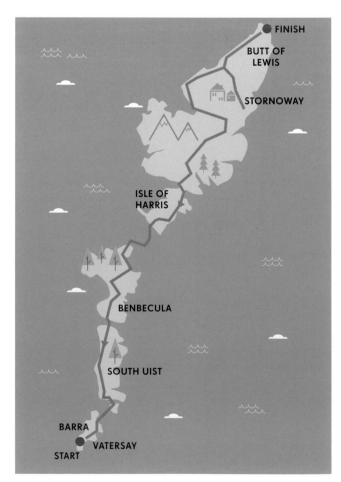

North Atlantic. I reasoned I could not complain about it raining, given where I was and that I'd been given one priceless gift: a vigorous tailwind. Over the next few days I passed numerous cyclists battling in the opposite direction who feigned disinterest in my sympathetic waves.

Barra's road network is essentially circular, so there are two ways around it. I took the route to Ardmhor (Aird Mhòr) that passed Barra Airport, voted the most scenic landing in the world for its cockle-strewn beach runway. I didn't see any planes. There weren't any cars for that matter until a few minutes before the Eriskay (Eiriosgaigh) ferry turned up.

This short hop took me onto a chain of islands – Eriskay, South Uist (Uibhist A Deas), Benbecula (Beinn Na Faoghla) and North Uist (Uibhist A Tuat) – with other-worldly landscapes. From the main road in South Uist, a ribbon of single-lane tarmac where few cars passed, the route was flat and watery. Hundreds of tiny lochans dotted the horizon. The water world was only broken by the looming peaks of Beinn Mhor (620m) and Hecla (606m), the highest points on South Uist, away to the east of the road.

Dawdling a little, my turns to the west took me to a strip of beach that was backed by machair, much-celebrated coastal grasslands, which were dotted with wildflowers. That said, with the wind and the oddness of the landscape, I gave in to the urge to ride and ride, sprinting across the causeway to Benbecula, and in turn to North Uist, rather than pausing and being a proper cycle tourist. The only distraction breaking the rhythm of the turning wheels, the rain in my face, and the splash of the road, were signs on the causeways warning of otters crossing.

## EXPLORE THE REGION

The islands can be traversed in as little as three days, but more time allows for detours and to explore alternative routes on Barra, to detour to the west of Benbecula and pause at Balranald RSPB Bird Reserve on North Uist. A convenient overnight stop is at the hostel on Berneray (Bearnaraigh), from where the ferry across the Sound of Harris (Caolas na Hearad) leaves.

*Clockwise from top: Callanish standing stones on the Isle of Harris; a weaver's loom on Lewis; Tarbet harbour and the local catch. Previous page: the Golden Road on Harris*

Once on Harris (Na Hearadh) I returned just a little to civilisation, the island being well-connected to the mainland via Skye (an t-Eilean Sgiathanach) and the ferry to Tarbert (An Tairbeart). I turned right along the Golden Rd, so named for the high cost of its construction, to yellow-sand beaches and sweeping views on the west coast.

The climb out of Tarbert over to Lewis (Leodhais) is one of the finest rides in the British Isles, an initially tough haul giving way to a glorious rolling pedal through mountains, past sea-lochs and hugely tempting roads snaking off, mainly (according to the map) to long-distance dead ends. Somewhere, quite unexpectedly, I passed a sign saying that I had arrived in Lewis: in name an island, in reality a distinctly different part of the same piece of rock. Weavers' cottages started to appear by the roadside, where the Hebrides' most famous export – tweed – is still produced.

There's more to the Hebrides than just quiet roads and wildlife. The islands have millennia-old history that's easily explored, such as the Barpa Langass chambered cairn on North Uist. On Lewis there's Garenin (Na Gearrannan) Blackhouse Village and, most remarkable of all, the Callanish Standing Stones.

The last leg to the Butt involved an out-and-back run to end of the island before returning to Stornoway (Steornabhagh). After so much solitude the size of the islands' largest settlement came as a shock, but being able to have a pint or two was a fine reward for wonderful, hard miles in the rain.

I rode the high road over the mountains to Inverness to pick up the sleeper train home. My bike travelled with boxes of fresh crab bound for London restaurants. **TH**

*"The only distraction breaking the rhythm of the turning wheels were signs on the causeways warning of otters crossing"*

## TOOLKIT

**Start** // Vatersay (Bhatarsaigh)
**End** // Butt of Lewis (Rubha Robhanais)
**Distance** // 150 miles (241km)
**Getting there** // Caledonian Macbrayne (www.calmac. co.uk) offers a Hopscotch ticket covering ferry travel from Oban to Barra, up through the islands and from Stornoway back to Ullapool. Cyclists can generally turn up and go.
**When to ride** // March to September, while not necessarily dry, are the brightest and warmest months. They're also the most popular, so book accommodation in advance.
**What to take** // This route is all on paved roads, but a touring bike is best for long days in the saddle and will allow for the carrying of pannier bags.
**More info** // See www.visitouterhebrides.co.uk for more information on planning a trip to the islands.

*Opposite:Taroko Gorge, Taiwan*

# MORE LIKE THIS
## ISLAND RIDES

### CROATIA ISLAND-HOPPING

Bikes, islands, ferries, beaches, repeat: if you like the sound of island-hopping but crave warmer weather than what's on offer in the North Atlantic, consider Croatia. From the Dalmatian port city of Split, ferries dart out towards Adriatic islands. A wonderful route offered by Cycling Croatia first explores Brač, Hvar and Korčula, then crosses the Pelješac peninsula before arriving at the finish point of Dubrovnik. There are hills to work up a sweat, deep blue waters to swim in, and fabulous seafood and wine to help revive tired muscles.
**Start // Split**
**End // Dubrovnik**
**More info // Cycling Croatia (www. cyclingcroatia.com)**

### NEW IRELAND PROVINCE, PAPUA NEW GUINEA

Remote island cycling of a different kind is on the menu on the little-known island of New Ireland, part of the archipelago making up Papua New Guinea. A flight from the capital, Port Moresby takes you to Kavieng, the main town on the island. From here it's a five-day, 164-mile (264km) ride along the Boluminski Hwy to Namatanai, passing caves, beaches and swimming holes, and stopping in local village guesthouses along the way. Where the tarmac (some of the best in PNG) ends, what the tourist office describes as a 'very bright' crushed-coral roadway takes over. Surely few cyclists could resist taking on such a route.
**Start // Kavieng**
**End // Namatanai**
**Distance // 164 miles (264km)**

### TAIWAN

What would be on a list of requirements for cycling nirvana? Great city, road- and off-road routes to suit all abilities? Friendly, cycling-mad locals? Easy to arrange bike hire and transport? Anything else? How about some of Asia's finest scenery, great beaches and a destination that will raise eyebrows. For all of this, look no further than Taiwan. Cycling is big here, from the busy streets of Taipei to the near-deserted east coast. Inland, spectacular valleys and rocky gorges – including the iconic Taroko and Mugua River Gorges – reward those prepared to take on big ascents. There is a fast-growing network of bike paths and off-road trails, especially on the east side of the island, and you can expect roadside encouragement whatever you're attempting. One of the most popular intermediate rides in Taiwan is to travel from Hualien to Taitung on the east coast and through the East Rift Valley on Hwy 11, 9 and other scenic roads.
**More info // To read about a couple's ride through Taiwan's east coast, see www.acruisingcouple.com/2013/04/ cycling-taiwan-east-coast.**

# ALL ALONG THE LOIRE

*Smooth, effortless riding along a grand river, from castle to castle, enchanted garden to walled wonderland, boutique wine to artisanal produce – so French, so perfect.*

OK, cliché alert: I'm sitting at the edge of Île d'Or, a small riverine island connected to both sides of the Loire by a lovely stone bridge. The town of Amboise with its 15th-century castle spreads out along the opposite shore. I have a baguette, a small (-ish!) wheel of soft cheese and a bottle of wine. A single cold beer too. And the bemusing, yet satisfying effects of a recently consumed mille feuille. I don't think I've ever been happier. Let's set the scene.

I began in Angers, visiting friends and settling into the long biking holiday I was about to embark on – around the coast of Brittany then a diagonal from Nantes right across France to

Perpignan on the Spanish border before continuing to Barcelona to wrap up the journey.

Angers is not a first port of call for tourists, yet it has a beautiful city centre, medieval walls and castle (which contains the Apocalypse Tapestry, the largest of its type in the world) and, at the confluence of a couple of rivers that join the Loire, a certain ... connectedness. I felt connected in any case, but I suppose that might have been holiday bliss.

I wasn't a newbie to the bike, but 6 miles (10km) a day commuting isn't a guarantee that 62 miles (100km) a day is going to be easygoing. So a small warm-up trip was in order, and the

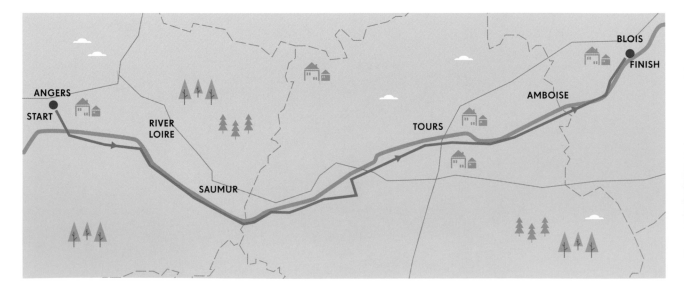

Loire beckoned.

The Loire is the longest river in France at around 621 miles (1000km). It has quicksand. And castles, so many castles. But better still, a ride along a river means no hills, just the occasional gentle undulation.

I set off.

The first day was a 31-mile (50km) ride to Saumur. Getting out of Angers, a relatively large city, has its issues, but eventually you catch sight of a small branch of the Loire, about 4 miles (6km) from the town centre. You cross it and then come to the Loire proper and the width of the river is a surprise – about 250m across at this point. The first half of the ride is inland from the river, on a mix of roads, none of which are scarily busy. The last half of the ride is along the bank of the river. It's wide and quick-flowing and you feel like you're riding faster as it disappears in the opposite direction. Saumur arrives in a flash.

Saumur has its own grand castle and a military equestrian history – you'll feel right at home on your iron horse. The camping ground (Chantepie) about 3 miles (5km) before town is a little bit luxurious – particularly the view from high, looking out across the river. Once the tent is up, it's a casual ride into town, with a stop at the rustic mushroom museum. And for a bottle of sparkling wine from Veuve Amiot.

Rising as the sun lights the tent, I head back on the road.

*"I walked through Amboise, gathering supplies – wine, beer, cheese and bread. Things get dreamy from here"*

It's 43 miles (70km) to Tours but there are two potential detours – both castles. Chinon and Azay-le-Rideau. I opted for Azay-le-Rideau, a 500-year-old classic fairy-tale construction perched in the middle of the Indre River. It's impossibly perfect. It adds about 6 worthwhile miles (10km) to the ride. Apart from the detour the route again meanders alongside the river. Tours is good town to base yourself in if you want to see all the castles of the Loire. As a part of my warm-up ride it was just an overnight, though. Next was Amboise.

The ride from Tours to Amboise starts with a few gentle miles on a riverside bike path. The next 9 miles (15 km) are busier, but French drivers are generally careful of cyclists. Riding through Montlouis and Lussault, old river towns, is a pleasure of its own and sets the scene for the beauty of Amboise, which takes it up a notch.

Amboise has a castle, to be sure, and it has the requisite medieval buildings as well. But it's the way it's put together. The buildings nest into the rise from the river bank, surrounding the

## FROM CYCLING TO CAVING

If you liked the mushroom museum and want more underground adventures, take a detour from Saumur to the troglodyte village of Rochemenier. The region around Saumur is well known for its cave-dwelling hobbyists, you'll notice houses that appear to bloom from the side of hillsides more than once on a ride along the Loire. Rochemenier gives you a chance to peek inside and get a sense of cool cave living.

*Left to right: bridges over the Loire at Angers; the old town of Amboise; bread and wine. Previous page: Château d'Azay-le-Rideau, near the Loire River*

castle and making a grand wall that looks over the river. The camping ground is on a small island in the Loire and this view is yours for next to nothing.

I walked through Amboise, gathering supplies – the wine, beer and cheese, next I needed bread. Things get dreamy from here. The bakery was bright and unrustic, at odds with the town's design, but the fare … I ordered my baguette and spied the mille feuille. I'm an aficionado, I couldn't resist.

As I left the bakery I took a bite. It was tremendous. It was earth shattering. I finished it in a flash and returned to the shop. In my broken French I told the woman that I'd tasted mille feuille all around France but that hers was the greatest mille feuille of them all.

She looked at me with a straight face, no smile, no give, and said, 'I know.'

I returned to my tent (with a second mille feuille for dessert) and let it all soak in.

The next day was a ride to Blois, which had the river in view constantly. Another detour beckoned, the Château de Chenonceau, but I was in a hurry now to return to Angers. Riding these few days was the kick-start I needed and I was raring to go on my longer trek. Of course, in hindsight, the few days of easy riding and majestic scenery on the Loire was more a highlight than a warm-up. **BH**

## TOOLKIT

**Start** // Angers
**End** // Blois
**Distance** // 114 miles (183km)
**Getting there** // Trains from Paris will take you to/from Angers and Blois.
**Where to stay** // Camping grounds are many along the Loire. If you can travel light, there's a definite allure to bringing your home with you on the bike.
**When to ride** // April to May; you'll beat the summer holiday traffic and heat.
**How to ride** // You can ride the Loire in either direction, and there's plenty of opportunity to add to the journey with numerous chateau and towns in the valley to catch your eye. Ride it as a circuit and vary your route on the way back – it would be a very comfortable week of cycling.

*Opposite: riding the Rhine as it
flows through Basel, Switzerland*

# MORE LIKE THIS
## RIVER RIDES

### PO RIVER, ITALY

Pedal the Po from Turin to Venice to cross
northern Italy from the Alps to the Adriatic.
The nascent route has been nicknamed
VenTo and it forms part of the plan for
the EuroVelo 8 route (EuroVelo is a pan-
European network linking long-distance
cycle paths), the full length of which
girdles the Mediterranean from Cádiz to
Athens. This Italian section reveals such
gems as the Renaissance city of Ferrara
and La Bella Addormentata, the sleeping
beauty city of Mantua. Cyclists can expect
fabulous food (the Po River delta is known
for its rice fields) and with more than 200
bike-friendly B&Bs, hotels and campsites,
not to mention the flat route, it's an
appealing adventure for cyclists of modest
ambitions.
**Start //** Turin
**End //** Venice
**Distance //** 390 miles (628km)
**More info //** www.eurovelo.org;
www.eurovelo8.com

### THE RHINE CYCLE ROUTE

Similar to the Po River route, the Rhine
Cycle Trail is suitable for cyclists of all
levels of fitness and ages. And it's also
part of a EuroVelo route, in this instance 15.
Riding along one of Europe's longest rivers
isn't something that many people will do in
a single trip. Instead, pick out the tastiest
portions of Switzerland, France, Germany
or the Netherlands and spend a week or
two on them. Choose from nine UNESCO
World Heritage sites, including the city of
Strasbourg, Dutch windmills, Cologne's
cathedral, and the entire Middle Rhine
Valley between Bingen and Koblenz. And
why not stop to sample some Riesling wines
around Colmar in Alsace?
**Start //** Andermatt, Switzerland
**End //** Rotterdam, Netherlands
**Distance //** 765 miles (1231km)
**More info //** www.rhinecycleroute.eu

### MISSISSIPPI RIVER TRAIL, USA

This river fascinated Mark Twain and Henry
David Thoreau. But rather than a raft you'll
have a bicycle and the challenge will be
all the greater. The Mississippi River Trail
starts in Itasca State Park in Minnesota
and meets the Gulf of Mexico 3000 miles
(4828km) to the south. Along the way there
will be ten US states, and riders will have
to take the rough with the smooth. The
River Trail is most developed in Minnesota,
using the shoulders of quiet roads and
byways. Minneapolis, north of Minnesota's
state capital St Paul, is one of the most
cycle-friendly cities in the US. By the time
the river has crossed into northeast Iowa it
has broadened and the scenery becomes
more majestic. In Missouri the trail passes
through Twain's home town of Hannibal.
And then the tenor of the trip changes as
the route reaches the Deep South states of
Mississippi and Louisiana.
**Start //** Itasca State Park, Minnesota
**End //** Venice, Louisiana
**Distance //** 3000 miles (4818km)
**More info //** www.mississippirivertrail.org

# BEACHES
# AND BICYCLES
# IN ADELAIDE

*During the Tour Down Under, the South Australian capital is a magnet
for cycling fans and this short circuit shows off the region's highlights.*

We're at one of Adelaide's bustling restaurants, enjoying a glass of wine. The Tour Down Under has the city full to the brim and it's the night before our group ride. There's some animated discussion about the following day's challenges ahead: the climbing, the descents, the wildlife we might spot.

Some of my fellow riders have come from across the country, while others, like me, have come from different parts of the globe. I've come only as far as New Zealand but there are riders from Singapore, Japan, England and Germany. In fact, I'm only one of approximately 40,000 visitors here this week.

The Tour Down Under transforms this sleepy South Australian city with all the fanfare of a European Grand Tour. The nine-day race was first held in 1999, and in 2007 was the first event to gain UCI Pro Tour status outside of Europe – guaranteeing all of the world's top professional teams would be present. Indeed, even the once-mighty Lance Armstrong used the Tour Down Under as his comeback race in 2008. Adelaide, once a year, becomes the hottest cycling destination on the planet. I'm eager to see if it lives up to the hype.

The morning dawns clear and warm. I'm mentally checking off everything I need – shoes, kit, sunscreen, snacks, helmet, coffee. Definitely more coffee. Luckily someone had already thought this through, as the departure point for the ride – The Glasshouse – is also one of Adelaide's top cafes. While the barista works on the

fuel we need to kickstart our metabolisms, introductions are made and friends reunited. There is a small mountain of bikes leaning against the wall and still more riders are rolling up. Although there are smiles all round, some are more nervous than others.

I can soon see why: the route we have planned is a challenging one. We head straight out for the hills. The city rolls past us and we navigate the outer suburbs along Greenhill Rd toward Mt

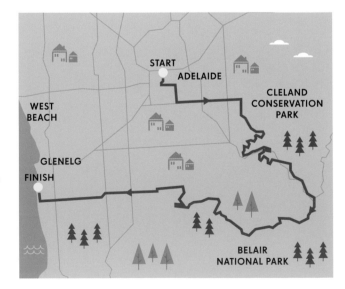

Osmond, the first climb of the day. It seems like only a few miles have passed before the 18% climb has us in its grip. Despite the gradient, a rhythm is surprisingly easy to find and the view that emerges as we approach the top makes the toil worth it. The conversations and chatter continue without pause as the road winds skyward.

We discuss our favourite riding spots – from the Alps in Europe, to the flatlands of Singapore, to the remote far north of my own home turf. Local tips, gear selections, best (and worst) riding food, favourite bikes. By the end of the first climb I've added at least three countries and two bikes to my 'must-ride' list.

The road rolls on through the mountainside. The climbs around here are long but beguiling. Whoever carved these roads did a good job. Everyone is in good spirits. There are words of encouragement, the occasional helping hand, and celebrations when the road begins to flatten out. A quick stop at the top of the longer climbs gives us some respite and a chance for everyone to regroup.

In the moments of quiet we contemplate the surroundings. From the top of the climbs we're rewarded with sweeping views over the city and coastline below. Gum trees provide some shade and the smell of eucalyptus wafts on the breeze. We make our way up Mt Barker. This long steady climb traces a disused section of highway, now closed to car traffic and designated as a bike lane. There are cyclists as far as the eye can see and, without the worry of cars, a chance to absorb the full experience of the Adelaide Hills.

I get overly excited at the sight of two large kangaroos sitting by the side of the road, close enough to touch. The Australians laugh

## CAUTION: ANIMALS CROSSING

The Adelaide hills and surrounding region host an abundance of wildlife. Kangaroos, koalas, snakes, lizards, echidnas, any number of birds and other creatures are easily spotted. Take care, especially when riding down fast descents or on roads with blind corners: an injury from hitting a kangaroo is not a story you want to take home! While they may be beautiful to look at, under no circumstances should you approach any wild animal.

*Clockwise from top: riding two abreast; a cafe stop before the big ride; Australia's beautiful morning light. Previous page: pedalling into the Adelaide Hills*

at me. The kangaroos also seem to give a mocking glance. But I feel I can tick something off my tourist achievement list.

We roll through Belair National Park, eyes darting between the road and trees as we hope to catch a glimpse of a koala. We had been lucky enough to spot one the day before. They probably heard us coming, as they keep well hidden today.

After each of the climbs come the descents. Steep, twisting ribbons of tarmac. Our train of riders flies down them. Pedal, float, lean, repeat. The smiles get even wider.

The weather in Adelaide can be fickle, and halfway through the ride the sky begins to darken, and a few spots of rain make an appearance. An unseasonably chilly wind rustles the trees. A gilet would have been a welcome addition at this point. The pace quickens as we try to stay warm.

We're hurtling down Windy Point. Twisting, turning, dropping toward the ocean. There's little opportunity to savour the view: this road isn't as smooth, and a few potholes and cracks in the surface add an extra challenge to an already fast descent. Remarkably, the clouds have blown over. A few sighs of relief. A flat sprint to the finish.

Finally, it's there, the beach spreads wide in front of us. This is where our ride ends. We roll gently toward the crowds at Glenelg, the flat bike path a welcome relief to protesting legs.

Cerulean ocean to the left, emerald hills to the right. An urban playground behind us and a beachside town in front. It's hard to believe that in one short morning we've experienced such a perfect melange of riding. **EB**

*"From the top of the climbs we're rewarded with sweeping views over the city and coastline below"*

### TOOLKIT

**Start //** Gouger St (King William end)
**End //** Glenelg
**Distance //** 37 miles (60km)
**How to get there //** Adelaide International Airport is located 4 miles (6km) west of the city
**Where to stay //** There are accommodation options for every budget. Book early for the Tour Down Under week and expect prices to be slightly higher than normal
**Climate //** Usually temperate, Adelaide can experience exceptionally hot weather during the Tour Down Under each January. Be prepared for anything between 20°C to 45°C (68°F to 113°F)
**More details //** www.southaustralia.com
**More rides //** There's usually a series of sportive rides before the race, see www.tourdownunder.com.au

*Opposite: Hot-air balloons above*
*Canowindra in New South Wales*

# MORE LIKE THIS
# ANTIPODEAN RIDES

## NEWCREST ORANGE
## CHALLENGE, AUSTRALIA

A nod to the spring classics and designed
to test the legs of even the most seasoned
rouleur, the Newcrest Orange Challenge
loop takes in over 2000m of climbing over
106 miles (170km). The event is run as a
fully supported Gran Fondo and riders are
given a total of eight hours to complete
the journey. However, anyone with strong
legs and a keen sense of adventure
can follow the route any time. The loop
circumnavigates Mt Canabolos, known to
locals as 'The Nob' and passes through
Cudal, Canowindra and Mandurama.
**Start/End // Orange**
**Distance // 106 miles (170km)**

## THE FORGOTTEN WORLD
## HIGHWAY, NEW ZEALAND

Following the road carved by early
pioneers, take in abandoned townships,
the 'republic' of Whangamomona (don't
forget to get your passport stamped
and a photo with the President), rugged
countryside and prehistoric landscapes.
Start the adventure in Stratford, named
for its apparent similarities to Stratford-
Upon-Avon, situated below the spectacular
snow-capped Mt Taranaki. From here the
Forgotten World Hwy begins surrounded
by farmland, but lush green valleys, raging
rivers, wooden-roofed tunnels, narrow
bridges and unsealed roads all feature
on this route. Riders will need to be well
prepared or travel with a support vehicle,
as there are very few opportunities to
restock supplies along the way.
**Start // Stratford, Taranaki**
**End // Taumaranui**
**Distance // 93 miles (150km)**
**over two days**

## AUCKLAND TO PIHA, NEW ZEALAND

What it lacks in distance this ride makes up
for in leg-draining climbs and breathtaking
views. There is a very good reason it has
become a yardstick for Auckland cyclist's
needing to test their form. Piha is a tiny
surfing town nestled on the west coast of
Auckland's Waikatere Ranges, famous for
its pounding surf, rugged coastline and
glistening black sand. The aptly named
Scenic Drive road to Piha twists and winds
its way up through subtropical rainforest,
before plummeting down a heart-pounding
descent to the beach. The road is narrow,
challenging, requires a high-level of
attention and strong legs, but also rewards
riders with postcard-worthy views over the
city, coastline and beyond. For an added
challenge drop down to Karekare beach on
the way (as seen in the film *The Piano*).
**Start // Auckland**
**End // Piha**
**Distance // 25 miles (40km)**

# THE OLD GHOST ROAD

*New Zealand's longest singletrack links two old gold mining routes to form a challenging but unforgettable multi-day adventure among rugged West Coast mountain ranges.*

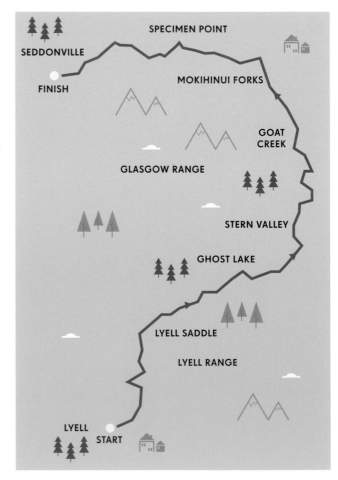

Who could resist the prospect of a challenging new cycle trail through some of New Zealand's wildest, untouched wilderness? The Old Ghost Road story begins with the rediscovery of a never-completed road between Lyell (in the Buller Gorge between Nelson and Westport) and Seddonville on the West Coast. Resurrecting the original sections and bridging the gap in between has proven one of the great track-building feats of the modern era.

The 53-mile (85km) trail officially opened late in 2015. Like rats up a drainpipe, Sarah and I rushed to be among the first to cycle it, setting off from Lyell within 24 hours of the official ribbon-cutting ceremony.

Unless you seek out the tiny cemetery hidden in the forest, you'd hardly believe Lyell was once a thriving gold town. The trail picks up an old dray road climbing gently into the thickly forested valley beyond, occasionally passing more relics of the gold rushes. We dismount our bikes to gingerly pick our way across two massive slips, dramatic evidence of major earthquakes, and scramble through rocky fords.

It's an 800m climb over 11 miles (18km) to reach Lyell Saddle Hut, one of four new bunkhouses built by the trail guardians, the Mokihinui-Lyell Backcountry Trust. In a clearing with views of the Glasgow Range, it's a magical spot to contemplate the alpine crossing ahead, with the possible bonus of hearing kiwi during the night. All four huts are geared up with bike tools, crockery and cooking pots, lessening riders' loads.

Just beyond the saddle, marked by a broken anvil, is the point where the old road builders threw in the towel. The proposed route down the south branch of the Mokihinui River proved impenetrable for the modern-day trail builders, too, but with the help of a

helicopter they scoped an alternative route over the tops.

Emerging above the bushline after a taxing grind up through luminous green forest, the track breaks out onto the open flanks of Mt Montgomery, a 'wow' situation if ever there was one. Those without a head for heights should probably turn back now, for here riders follow an improbable goat track blasted into the precipitous slopes of Rocky Tor. Alternatively you could get off and walk until the track resumes 'normal operation' down through more verdant forest towards Ghost Lake Hut.

The reality of Ghost Lake exceeded its hyped-up promise. The lake itself is a small, alpine tarn, bejewelled with colourful plant life. Alongside is a stand of alpine beech, and the adjacent hut, perched high on a bluff, affords vistas across mountainous wilderness and the rural plains around Murchison. It's a somewhat peculiar but utterly inspiring place to find yourself on a bicycle, but so flows the magic of the Old Ghost Road.

From the hut you can clearly make out the track heading in the direction of Stern Valley, some 800m below. Some menacing switchbacks are followed by a push on to razor-edged Skyline Ridge that doubles the jeopardy with dangerously distracting views.

Then, there are the steps. In a major 'uh-oh' moment that must have had the trail builders scratching their heads, it was decided that the only sensible way to descend the 60m off the ridge was via the now-named Skyline Steps. It's some relief when the trail resumes through sublime forest, laden with oddball rock formations, and along Stern Creek that tumbles over a gushing waterfall. The relatively smooth, sweeping terrain is welcome after the tricky, rocky stuff on top.

## A LINE ON A MAP...

The discovery of an old survey map provided the genesis for the Old Ghost Road. Drawn in 1886, it proposed a route connecting the Buller and Mokihinui gold fields. Sorties into the backcountry 130 years later revealed that roads had been started at each end but stopped abruptly deep in the wilderness. It would take nine years, NZ$6 million, 150,000 man-hours (including almost 27,000 of volunteer labour) to complete what the old-timers had started.

*Clockwise from top: rugged riding; beating the Boneyard; waterfalls are a familiar feature of riding in New Zealand. Previous page: the Skyline Steps – you might need to walk some sections of the Old Ghost Road*

Beyond Stern Valley Hut is the Earnest Valley, arguably the most astonishing sight on the whole trail. Around the halfway point, it appears at first as a tranquil mountain idyll, encircled by soaring peaks and graced with pretty alpine tarns and gardens. But then you notice a certain rippling of the landscape: mountains tilted and sheared by tectonic forces that crush boulders and scatter the basin with debris. But surely that's not actually the track zigzagging up through the spectacularly collapsed hillside known as the Boneyard, complete with car-sized boulders teetering precariously?

Moving quickly on. The next landmark is Solemn Saddle, from where the trail breaks through into a new river system, the Mohikinui. Backdropped by multiple mountain ranges, the fast, flowing descent to Goat Creek is a great place to purge some adrenaline and break out the GoPro.

On the valley floor, the track cruises through towering podocarp forest with ferny undergrowth and twittering birdlife. At Mokihinui Forks, the south and north river branches meet in a turbulent junction, but sandfly attacks may prevent lengthy admiration. The Old Ghost Road then follows the main branch to Specimen Point, a magnificent spot for the final hut, with grandstand views over a picturesque bend in the river that swirls, pools and cascades in a constant thrum of white water.

The home stretch of trail sidles high along the river gorge, with impressive bridges spanning the ominously named Suicide Slips. Relics from gold mining times can be seen here and there, testament to yet more great aspirations, toil, danger and failure. In more recent times the Mokihinui River was the scene of a great victory, when it was saved from being dammed, paving the way for the old road builders' dreams to be realised. **LS**

## *"Surely that's not actually the track zigzagging up through the collapsed hillside known as the Boneyard?"*

### TOOLKIT

**Start** // Lyell, Buller Gorge (50 minutes' drive from Westport)
**End** // Seddonville, West Coast (40 minutes' drive from Westport)
**Distance** // 53 miles (85km)
**When to ride** // Summer and autumn, although bad weather can make the trail dangerous at any time of year.
**Where to stay** // The four huts available must be booked in advance.
**Terrain** // Track surface varies and is very rugged in parts; expect to push your bike in some sections.
**Rider ability** // This is an advanced trail suitable only for fit, experienced mountain bikers, with sound mechanical skills.
**More info** // See www.oldghostroad.org.nz for essential hut bookings, gear lists and trail conditions, plus details on bike hire, guided tours, shuttles and heli-transport.

*Opposite: mountain bikes are permitted on New Zealand's Heaphy Track for some of the year*

# MORE LIKE THIS
# MOUNTAIN BIKE RIDES

### DOWNIEVILLE, USA

From ghost towns to railroads, California's gold rush has left many lasting mementos. One of the most thrilling is the web of trails in the north of Gold Country in the Sierra Nevada, California – specifically the Downieville Downhill trail. This dusty delight weaves around pine trees and rocks, over bridges and under shady canopies. At 17 miles (27km), it's one of the longest singletrack descents in the world and, lying a couple of hours northwest of Lake Tahoe, it's surrounded by miles of more excellent riding. Trails tend towards the narrow and rocky, with some exposure to cliff edges. Outfitters in Downieville can supply shuttles to the top of the trail and rental bikes.

**Start // Packer Saddle**
**End // Downieville**
**Distance // 18.5 miles (30km)**

### HEAPHY TRACK, NEW ZEALAND

From May to September, over the Southern Hemisphere's winter months, mountain bikers are permitted to ride one of New Zealand's treasured Great Walks. The Heaphy Track through Kahurangi National Park in the northwest of the South Island was where the Department of Conservation trialled multi-use trails through a national park for the first time, many years after the gold rush of the west coast saw 19th-century prospectors tramping through these beech-forested hills. Mountain bikers should expect to spend two nights on the trail, in order to experience this wild and wonderful place. In such a precious environment – the Heaphy passes through intensely varied habitats and landscapes – there are rules to follow: no groups larger than six, overnight accommodation only in huts (remove your saddle from the bike to stop kea parrots destroying it), and no night riding in order to protect the nocturnal kiwi and the giant (and carnivorous) land snail.

**Start // Collingwood**
**End // Karamea**
**Distance // 50 miles (80km)**
**More info // www.doct.gov.nz/ heaphytrack**

### LAKE GARDA, ITALY

It wasn't gold seekers who created many of the trails in the mountains surrounding the north tip of Lake Garda but soldiers and engineers. In WWI and WWII they blasted tunnels through rock and forged paths to lookouts. Today many of those routes are trails for mountain bikers and hikers, making the town of Riva del Garda a European mountain-bike hotspot – the town hosts a long-standing mountain bike festival in May. And, helpfully, there are several outfitters with bikes for hire. This is one place where a local guide or a very good map will be required to find the best trails, though there are some well-known singletrack descents, such as trail 601, which descends 2000m in 7.5 miles (12km) – don't let the lake views distract you from this technically difficult trail! Try to stay in Torbole or Riva del Garda.

**Start // Monte Altissimo (for trail 601)**
**End // Torbole**
**Distance // 7.5 miles (12km)**

# AUSTRALIA'S ATHERTON TABLELANDS

*Rolling through rainforests, across the tropical tablelands that tower above the sun-splashed beaches of Cairns, a sensational suite of mountain-bike trails await the world.*

Even the flora is feisty in Tropical North Queensland. I've been bucked from my bike in many colourful ways, but only once has a plant pulled me from the saddle. The triffid attack happened while riding rainforest trails in the hinterland high above the beaches of Australia's Coral Sea coast, when a stray strand of the wicked Wait-A-While vine snared my torso with its hooked spine and dragged me down. It became suddenly obvious how this vine got its name.

This is the real Australia – a gritty, wild place, where trails creep past creeks with crocodile warning signs and anything can, and – judging by anecdotes from local cyclists – often does, happen. I've

even heard tales of a rider being booted off his bike by a bird – a cassowary – a primeval-looking, human-sized rooster of a species that stalk the forests and foreshore of this region like leftover dinosaurs in an Arthur Conan Doyle story.

The riding, though, is sublime. And like the Wait-A-While, this place is hard to shake off once you're hooked. For years I kept returning to ride the Triple-R – Australia's oldest mountain-bike race – and razz around steamy jungle trails at Smithfield, but it took a while to realise that the cream of the North Queensland scene was floating on the top, with the development of a huge highlands hubs-and-links system.

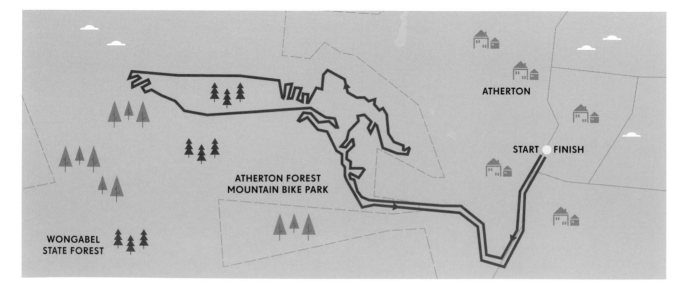

A grand vision is unfolding here, which is turning the Tablelands into a world-class mountain-bike destination. The concept revolves around a singletrack-dominated trail system at Atherton, around Mt Baldy, and extra tracks in places, including Mareeba and Herberton, with dirt roads joining the dots.

Between these hubs, the original MTB park at Smithfields, and an additional smattering of tracks and trails around Port Douglas, Daintree and the Cassowary Coast, the region boasts over 435 miles (700km) of documented rideable off-road routes. It's this kind of offering that has attracted mountain-biking's biggest events – the World Cup and the World Championships – to the region.

Because these aren't average trails. The tropical tracks slice through great green sweaty swathes of World Heritage–listed rainforest, throwing everything at riders from snarly tree roots to hand-sized spiders. The first dash of the day is the cobweb-clearing ride – not for the faint hearted.

Yet, every morning at 6am, a rotating mob of mountain bikers meets at a cafe in Atherton to ride up Rifle Range Rd and launch themselves into orbit around a still-expanding trail universe, currently comprising 40 miles (65km) of singletrack.

We start on Ridgy Didge, Atherton's original professionally sculpted trail, built when Queensland Parks and Wildlife began investing in the creation of this mountain biking mecca. In Aussie slang, Ridgy Didge means 'the real deal' – something that's kosher – and this 4-mile (6.7km) loop epitomises everything that's epic about the area.

Climbing around switchbacks bathed in dappled dawn sunlight,

> *"This trail turns new mountain bikers into lifelong converts but it also challenges really good riders"*

we hoon around the route until the arresting view at Leasie's Lookout demands that we take a breather, and drink in the verdant vista across the tablelands.

'Atherton is now one of the greatest bike parks in Australia,' enthuses local legend and Mountain-bike Hall of Famer, Glen Jacobs – who knows a thing or two about the country's best trails, having created of most of them, including this one.

'This is still my favourite Tablelands track,' says Jacobs. 'Partly because it was the first, but also because it has everything, from uphill berms and switchbacks that make the climbing as much fun as the descents, to some really fast and flowy downhill sections. This trail turns new mountain bikers into lifelong converts, but it also challenges really good riders, because if you're not careful you can overcook it.'

Ridgy Didge segues with Bandy-Bandy, a challenging 1.6-mile (2.6km) trail with a technical climb that rewards with another magical outlook. This is one of three tracks named after snakes, which reveals the nature of the local wildlife, but also reflects the feel of the trails, which slide and glide through the trees with serpentine grace, occasionally delivering a viper's nip along the way.

Both circuits pass through the spaghetti junction that forms the

network's nucleus, the 'Roundabout', from where trails spin off in all directions. The longest is Stairway to Heaven, which features almost 7 miles (11km) of continuous singletrack, wending around endless eucalypt-fringed elbows, up and over a ridgeline offering amazing views across the Great Dividing Range, and ultimately arriving at Three-ways, where downhill devotees have several options to sink their tyres into.

Ricochet is a fast and furious 1-mile (1.5km) descending trail that shoots towards Rifle Range, bouncing around big-arse berms and serving up numerous technical treats, including jumps. Yahoo Wahoo is slightly gentler, but it's still gravity assisted for 75% of its 2-mile (3km) length, punctuated by the odd uphill pinch.

Crucially, Atherton has embraced its new incarnation as a mountain bikers' magnet. When we return to the cafe for a post-ride caffeine blast, staff are utterly unfazed by our mud-splattered appearance, even when a leech detaches from my leg and sends a trail of blood across the floor.

The trails are well used by events, including Far North Queensland's notoriously cruel Crocodile Trophy – an epic 8-stage 404-mile (650km) race, rated among the planet's toughest MTB challenges – which spends two entire days in Atherton.

And there's even talk of staging a new multiday race, climbing from Smithfields in Cairns to do a Tablelands traverse, and ending with a gravity-assisted rampage from Mt Molloy, down the infamous Bump Track, to finish on Four Mile Beach at Port Douglas. Now that would be epic. **PK**

## WORLD CHAMPS

In 1996, Cairns skidded onto the mountain-biking map by staging the UCI World MTB Championships. Glen Jacobs wasn't solely responsible for this coup, but his revolutionary route designs influenced a still-evolving sport, and the event launched his career as a globetrotting trail architect. Now he's back where it began, working on the Atherton trails and redesigning Cairn's Smithfield MTB park for the World Championships, which return to the tropics in 2017.

*Left to right: Hotel Eacham in the Atherton Tablelands; mountain biking the Atherton Tablelands, Millaa Millaa Falls*

## TOOLKIT

**Start/End** // Atherton
**Distance** // 15 miles (24km)
**Getting there** // Access the Atherton Tablelands via Cairns, which has an international airport served by major carriers.
**When to ride** // June to September offers the best conditions. Temperatures get sticky during the day year-round – the ideal time for riding is early morning and late afternoon.
**Where to swim** // Cool down between rides in the plunge pool beneath Millaa Millaa Falls, or in the green waters of volcano-created Lake Eacham. Always obey warning signs when swimming in Tropical North Queensland, where killer crocodiles lurk.
**What to take** // A dual-suspension bike is recommended, with tubeless tyres.
**More info** // www.ridecairns.com; www.tablelandstrails.com

*Opposite: mountain bikers admire
the view in Morzine Bike Park*

# MORE LIKE THIS
## MOUNTAIN BIKE RIDES

### THE SEVEN STANES, SCOTLAND

Spread across the south of Scotland, the
Seven Stanes are a septuplet of mountain-
biking hubs that collectively offer some of
the best cross-country riding in Europe.
Like Atherton – and unlike their continental
counterparts, which are mostly based
around ski resorts – these MTB parks
are dedicated to bikes year-round, and
although they feature plenty of fast and
technical descents, there are no lazy-arse
lifts and you have to earn your downhill
turns by putting in the grunt during ascents.
Ride the phenomenal Glentress Trail, an
18.5-mile (30km) black run, often named
Britain's best trail. Also explore family-
friendly conditions at Glentrool in Galloway
Forest; rocky and technical terrain at
Kirroughtree; coastal tracks at Dalbeattie;
a woodland wonderland at Mabie Forest;
brilliant blue and red runs at Newcastleton,
on the England–Scotland border; and a
mixed bag of treats at the village of Ae.
**Start/End // Glentress Peel Centre
Trailhead**
**Distance //** 18.5 miles (30km)
**More info //** www.
7stanesmountainbiking.com

### PORTES DU SOLEIL,
### FRANCE/SWITZERLAND

For those who prefer to mix up their cross-
country runs with some lift-assisted downhill
(DH) action, the Portes du Soleil area in
the Franco Swiss Alps boasts 12 mountain
resorts with four linked mountain-bike
parks and over 50 DH trails. As the resorts
are linked, so too are the lift passes, with
access to 21 bike-friendly lifts and more
than 404 miles (650km) of tracks. This
enables you to explore Châtel Bike Park,
the 'European Whistler', with 20 DH tracks;
the Les Gets Park, with 12 DH tracks, six
all-mountain cross-country routes and the
Canyon freeride slope (plus some trails for
beginners); Morzine Bike Park, with five DH
tracks and a range of trails suitable for less
experienced riders; and Montriond-Avoriaz
with a mixture of DH trails. The Pass'Portes
du Soleil weekend kicks off the MTB
season, with an epic 50-mile (80km) all-
mountain classic course, featuring 6500m
of descent (and only 1000m of climbing).
**Start/End // Morzine**
**Distance //** 50 miles (80km)
**More info //** en.portesdusoleil.com/
summer; www.passportesdusoleil.com

### KOKOPELLI TRAIL, FRUITA, US

Moab is the most famous mountain-
bike friendly 'trail town' in the world, but
many Stateside rough riders rate juicy
Fruita in Colorado even higher, and not
just because it's easier to access. The
town is surrounded by hundreds of miles
of fast and flowing canyon- ridge- and
desert-style singletrack, with myriad route
options available within the North Fruita
Desert/18 Rd trail system and at the
Kokopelli Trailhead region. Nearby Loma
is the starting point of the Kokopelli Trail,
a 142-mile (229km) stretch of continuous
double- and singletrack trail that flows all
the way to Moab.
**Start // Loma**
**End // Moab**
**Distance //** 142 miles (229km)
**More info //** www.otesports.com

# THE ACHERON WAY

*Take a challenging day-ride amid some of the world's tallest trees to encounter unique wildlife and witness the rebirth of a town in the Australian state of Victoria.*

Saturday dawns on a winter weekend in Warburton, Australia. The former logging town, an end of the (paved) road sort of place, lies in a steep-sided forest valley; low clouds streak the green-grey treetops. The Yarra River, which broadens as it reaches Melbourne, runs through its centre.

I carry my road bike down from my motel room and make my final checks: pump, two tubes, puncture repair kit, multi-tool, water, cake. Before I set off, I see Franz, the barrel-chested owner of the motel, who has cycled and photographed this part of Victoria for decades. I tell him where I'm planning to go and he lets me in to a couple of local secrets.

Then, in the cool air, I follow the Woods Point Rd east out of Warburton along the floor of the valley. It undulates through a couple of townships before turning left, about 30 minutes later. As soon as I round the corner, the road pitches up. It's a steady gradient, so I settle into a comfortable gear — I know already that this is a big climb. The sparsely populated valley floor has been

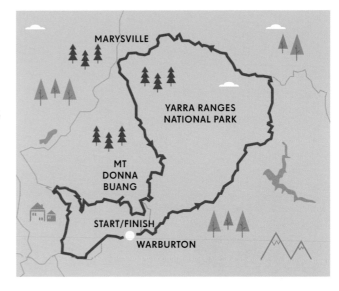

replaced by dense forest – I'm in the Yarra Ranges National Park now. On either side of me are mountain ash trees, manna gum trees, mountain grey gums and myrtle beeches, rising above an understory of 12ft ferns. The mountain ash eucalypts are among the tallest and fastest-growing flowering plants in the world, topping out at more than 100m. It's not unusual to feel dwarfed by the Australian landscape, but here I'm dwarfed by the trees.

The road curves around the contours of the Reefton Spur. I pedal higher and higher. At breaks in the trees, on corners, I glimpse wave after wave of green, as far as I can see. Another sort of wave breaks over me – trepidation. What if I break my chain and can't fix it? What if I tear a tyre, or simply run out of steam?

A pair of crimson rosellas, foraging on the verge, provide a distraction. They burst upwards and fly alongside me – streamlined red bodies, straight blue wings a blur – before peeling off into the undergrowth, like vivid Spitfires. These raucous and social parrots are common companions on these roads. Higher in the tree canopy, large flocks of white cockatoos flap haphazardly from ridge to ridge, cawing loudly to each other. A rarer sight are yellow-tailed black cockatoos; larger birds, they tend to fly slowly and more purposefully, like WWII bombers.

I'm breathing deeply but steadily. This is a 12.5 mile (20km) climb and eventually it levels out before meeting a junction. I turn left to Marysville. This road (slightly busier, meaning one or two cars, or a logging truck) runs along the spine of a ridge, dipping and rising, never straight. Up here I get a glimpse of something terrible but curiously beautiful: entire hillsides of dead trees, the colour of grey-white bone. Scoured of foliage by flame, the upward-stretching

*"From June to October this gravel road is a traffic-free treat for cyclists; great scrolls of bark are strewn across it"*

branches that crown the tall, straight trunks are sculptural. This is the aftermath of Black Saturday. On 7 February 2009, after days of withering heat (in Melbourne the temperature exceeded 46°C) bush fires ignited across this part of Victoria. Fanned by 100km/h winds, fires of 1200°C, with flames 100m tall, roared through the Kinglake-Marysville region, where 159 people died.

Since then the surviving trees are bursting with new life, green shoots growing from charred trunks. Young trees have grown up to the knees of the forest giants. Birds and animals are returning.

Through this landscape in transition, the road begins to drop into Marysville. This is a steep, long and fast descent – check brake pads, cables and quick releases first. As I slalom around the bends, I shift my weight to the outside pedal for grip, raising the inner pedal and leaning my knee towards the tarmac. The road steepens just before it reaches Marysville and then tilts uphill into the main street. When the fire swept through, only seven businesses were left standing and just 33 houses were habitable, 400 were destroyed. For personal accounts of Black Saturday, stop by the Phoenix Museum in the tourist information centre.

After topping up my water bottles at Fraga's Cafe and wolfing down a baguette, I continue south on the main road. This is the busiest stretch of the route but it doesn't last long – I'm looking for

## LEADBEATER'S POSSUM

One forest resident that you probably won't spot is the Leadbeater's possum, also known as the fairy possum. This mini-marsupial, weighing between 100 and 160g, and fitting into the palm of a hand, is one of the world's most endangered creatures. The mountain ash forests of the Central Highlands are its habitat – it lives in colonies of about a dozen animals but only one pair will breed – with the possum making its home in high-rise hollow trees.

*Left to right: rushing water and giant mountain ash trees in the Yarra Ranges; a Leadbeater's or Fairy possum in the wild. Previous page: the gravel descent on the Acheron Way*

a left turn onto the Acheron Way. Swing off the highway here and you're back in the shady forest. A couple of years ago when I first rode this logging road, which runs beside the Acheron River, I saw a red-bellied black snake, hunting for frogs. Now if I stop, I watch where I put my feet.

The Acheron Way turns into a gravel road as it climbs up over the Acheron Gap at 756m and down the other side. After a dusty, helter-skelter descent, and back on the Warburton side of the Ranges, I rejoin the tarmac at the Rainforest Gallery, a 15m-high walkway through the forest canopy. Warburton is a short descent away, but if you've still got some zip left in your legs, turn right to head up Mt Donna Buang, one of Australian cycling's iconic climbs. It's another long but gradual ascent, with views over the Yarra Valley. Half a mile (1km) from the summit, I follow Franz's first tip and turn left onto the C505. There's a gate across the entrance: in the winter Parks Victoria closes this gravel road, which means that from June to October it's a traffic-free treat for cyclists. Great scrolls of bark are strewn across the descent, and the wildlife has grown unaccustomed to people. I stop to watch a lyrebird, a famous mimic, disappear into the undergrowth.

After a 6-mile (10km) descent, I turn left at the next junction towards Launching Place, keeping an eye out for Franz's second suggestion. It's easy to miss: on a fast descent I spot the crossing point for the O'Shannassy Aqueduct Trail. This little-used track for walkers and cyclists follows the route of a now-disused aqueduct that was opened in 1914 to deliver water from Warburton's reservoir to Melbourne, 51 miles (82km) away, and I follow the flat track back to Warburton for 6 miles (10km): fire and water in one day. **RB**

## TOOLKIT

**Start/End //** Warburton
**Distance //** 93 miles (150km)
**Getting there //** Warburton is about a 90 minute drive northeast from Melbourne. Even better, the Lilydale–Warburton Rail Trail allows you to cycle 25 miles (40km) from Lilydale train station (on the Melbourne line).
**Tour //** You can take some of the hard work out of the ride by signing up with Soigneur (www.soigneur.cc), a Melbourne-based tour operator that escorts cyclists on rides, including this route.
**Where to stay //** There's a motel and two hotels in Warburton. If you break the ride at Marysville there are a couple of new hotels in the town.
**What to take //** Carry spare inner tubes, food, water (to be replenished at Marysville), tools and sunscreen.

*Opposite: The Great Ocean Road
along Victoria's south coast*

# MORE LIKE THIS
# VICTORIAN ROAD RIDES

### THE 7 PEAKS RIDE

Each year Parks Victoria challenges cyclists to climb seven of the toughest road climbs in Australia, all of them in Victoria's High Country. At the top of each you can get your 7 Peaks passport stamped, and riders who have completed more than four are entered into a prize draw. Four of the climbs are close to the beautiful town of Bright: Mt Hotham, Mt Buffalo, Falls Creek and Dinner Plain. Mt Buller (see p104) near Mansfield is another. The sixth climb is Lake Mountain, which starts from Marysville. And the final climb is short but very steep Mt Baw Baw to the southeast. All are achievable for a fit cyclist and riders generally have five months of warm weather to attempt all seven.
**Start/End // Individual climbs range from 6 miles to18.5 miles (10km to 30km) but would typically be part of a longer ride.**
**More info // www.7peaks.com.au**

### AROUND THE BAY IN A DAY

Australia's largest mass participation bike ride was first held in 1993. Although much of the route around Melbourne's Port Phillip Bay is rideable throughout the year (the Mornington Peninsula, the eastern end of the croissant-shaped route, is particularly popular with weekend cyclists), this is the only time you will ride in the company of 15,000 other cyclists. The full loop is 155 miles (250km), with participants catching the ferry between Sorrento at the tip of the Mornington Peninsula to Queenscliff at the tip of the Bellarine Peninsula. Groups start and finish at Alexandra Gardens in Melbourne, but head off in different directions, east and west. Many of the roads are closed to cars for the ride.
**Start/End // Alexandra Gardens**
**Distance // 155 miles (250km)**
**More info // www.bicyclenetwork.com. au/around-the-bay**

### GREAT VICTORIAN BIKE RIDE

The GVBR was founded in the mid-1980s and has grown to become an annual fixture on the cycling calendar. Think of it less as quiet, solitary ramble through the countryside and more of a travelling jamboree on wheels, with thousands of other cyclists. The ride covers approximately 340 miles (550km) over eight or nine days so distances aren't daunting; nobody cares much what you ride (or wear). The GVBR ranges over a different corner of Victoria each year (in 2015 it explored some of Victoria's classic gold-rush towns, in 2016 it's from the Grampians to the Great Ocean Road), with luggage being carried on ahead in dozens of trucks, leaving you free to enjoy the ride. Tent cities spring up in each host town, which compete to offer the warmest welcome.
**Start // The Grampians (2016 ride)**
**End // Great Ocean Rd (2016 ride)**
**Distance // typically around 340 miles (550km)**
**More info // www.bicyclenetwork. au/racv-great-victorian-bike-ride/**

# THE MUNDA BIDDI TRAIL

*Western Australia's 621-mile (1000km) Munda Biddi Trail is one of the world's longest, dedicated, off-road cycling tracks and a challenging wilderness adventure.*

t's 8.15am and the air is starting to warm up in this wild and thickly wooded patch of south-west Western Australia (WA). Shafts of sunlight stream through breaks in the jarrah canopy to illuminate wildflowers alongside the narrow dirt paths that our little convoy has been following for the past five days.

The distant 'kerrreee-kerrreee' calls of red-tailed black cockatoos can be heard through the gum leaves. My morning coffee, brewed on a camp stove, has barely kicked in, but already I am knee-deep in water and clambering across rocks in a shallow, but fast-flowing section of WA's Murray River. We are about 3 miles (5km) south of Dwellingup, and I am half pushing, half carrying my mountain bike. My legs are sore for the fourth morning, but I have a great fat grin daubed across my face.

This is not how I pictured this week turning out, when our team of four set out from Mundaring, east of Perth. From getting lost on badly signposted dirt roads, and navigating steep, rutted sections of trail, to climbing constantly undulating hills – frequently leaping into waterholes, rivers, pools and cascades – and just coping with the technical complexity of up to 37 miles (60km) a day of difficult terrain, there's been much more scope for serious adventure than I could have anticipated. The 207-mile (333km) section of Munda Biddi that we were attempting over seven days, I quickly discovered, is hard work.

This northern section of the Munda Biddi ('path through the forest' in one of the local Nyungar dialects) winds over 309 miles (498km) from Mundaring, in the Darling Range, to Nannup on the Blackwood River. It zips through thick forest and open patches of dry bushland, river valleys, and along a massive escarpment that

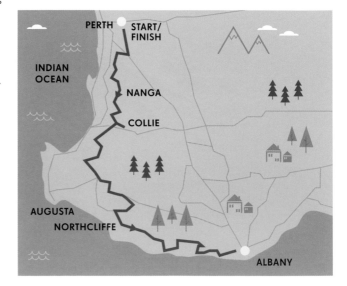

looks out over an 18.5-mile (30km) wide coastal plain to the Indian Ocean. 'It's a cycling wilderness experience that's probably the best you'll get in Australia,' says Munda Biddi Trail Foundation (MBTF) volunteer Stewart Parkinson. 'In some of the state forests, you're going into areas that are totally uninhabited. It's quite primeval.' The complete Munda Biddi Trail wends all the way down through the stately karri forests of the south via Walpole and Denmark to Albany.

'What makes the Munda Biddi unique is that it's one trail, it has got purpose-built huts, and it is effectively wilderness,' says Ron Colman, chairman of the MBTF. The trail is designed so that every 25 miles (40km) or so there is either a town or a hut. The idea is that you stop in to restock on food supplies (so you never have to carry more than a couple of days' worth), carry out any repairs (on both bikes and weary bodies), get a shower and sleep in a bed.

At the end of the third day, and 85 miles (137km) into our journey, we roll into the Dandalup campsite. On top of a vast escarpment – the Darling Range – and facing the coast, this hut has stunning views along the northern part of the trail. From here you can see across 18.5 miles (30km) of coastal plains to the sea. A charming uphill section of narrow trail twists and turns through open woodland, studded with primitive-looking, multi-headed grass trees. There is a decking area, so we stop to take in the view. Later we watch the sun set over the ocean.

The northern part of the trail up to Dandalup features the greatest concentration of sections graded 'challenging' and 'medium' by the MBTF – meaning they are steep and the trail condition can be poor. But the great thing about the Munda Biddi is that there are many entry points from roads, so you can devise a

## FIRE-LOOKOUT TREES

In the 1940s in Pemberton, which the trail passes, pegs were embedded in eight local karri trees (the third tallest species in the world) to create nature's own fire-lookout towers. Two of these trees – the Diamond Tree, the Gloucester Tree – can still be climbed. The Dave Evans Bicentennial Tree, which reaches the dizzying height of 75m with 165 pegs spiralling up the trunk, was made a fire lookout in the 1980s.

*Clockwise from top: a cockpit view near Dundalup; a Western Shingleback; Tom's crossing on the Munda Biddi; waterfalls near Baden Powell Camp*

trip to suit fitness levels and thirst for excitement.

It's the end of the sixth day of riding – and 141 miles (227km) into our journey – and by now I have lost track of the dates or the days of the week. Our lives out here are driven by rhythms: the sun rising, passing across the sky and setting again each day; the packing up of our gear and saddling it to the bike each morning; the wheels and spokes as they spin, and the repetitive crunch of the pea gravel; the constant eating to fuel the pistons that our legs have become (nuts, chocolate, trail bars, sweets, bread, peanut butter, Gatorade); and the rhythms of the bush, as the rustling and buzzing rises into a crescendo and falls away again each day. At points I feel totally unplugged from civilisation.

The next day is our last on the trail. The final stretch into the coalmining town of Collie is more open, flanked by farmland, and even though it's late spring and the wildflower season is waning, there's still a sprinkling of flame peas, Woodbridge Poison, pom poms, fringe lilies and other blooms. Our convoy makes a sudden stop at one point to avoid two feisty western shingleback lizards sunning themselves on the path and flashing their tongues at us. We are joined later by a large and noisy flock of wheeling red-tailed black cockatoos. It seems as if they've come to bid us goodbye.

'What I enjoy about cycling,' says one of our crew. 'is that you are going fast enough that you feel like you're actually going somewhere, but you're also right in the environment, not like being in a car.' I have to say that I'm starting to agree, and as we roll into Collie I'm already thinking about where my next mountain biking adventure might be. **JP**

*Previous page: cooling off in a pond at Lane Pool Reserve, outside Perth*

## TOOLKIT

**Start/End** // Mundaring in the Perth Hills, Albany
**Distance** // 621 miles (1000km)
**Where to stay** // There's a wide range of accommodation available, from campsites to B&Bs, depending on your budget and preference.
**What to take** // A mountain bike, or at least a bike with wide, knobbly tyres will tackle the gravel. Be equipped to perform on-the-road bike maintenance, bring spare chain links, spokes and inner tubes (also a puncture repair kit).
**When to ride** // You'll need about three weeks to do the full 1000km trail, longer if you take rest days– but most riders just come for a day or two. Summer (January and February) is hot and not ideal for cycling. Spring and autumn are better and the winter (July, August) is also typically mild.
**More info** // www.mundabiddi.org.au

*Opposite: riding the green
route of the Via Dinarica*

# MORE LIKE THIS
# LONG-DISTANCE RIDES

### NC500, SCOTLAND

Launched in 2015, this new trail follows the crenellated coastline of northern Scotland, using quiet roads and byways. Like Munda Biddi, it delivers you into a little-explored (though not underrated) part of the country, starting from Inverness. Heading clockwise, you'll reach the west coast at Applecross to discover some of Britain's most stunning (if chilly) white-sand beaches heading north up the west coast. Fishing villages provide accommodation. Then the NC500 trails round the top of Scotland, passing John O'Groats before heading down the east coast back to Inverness. There are plenty of Scottish diversions along the way: ruined castles, ceilidh bars, whisky distilleries and even a Munro mountain or two.
**Start/End //** Inverness
**Distance //** 500 miles (805km)
**More info //** www.northcoast500.com

### GREAT ALLEGHENY PASSAGE, USA

Pennsylvania a cycling hotspot? Yes, really. Far from the fanfare of the cycle-mad coasts, PA has developed some excellent routes and trails, including more than 90 rail trails. Chief among these is the Great Allegheny Passage through the Allegheny Mountains and it's one of the longest in the US. Embark from Pittsburgh and pedal southeast towards Cumberland in West Virginia. The trail is on graded gravel paths and you'll be riding through forest and staying in such welcoming local communities as Confluence and Rockwood. From Cumberland you can jump on the 185-mile (298km) Chesapeake and Ohio Canal Towpath all the way to Washington DC. (Of course, if you really want to get away from traffic, there are few better places in the state than Amish Country around Lancaster over to the east.)
**Start //** Pittsburgh, Pennsylvania
**End //** Cumberland, West Virginia
**Distance //** 150 miles (241km)
**More info //** www.gaptrail.org

### VIA DINARICA, SOUTHEAST EUROPE

This project dwarfs even Munda Biddi – not in terms of distance, perhaps, but in its ambition. The idea behind Via Dinarica is to connect walking and cycling routes across seven countries: Albania, Bosnia and Hercegovina, Croatia, Kosovo, Montenegro, Serbia and Slovenia. There are three routes across the Dinaric Alps: blue for a bay-hopping walk along the coast, white for the hardcore hikers, across the spine of the limestone spine of the range. But it's the green route that is designed for cyclists, skirting the mountains through inland forests and villages. It connects hundreds of miles of bike paths with accommodation in rural guesthouses and mountain huts along the way, but note that this is still very much a work in progress, with the project only starting in 2012, supported by the UN and USAID. But it will surely develop into an enthralling way to experience this little-known corner of Europe.
**Start/End //** Any point between Albania and Slovenia
**Distance //** 600 miles (966km)
**More info //** www.viadinarica.com

# ALPS 2 OCEAN
# CYCLE TRAIL

*New Zealand's longest cycle trail serves up colossal, colourful vistas on its way from the Southern Alps to the Pacific Coast town of Oamaru.*

N ew Zealanders have long been mad for mountain biking. But when, in 2009, the government injected NZ$50 million to build a nationwide cycle trail network and it was matched by another $50 million from community groups, it was spades and diggers at dawn in the battle to become the world's ultimate off-road cycling destination.

The fruits of this funding are the New Zealand Cycle Trail's 23 'Great Rides', ranging from day-trips to multi-day epics, some following old byways and others cutting new paths through previously inaccessible wilderness. I have now ridden 22 and while there's the odd lemon among them, the majority are fat, juicy cherries on a riding pie that already boasted such internationally renowned trail centres as Rotorua's Redwoods and Wellington's Makara Peak.

The South Island's Alps 2 Ocean (A2O) is one of the best – an instant classic that can be enjoyed by almost anyone.

Stretching more than 186 miles (300km) from mountains to sea, divided into nine sections ridden individually or in full over four to six days, its merits are many and varied. First up, there's the starting point: at the foot of New Zealand's highest peak, Aoraki (Mt Cook; 3724m), amid the splendour of the Southern Alps.

The A2O heads down the lower Hooker Valley and soon meets an impasse at the Tasman River. It's a quick helicopter hop to the other side, from where the trail recommences through fairly rocky terrain along the Tasman delta. The broad, braided river channels are a spectacular sight, backdropped by the Ben Ohau Range that remains in view downriver to Lake Pukaki, where the trail follows the smoother Braemar Rd towards Twizel.

There's an alternative start at Lake Tekapo, from where the trail parallels the first of many powder-blue, hydropower canals through

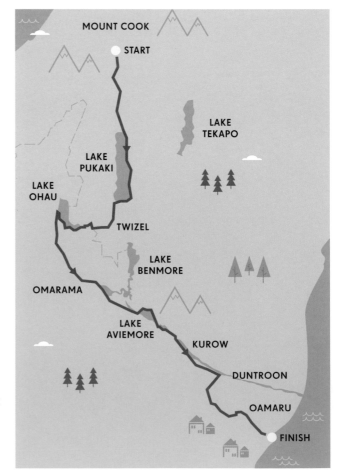

golden tussockland, past the supremely positioned Tekapo B Power Station, to meet the main trail on Braemar Rd. Lake Tekapo itself is a must-see, the almost impossibly turquoise jewel in the heart of the famed Mackenzie Country. Above the lake is Mt John Observatory, the focal point of the Aoraki Mackenzie International Dark Sky Reserve, a magnet for astronomers and amateur stargazers alike. But big skies, day and night, are a constant on the A2O.

The town of Twizel was established in 1968 for workers on the Waitaki hydroelectric power station. Defiantly surviving beyond its use-by date only to play second fiddle to the national park village of Aoraki/Mt Cook, today it's undergoing a bit of a micro-boom. Close to major crossroads, more or less in the middle of everything, it's a solid service town for passing A2O riders, and also a pleasant home-base for day rides on and around the trail.

One of the A2O's best day rides is from Twizel to Lake Ohau: a leisurely cruise along pretty country roads and another intensely blue canal, then beside the lake to longstanding Lake Ohau Lodge, with an atmospheric restaurant, bar, and killer mountain views.

From there, the A2O heads up and over an old moraine terrace, then down the quintessentially rural Quailburn Road towards the town of Omarama. The climb over the hill is a bit of a grind, but rewards with panoramic views over one of New Zealand's most celebrated landscapes.

As well as a merino ram sculpture on the main highway, Omarama boasts benign skies, encouraging glider flying for which it is thankfully more famous. Scenic flights are all go, as are the town's wooden hot tubs, tucked into tussocky gardens. Around the A2O's halfway point, a therapeutic soak holds considerable appeal.

Omarama signals the start of the trail's gentle descent down the

## ELECTRIFYING VIEWS

The Waitaki Hydro Electric Scheme is a constant companion for nearly two-thirds of the A2O journey, imbuing it with considerable colour and texture. Lakes and canals brim with surreal blue waters, contrasting starkly with the surrounding golden tussock and flinty grey ranges, while eight powerhouses and dams lend industrial elegance. The power stations also offer elevated vantage points over the landscape, with Benmore near Otematata, and Tekapo B overlooking Lake Pukaki, two particularly spectacular lookouts.

*Clockwise from top: lake country; be prepared for all sorts of weather. Previous page: parts of the route are roughly surfaced and mountain bikes might be advisable*

Waitaki Valley, funneling riders towards the sea. The upper valley is home to three pretty hydro lakes, the first of which is Benmore, New Zealand's largest manmade lake. Benmore Dam is a beauty, and an awesome place for a picnic and a few snaps with the camera.

A picturesque road follows the shore of Lake Aviemore where we stopped for a cooling dunk and lingered in the shade of the willows. Beyond the much smaller Lake Waitaki is Kurow, another logical overnight stop with warm hospitality and the bonus of the Vintner's Drop. Home to boutique Ostler winery, it's a rare opportunity to try wines from the Waitaki's propitious but tricky terroir. And then there are the medicinal benefits, of course.

Near Kurow, the Waitaki River is released from its concrete confines and flows in its naturally braided fashion over broad alluvial plains, all the way to the ocean. Down the line, though, at Duntroon, the Alps 2 Ocean detours away from the river into rolling hills with hidden delights.

Yes, what could be merely a gentle pedal through idyllic countryside quickly ramps up with the emergence of a series of unexpected limestone boulders and escarpments. One particular cluster, Elephant Rocks, lie like oddly cast, oversized knucklebones scattered across a paddock filled with sheep nibbling neatly. By the time you've worked out a few more camera angles, scoffed your sandwich, and had a lie-down in one of the rocks' warm, smooth cradles, a good hour will have whiled away.

From here it's only around 31 miles (50km) to Oamaru, with the trail tracking hither and thither along an old railway line and passing through a spooky tunnel. Then it's a cruisy downhill swoop to Oamaru's manicured public gardens, emerging through them to the town's waterfront. The harbourside park, along the town's magnificent Victorian Precinct, is a great place to savour a cold beer after a celebratory toe-dip in the Pacific Ocean. **SB**

*"Mt John Observatory, in the Dark Sky Reserve, is a magnet for astronomers and amateur stargazers"*

## TOOLKIT

**Start** // Aoraki (Mt Cook) Village or Lake Tekapo (4 hours' drive from Christchurch; 3 hours' drive from Queenstown)
**End** // Oamaru (3.5 hours' drive from Queenstown, 90 minutes' drive from Dunedin)
**Distance** // 187 miles (301km)
**Getting around** // This trail is well supported by tour companies offering bike hire, shuttles, luggage transfers and accommodation, many of which are detailed on the trail's website.
**What to take** // A mountain bike with knobbly tires.
**Terrain** // Varied, but predominantly wide and smooth with some rougher, hilly stuff.
**Weather** // Changeable, particularly around the Southern Alps and high country, which may be blanketed in snow in winter. Check the forecast and track conditions before setting off, and take clothing for all eventualities.
**More info** // www.alps2ocean.com

*Opposite: stop to ride at Queenstown*
*Mountain Bike Park, New Zealand*

# MORE LIKE THIS
## NEW ZEALAND RIDES

### MOUNTAINS TO SEA, NORTH ISLAND, NEW ZEALAND

The North Island's version of the Alps 2 Ocean is the similarly named Mountains to Sea, which starts on the slopes of Mt Ruapehu in volcanic Tongariro National Park. Altogether it's a much more gnarly adventure, taking riders through hilly backcountry, remote valleys in Whanganui National Park, and the along the Whanganui River, all the way to the Tasman Sea. This journey is particularly rich in natural and cultural heritage, featuring such sights as an old cobbled road, towering bluffs, Māori meeting houses and the isolated Bridge to Nowhere. Off-the-bike activities include hiking, kayaking and a jet boat ride down the river. Completing the full trail requires good planning, dry conditions, reasonable fitness and off-road bike skills.
**Start // Mt Ruapehu**
**End // Tasman Sea**
**Distance // 184.5 miles (297km)**

### GREAT LAKE TRAIL, NORTH ISLAND, NEW ZEALAND

Skirting the shores of New Zealand's largest lake not far from downtown Taupo, this trail dishes up an enviable mix of lush forest and wetlands, waterfalls, beaches, plus panoramic views of Tongariro National Park's volcanoes. Although most of the trail is smooth and flowing, some moderate hill climbs make it most suitable for reasonably fit riders. The whole ride can be spread over two days, or broken into shorter sections of various lengths and difficulty using local shuttles and a water taxi. Starting at pretty Kinloch, the deservedly popular W2K Track climbs around a bushy headland between Whangamata and Whakaipo Bays, with the option of a return ride known as the Headland Loop. Both options take around half a day.
**Start/End // Kinloch**
**Distance // 44 miles (71km)**

### QUEENSTOWN TRAILS, SOUTH ISLAND, NEW ZEALAND

Proving the saying that getting there is half the fun, this extensive trail network is a richly rewarding way to reach many of the Queenstown region's must-see attractions while soaking up sublime Central Otago scenery. Linking Queenstown, Arrowtown and the Gibbston Valley, trails range from easy lakeside jaunts to ambitious cross-country treks, offering adventures for cyclists of almost every ability and interest. Options include the family-friendly Lake Hayes Loop, and the Gibbston River Ride, an easy wine-tour through the 'Valley of the Vines' beginning at the iconic Kawarau bungy jump bridge.

Handy bike hire depots, open terrain and clear signage make planning and navigation a breeze, while wide, smooth paths means riders can keep their eyes front and camera at the ready.
**Start // Queenstown**
**Distance // 75 miles (120km) of trails**
**Details // www.queenstowntrail.co.nz**

# TASMANIA'S WILD WEST

*Tasmania's untamed west coast offers some of the most exciting, technical and raw cross-country mountain biking conditions – a true ride on the wild side.*

The rainforest claws at my face with cold, clammy fingers as I get up out of the saddle and dig deep, battling hard to keep the cranks going round so I can gain ground during the twisty and technical ascent between Mt Black and Mt Murchison. Since turning off the sealed road from Tullah and onto the serpentine singletrack, every metre has been hard-fought, like territory won during a muddy, bloody skirmish.

This is proper cross-country mountain biking, through genuine wilderness, where there are no lifts or easy drive-and-drop points, and every glorious downhill run has to be earned before it can be burned. No-one is here to hold your hand – except, perhaps,

the thoughtful individual who left a sign at the apex of the climb, warning: 'Bees! Keep your mouth shut!'

That seems like advice worth listening to. Mobile phone reception is little more than a rumour here – as it is along much of the wild western flank of Tasmania – and swallowing a bee could really ruin my day. But keeping one's cakehole shut during the delicious descent that follows such a tortuous climb is easier said than done.

As the valley suddenly opens up in front of me, I involuntarily whoop my way down the thrilling bumpfest of a trail, bouncing over the nuggetty, rubbly and root-covered terrain that shakes my body

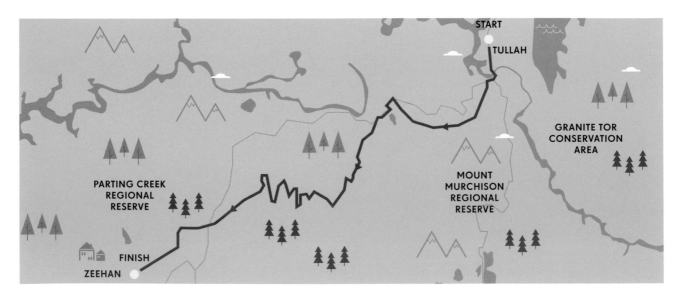

and bike almost to bits and covers both of us in a dusty cloak of track powder.

The drop-offs and washed-out sections are technical enough to keep even the confident riders in our group right on their toes during this dramatic downhill stretch. The terrain is super sketchy, so it's wise to keep a finger hovering over the anchor lever while wending around bends and hopping over potholes, controlling the temptation to simply let loose and just hang on for the ride.

Having managed to avoid both bees and broken bones, my bike and I get a good rinsing during a deceptively deep creek crossing at the bottom, and I pedal across the first flat piece of track of the day, beaming at the thought that this trail is only just getting started, and the best is still ahead.

After following a roundabout route to the road, we hang a left and roll into Rosebery – a remote mining town on Lake Pieman that still has, like many of western Tassie's settlements, a genuine frontier feel to it. Wide empty streets and drinking holes dominated by tough mining men bestow these towns with a look and ambience reminiscent of America's Old West. On most somnambulant Sundays, you could imagine tumbleweed blowing down the main street, but today there's a pedalling posse of mountain bikers rolling through town. We don't linger, though. The tree-lined trails are calling.

Sparsely populated and for the most part defiantly untamed, the west coast of Tasmania has always been a fearfully wild place. It's

*"There's something epic about hoisting a bike over your shoulder and attempting to negotiate a narrow swing-bridge"*

no accident that the British built the very worst penal establishment in the entire empire right here, where the entrance from the sea was known as Hell's Gate.

This coast is where the notorious cannibal convict Alexander Pearce did his worst, munching his way through several fellow escapees after twice absconding from Sarah Island in Macquarie Harbour in the 19th century (authorities didn't believe he'd eaten the other prisoners the first time he was captured – thinking he was covering for them – and they sent him back for seconds).

My riding buddies are a dirt-encrusted, sweaty and smelly bunch, and I have no intention of gnawing on any of them, so I chomp on some carb-loaded trail tucker instead – essential fuel for the forest fun that lies ahead. Just south of Rosebery is Williamsford Car Park, and from here we begin a 3.5-mile (5.5km) section of singletrack that has everyone hollering and horsing around.

This downhill run has a far gentler gradient, but there are booby traps aplenty beneath the leaf litter that covers the trail, with sneaky sleepers left behind by the historic North East Dundas Tramway lying in wait to catch careless riders out. These surprise

## WILDSIDE

Every other year between 2002 and 2016, an epic 4-day mountain bike race – the appropriately titled Wildside (www. wildsidemtb.com) – has roared through the forests and beaches of Tasmania west coast. It's been one of the biggest and best shindigs on the Australian MTB calendar, but organisers are currently taking a breather. We've heard that several times in the past, however, only for the popular event to emerge like a fat-tyred phoenix from the flames. Stay alert.

*Left to right: Montezuma Falls; the suspension bridge across the river at Montezuma Falls; a pitstop on day two of the Wildside; pedalling hard on the Wildside. Previous page: snow gum trees in western Tasmania*

## TOOLKIT

**Start //** Tullah
**End //** Zeehan
**Distance //** 23.5 miles (38km)
**Tour //** This route was Day 2 of the epic Wildside MTB race (see box) – usually regarded as the best stage for 'real mountain bikers' – but you don't need to be participating in an event to cycle these trails, which are always open to the public.
**What to take //** A friend, a first-aid kit, plenty of spares, and a map and a GPS unit. These trails are unsigned and technical, and mobile phone reception is sketchy.
**When to ride //** You can cycle these trails year-round, but some of the swamps turn into bike-bashing man-eaters after heavy rain. Summer (December to February) is best.
**More info //** www.tassietrails.org

speedbumps are guaranteed to send you unceremoniously over the hangers if you hit them full pelt, which adds an element of excitement to an already red-carpet quality doubletrack trail that flows all the way to the most iconic feature of the entire ride: a 100m suspension bridge crossing the river beside the misty mess of Montezuma Falls.

As tasty as the trail has been up to this point, there's something undeniably epic about hoisting a bike over your shoulder and attempting to negotiate a narrow swing-bridge – especially one that spans such a glorious ravine, right in front of fantastic falls that cacophonously cascade across 104m of vertical rock. Regardless of realities, it makes you feel like a proper pedalling pioneer and puts a spring in your cadence – which is just as well, because from here on, the trail goes bloody bonkers.

From Montezuma Falls to Melba Flats, the track becomes petulant and unpredictable, one minute delighting with sweet singletrack, and the next snarling with swamps that suck and swallow wheels, and fill your shoes and soul with dark matter. The first 4 miles (6km) are uphill, after which there's 5 miles (8km) of descent, along a trail that improves the closer you get to Melba.

The final section of track, a 5-mile (8km) scoot, involves jumping yet more sleepers, while steaming along the old route of the long-extinct Emu Bay Railway into Zeehan. The trail ends here, with a celebratory Boags beer in the Wild West-esque saloon bar of the Central Hotel. **PK**

*Opposite: stage five of the Cape Epic race in South Africa, in Oak Valley*

# MORE LIKE THIS
## EPIC MTB RACES

### CAPE EPIC (TASTER), SOUTH AFRICA

Running for 400 miles (644km) or more, South Africa's 7-day Cape Epic is aptly named. This race is commonly regarded as the world's premiere mountain-bike event, one that every professional rough-rider wants to have on their CV. The full course travels from Cape Town to Durbanville, but with savage daily distances peppered with cruel climbs (nearly 15,000m of vertical gain), and strict cut-off times, it's a tough gig for non-elite bikers. But it's possible to independently pluck a single day from the course and get a self-guided taster. For example, try exploring the legendary trails of Welvanpas, near Wellington, where the 2016 Cape Epic tested competitors' mettle on such features as the Patatskloof climb, the Aap Duez (which has 29 switchbacks), and the infamous Cheese Grater. The Yellow route is probably the best option for intermediate riders.
**Start/End // Welvanpas Farm, near Wellington**
**Distance // 17 miles (27km)**
**More info // www.graveltravel.co.za; www.cape-epic.com**

### BC BIKE RACE (TASTER), CANADA

Spending 7 days almost entirely on singletrack is a prospect that gets most mountain bikers dribbling with excitement. Throw in a location like British Columbia – home to the legendary North Shore trails – and salivation gets serious. Unsurprisingly, since it boasts more singletrack than any other stage race in the world – the BC Bike race sells out very quickly. The route changes most years, but to get a taster, try hitting the Squamish trails, which have been the riders' favourite for the last five years. Tucked between Vancouver and Whistler, the Garibaldi Highlands here offer a network of world-class routes, including Rock N Roll, Rupert's, Skookum, Hoods in the Woods, Powerhouse Plunge and the legendary Half Nelson pump track.
**Start/End // Brennan Park, Squamish**
**Distance // 35 miles (56km)**
**More info // www.exploresquamish. com; www.bcbikerace.com**

### TRANSALP (TASTER), AUSTRIA/ SWITZERLAND/ITALY

Now into its 20th year, the Transalp is one of the toughest and longest-running multi-stage mountain bike challenges in the world, and it boasts an incredible amount of elevation gain to boot (somewhat inevitable, being in the Alps). The total distance, spread across 7 days and travelling from Imst in Austria to Arco on Italy's Lake Garda, is 325 miles (523km), with 17,750m of climbing. Day 2 passes through three countries, but possibly the best one-day taster is the Scuol to Livigno epic on day 3, where riders climb into the Alp Astras, round Alp Buffalora, ascend Passo del Gallo, pass through Stelvio National Park and negotiate the Mega-Flow-Downhill route from Passo Trela, over Trepalle and through the Val Torto to the shores of Lago di Livigno.
**Start // Scuol, Switzerland**
**End // Livigno, Italy**
**Distance // 45.5 miles (73km)**

# INDEX

Camel Trail, England 176
Ciclabile delle Dolomiti, Italy 86
Dingle Peninsula, Ireland 46
Guadalavaca to Banes, Cuba 26
Île de Ré, France 244-7, **244**
Loire, France 274, 274-7, **274**
Mai Chau, Vietnam 114-17, **115**
Manifold Track, England 176
Minuteman Bikeway, USA 82-5, **82**
Nantucket Island USA 46
Po River 278
San Juan Island, USA 42-5, **43**
Sonoma County, USA 98
Valle de Viñales, Cuba 26
Vieques Island, Puerto Rico 46
Ecuador 48-53
England
    Camel Trail, England 176
    Cornwall 176
    Devon Sea to Sea 260
    Icknield Way Trail 236
    London-Edinburgh-London 188
    London-Munich 194
    London-Quantock Hills 266
    Manifold Track 176
    Ridgeway, the 236
    Sea to Sea Cycle Route 256-9, **256**
    South Downs Way 232-5, **232**
    Tissington Track 176
Eritrea 12

**F**

family rides
    Camel Trail, England 176
    Cape Breton Island, Canada 248
    Conguillío National Park, Chile 54
    Danube River, Austria 172-5
    Lake Annecy, France 224
    Lake Constance 220-3
    Lake Geneva, Switzerland 224
    Lofoten Islands, Norway 248
    Quilotoa Loop, Ecuador 48-53, **48**
    Route of the Hiawatha, USA 86
    Sark, Channel Islands, UK 248
    Tissington Trail, England 176
    Vermont, USA 94-7, **94**
    White Rim Trail, USA 54
Fiora Valley, Italy 182
Forgotten World Hwy, New Zealand 286
Fort William, Scotland 80

France 138
    Alp D'Huez 200
    Atlantic coast 66
    Cévennes 262-5, 266, **263**
    Corsica 214-17, **215**
    Côte d'Azur 266
    Île de Ré 244-7, **244**
    Lake Annecy 224
    Loire 274-7, **274**
    Mont Ventoux 196-9, **196**
    Paris 242
    Paris-Brest-Paris 188
    Paris Roubaix 254
    Portes du Soleil 298
    Provence 230
    Rhine Cycle Route 278
    Samoens 104
Friendship Hwy, Tibet-Nepal 34, 144

**G**

Germany 66, 166-9, 220-3, 236, 278, **166**, **220**
Great Allegheny Passage, USA 40, 310
Great Divide Mountain Bike Route, USA 54
Great Lake Trail, New Zealand 316
Guatemala 194

**H**

Heaphy Track, New Zealand 292
High Atlas, Morocco 138
Himalaya, 134-7, 140-3, 144, 162, **134**, **140**

**I**

Iceland 126
Icknield Way Trail, England 236
Île de Ré, France 244-7, **244**
India 134-7, 162
Indonesia 150, 156
Ireland 46, 208-211, 212
Italy 132, 218
    24h of Finale Ligure 72
    Ciclabile delle Dolomiti 86
    Fiora Valley 182
    Lake Como 224
    Lake Garda 292
    Monte Amiata 178-181, **179**
    Po River 278

Sardinia 218
Strade Bianche 182
Transalp 322
VenTo 278

**J**

Japan 98, 110, 128-131

**K**

Karakoram Hwy, Pakistan-China 162
Kilimanjaro Circuit, Tanzania 12
Kokopelli Trail, USA 298
Kosovo 310
Kyoto, Japan 98
Kyrgyzstan 162

**L**

La Farola, Cuba 26
La Vélodyssée, France 66
Lake Annecy, France 224
Lake Como, Italy 224
Lake Constance 220-3, **220**
Lake Garda, Italy 292
Lake Geneva, Switzerland 224
Lesotho 12
Lofoten Islands, Norway 248
Loire, France 274-7, **274**
London 188, 194, 266
Lôn Las Cymru, Wales 260
Lycian Coast, Turkey 18

**M**

Mae Hong Son, Thailand 146-9, **147**
Mai Chau, Vietnam 114-17, **115**
Mammoth Bike Park, USA 104
Manali-Leh Hwy, India 162
Manifold Track, England 176
Mekong Delta, Vietnam 118
Melbourne, Australia 194, 242
Mexico City, Mexico 110
Minuteman Bikeway, USA 82-5, **82**
Mississippi River Trail, USA 278
Moab, USA 68-71, **69**
Mongolia 120-5, **121**
Mont Ventoux, France 196-9, **196**
Monte Amiata, Italy 178-181, **179**
Monte Bondone, Italy 182

**Epic Bike Rides of the World**
August 2016
Published by Lonely Planet Global Limited
ABN 36 005 607 983
www.lonelyplanet.com
10 9 8 7 6 5

Printed in Italy
ISBN 978 1 76034 083 4
© Lonely Planet 2016
© photographers as indicated 2016

Managing Director, Publishing Piers Pickard
Associate Publisher &
Commissioning Editor Robin Barton
Art Director Daniel Di Paolo
Designer Ben Brannan
Editors Karyn Noble, Ross Taylor
Print Production Larissa Frost, Nigel Longuet

**Lonely Planet Offices**

**Australia**
The Malt Store, Level 3,
551 Swanston St, Carlton,
Victoria 3053 T: 03 8379 8000

**Ireland**
Unit E, Digital Court,
The Digital Hub,
Rainsford St, Dublin 8

**USA**
124 Linden St, Oakland,
CA 94607
T: 510 250 6400

**Europe**
240 Blackfriars Rd,
London SE1 8NW
T: 020 3771 5100

**STAY IN TOUCH**
lonelyplanet.com/contact

**Authors** Andrea Sachs (**AS**) is a writer for the Washington Post. Andrew Bain (**AB**) has cycled around Australia, across the Himalayas and towed his kids over the Alps. He is the author of Lonely Planet's *A Year of Adventures*. Ben Handicott (**BH**) is a *bon viveur* who once published travel pictorial and reference books. Brendan Sainsbury (**BS**) is a former Cuba cycling guide. He has been researching and updating Lonely Planet's Cuba guidebook for over 10 years. Cass Gilbert (**CG**) has been obsessed by bicycle touring for the last 18 years. He's traversed Asia and the Middle East, bikepacked his way around the American South West, and ridden dirt roads from Alaska to Patagonia. Follow his travels at whileoutriding.com. Clover Stroud (**CS**) is a freelance journalist and author. David Else (**DE**) is a writer specialising in travel, trekking, cycling and walking. Emma Bryant (**EB**) is a writer and sports marketing professional based in Cambridge, New Zealand. She competes on road and track but is as happy rolling to the coffee shop as sprinting for the finish line. Ethan Gelber (**EG**) has pedalled more miles than he's driven. Twitter: @thetravelword. Jasper Winn (**JW**) writes about, photographs, and gives talks on long journeys by bicycle, on foot, with horses and in kayaks around the world. He's the author of *Paddle*, an account of sea kayaking the 1000 miles around Ireland (www.theslowadventure.com). John Pickrell (**JP**) is editor of *Australian Geographic* magazine, where a version of his story was first published. Kerry Christiani (**KC**) is a Lonely Planet writer. Lee Slater (**LS**) is a Lonely Planet writer. Lewis Blackwell (**LB**) is the author of many books on the environment and on creative matters, most recently *Rainforest*. He is also currently chair of the Natural History Museum's Wildlife Photographer of the Year. Luke Pegrum (**LP**) is a writer based in Western Australia. Matt Swaine (**MS**) commutes through the mean streets of Bristol on his Brompton and takes part in Audax rides on his Trek. He hopes his involvement in this book will help pay for a titanium frame he's been talking about for months. Max Leonard (**ML**) is the author of *Lanterne Rouge: the Last Man in the Tour de France*, published by Yellow Jersey Press. He'd like to thank *Soigneur* magazine, which originally commissioned a piece on *The Rider*. Mike Higgins (**MH**) is a journalist and editor who lives in Crystal Palace, south London. Nate Cavalieri (**NC**) is a San Francisco-based writer and cyclist. Patrick Kinsella (**PK**) is an editor, writer and director of Adventure Types, now based in Devon, England. Paul Bloomfield (**PB**) is a British writer and photographer who contributes to newspapers and magazines including the *Telegraph*, the *Times* and *Wanderlust*. Rob Penn (**RP**) is a journalist, TV presenter and author of the bestselling *It's All About the Bike: the Pursuit of Happiness on Two Wheels*. He is also a director of Bikecation (www.bikecation.co.uk). Robin Barton (**RB**) has ridden and raced mountain and road bikes on four continents. Sam Haddad (**SH**) lives in Brighton with her husband and two young sons. She's cycled all her life. She tweets at @shhhaddad & would like to thank Brittany Ferries for Île de Ré. Sarah Bennett (**SB**) is a Lonely Planet writer. Sarah P Gilbert (**SG**) is a Sydney-based writer who spends a lot of time in Argentina; she's working on her first book of non-fiction about Buenos Aires. Tom Hall (**TH**) is the Editorial Director of Lonely Planet who dreams of conquering the classic climbs of the Alps, but settles for slogging up Swain's Lane in north London most days. Wade Wallace (**WW**) is the founder of www.cyclingtips.com.au, where a version of his story was first published. **Cover and illustrations** by Ross Murray (www.rossmurray.com). **Maps** by Mariana Sameiro (marianasameiro.com).